Translated Tex

This series is designed to meet th
medieval history and others who wi   ......g
source material, but whose knowledge of Latin or Greek is not sufficient
to allow them to do so in the original language. Many important Late
Imperial and Dark Age texts are currently unavailable in translation and
it is hoped that TTH will help to fill this gap and to complement the
secondary literature in English which already exists. The series relates
principally to the period 300-800 AD and includes Late Imperial, Greek,
Byzantine and Syriac texts as well as source books illustrating a
particular period or theme. Each volume is a self-contained scholarly
translation with an introductory essay on the text and its author and
notes on the text indicating major problems of interpretation, including
textual difficulties.

Front cover drawing: Inscription from Tebessa, an example of Donatist iconography;
drawn by Gail Heather (source: Yvette Duval, *Loca Sanctorum Africae: Le culte des
martyrs en Afrique au IV° au VIF siècle* [Rome: École français de Rome, 1982]).

A full list of published titles in the Translated Texts for Historians series is available on request. The most recently published are shown below.

Caesarius of Arles: Life, Testament, Letters
Translated with notes and introduction by WILLIAM E. KLINGSHIRN
Volume 19: 176pp. 1994, ISBN 0-85323 368-3

The Lives of the Ninth-Century Popes (*Liber Pontificalis*)
Translated with an introduction and commentary by RAYMOND DAVIS
Volume 20: 360pp., 1995, ISBN 0-85323-479-5

Bede: On the Temple
Translated with notes by SEÁN CONNOLLY,
introduction by JENNIFER O'REILLY
Volume 21: 192pp., 1995, ISBN 0-85323-049-8

Pseudo-Dionysius of Tel-Mahre: *Chronicle*, Part III
Translated with notes and introduction by WITOLD WITAKOWSKI
Volume 22: 192pp., 1995, ISBN 0-85323-760-3

Venantius Fortunatus: Personal and Political Poems
Translated with notes and introduction by JUDITH GEORGE
Volume 23: 192pp., 1995, ISBN 0-85323-179-6

Donatist Martyr Stories: The Church in Conflict in Roman North Africa
Translated with notes and introduction by MAUREEN A. TILLEY
Volume 24: 144pp., 1996, ISBN 0 85323 931 2

Hilary of Poitiers: Conflicts of Conscience and Law in the Fourth-Century Church
Translated with Introduction and notes by LIONEL R. WICKHAM
Volume 25: 176pp., 1997, ISBN 0-85323-572-4

Lives of the Visigothic Fathers
Translated and edited by A. T. FEAR
Volume 26: 208pp., 1997, ISBN 0-85323-582-1

Optatus: Against the Donatists
Translated with Notes and Introduction by MARK J. EDWARDS
Volume 27: 220pp., 1997, ISBN 085323-752-2

For full details of Translated Texts for Historians, including prices and ordering information, please write to the following:
All countries, except the USA and Canada: Liverpool University Press, Senate House, Abercromby Square, Liverpool, L69 3BX, UK (*Tel* 0151-794 2233, *Fax* 0151-794 2235).
USA and Canada: University of Pennsylvania Press, 4200 Pine Street, Philadelphia, PA 19104-4011, USA (*Tel* (215) 898-6264, *Fax* (215) 898-0404).

Translated Texts for Historians
Volume 27

Optatus:
Against the Donatists

Translated and edited by MARK EDWARDS

Liverpool
University
Press

First published 1997 by
Liverpool University Press
Senate House, Abercromby Square
Liverpool, L69 3BX

British Library Cataloguing-in-Publication Data
A British Library CIP Record is available
ISBN 0-85323-752-2

Printed in the European Community by
Bell & Bain Limited, Glasgow

CONTENTS

vi

PREFACE

Thanks are due to the editors of the series for commissioning this volume, and especially to Mary Whitby, Gillian Clark and Robert Markus for comments on early drafts. Some of the indispensable items on the bibliography I owe to the vigilance of Henry Chadwick. I have also benefited from the assistance of Mark Allen and Sarah Cannon, and Christ Church has provided me not only with a computer and an office, but with funding for the preparation of camera-ready copy. The most important role in the production of the final text was played by my wife Mali, who, knowing both the regular operation and the foibles of computers better than I do, was able to reduce the anarchic typescript to a sober uniformity. Any remaining blemishes, where they are not inevitable, are mine.

Christ Church, February 1997.

CHRONOLOGY

A.D. 303	Edicts of Diocletian against Christianity
305	Abdication of Diocletian and Maximian. Accession of Galerius and Constantius
305/308	Protocol of Cirta against Caecilian
306	Constantine assumes power in Britian and Gaul, Maxentius in Italy and Africa
308	Maximian unsuccessfully attempts to depose Maxentius
?308	Pamphlet of Felix the deacon against a tyrannical ruler
308-10	Peace extended to Christians by Maxentius
311	Galerius repeals edicts of persecution; Caecilian elected Bishop of Carthage
312	Conversion of Constantine, who captures Rome and becomes sole ruler of west
313	Licinius becomes sole ruler of east and joins Constantine in toleration of Christians
313	Roman council upholds Caecilian's election
314	The party of Donatus appeals to Constantine. Council of Arles
315	Felix of Abthugni acquitted of collaboration
316	Constantine gives unqualified support to party of Caecilian

321	Constantine begins war against Licinius and relents somewhat toward the Donatists
324	Constantine becomes sole Emperor
330	Constantine builds new church at Cirta for catholics
337	Death of Constantine. Accession of Constans as ruler of Gaul and Italy
346	Macarius and Paulus sent to pacify Donatists
347	Constans exiles the Donatist bishops
348	Council of Carthage under Bishop Gratus approves actions of Macarius
362	Emperor Julian recalls exiled Donatist bishops
378	Death of Valens, under whom Optatus is said to have written
384	Accession of Pope Siricius, called contemporary by Optatus

INTRODUCTION

I. Constantine, the Empire and the Donatists

The history of the Donatists begins with the edict issued by the Emperor Diocletian on 23 February 303 A.D.[1] This, whatever its origin, entailed the demolition of Christian churches, with the confiscation and burning of the Scriptures - no small loss in an age before the printing-press, when books were scarce and the labour of producing them immense. In the eastern provinces at least,[2] the decree was followed by three others, the first of which provided for the arrest of Christian clergy, while the next required an offering to the gods as the precondition of their release, and the last imposed the duty of sacrifice on every Christian. The suddenness of the persecution alarmed the Church no less than its ferocity: for Diocletian, one of the most astute of Roman Emperors, had already held the throne for eighteen years without persecution, and the reasons for this inititiative were a matter of debate and speculation, then as now.

Diocletian abdicated only two years later. Nevertheless, he survived until 311, and he saw the persecution carried on in the east by two of his successors: first Galerius, who had held the rank of Caesar, or Crown Prince, under Diocletian; then Maximinus Daia, who seized the eastern throne a little before Galerius' death in 311. Galerius was believed by two contemporary historians - Lactantius and Eusebius, both Christians[3] - to have been the instigator of the first edict, yet after Diocletian's abdication in 305, the sufferings of the Church did not increase.[4] Only where Maximinus was the Caesar after 306, or Emperor

---

[1] On the edicts see now Corcoran (1996), 179-182.

[2] See De Ste-Croix (1954) and Corcoran (1996), pp. 181-2 on the variable enforcement of the edicts. Frend (1965) believes that there is some evidence of enforcement in the west.

[3] See Eusebius, *HE* IX; Lactantius, *Mort.*. They are believed, e.g. by Barnes (1981), but strong points have been made against their testimony by Davies (1989). Nothing in Optatus' text suggests that he had heard of Galerius.

[4] See De Ste-Croix (1954). On Maximinus' edicts, enforcing then revoking persecution, see Eusebius, *HE* IX.5 and IX.10.

after 311, was Diocletian's policy maintained with the same severity; and after 305 it was almost dormant in the west.[5]

Diocletian had delegated the rule of the western provinces to Maximian, who abdicated reluctantly with his colleague in 305. Between 303 and 305 the persecution had been harsh in Africa, where Maximian was most potent, but had been less intense in Gaul, where it was Constantius, the Caesar or Crown Prince, who held the reins.[6] After becoming Emperor (or Augustus) of the west, Constantius seems to have refrained from persecution until his death in 306. During the intervening year he was joined by his son Constantine, who had fled the court of Galerius on learning that he had not been appointed Caesar to his father.[7] On his death Constantius should have been succeeded by the official Caesar, one Severus; but Constantine lost no time in proclaiming his own succession, to the immediate acclaim of his father's troops.

According to Lactantius, one of Constantine's first acts was to repeal the recent laws against the Christians and restore to the church its confiscated property.[8] He was not, however, a Christian at that time, and by his own account had received no instruction in the new religion.[9] His subsequent devotion to the pagan cults suggests that he wished to emulate the piety of his father;[10] but Constantius had subscribed, however tepidly, to the policy of his colleagues, and Constantine himself

---

[5] See Lactantius, *Mort.* 8 and 15 on Constantius' clemency, verified by the absence of any inscriptions attesting enforcement of the edicts. The African persecution may have begun prematurely, after Diocletian's letter on the Manichees (*Collatio Mosaiacarum et Romanarum Legum* 15.3).

[6] One of the few written testimonies to the clemency of Constantius is found in the Donatists' letter to Constantine at Optatus I.22, though Barnes (1973) and (1975) offers a different interpretation of the *facinus* from which Gaul is exculpated (see text and notes below).

[7] Lactantius, *Mort.* 19. It appears to bave been the policy of Diocletian to avoid a dynastic succession, which would (and later did) entail forced marriages and internecine rivalries.

[8] Lactantius, *Mort.* 24--perhaps the strongest evidence that the *Mort.* is (among other things) an apology to Christians on behalf of Constantine.

[9] See *Orat.* 11. The difficulty of reconciling this with Eusebius' reference to Constantine's "paternal deity" at *VC* I.27 seems to me one of the strongest arguments against Davies (1991), together with those of Edwards (1995). In Edwards *et al.* (1997/8) I shall defend the authenticity of *Orat.*, proposing a date c. 314 A.D., a proper time (as the present volume indicates) for the Emperor to explain his own credentials.

[10] See *Panegyrici Latini* VI (VII) 7.3 on Constantius Pius, and 22.6 on Constantine's profuse foundation of temples. The one remaining panegyric on Constantius flatters him as a present god in a manner scarcely compatible with Christian devotion and eschewed by the later encomiasts of Constantine.

appears to have been the first Roman Emperor who made it lawful to be a Christian. Only Gaul and Britian were the immediate beneficiaries of this measure, for Constantine's usurpation had awakened the ambitions of Maximian's son Maxentius,who proclaimed himself the true Emperor of the west, and remained the master of Italy and Africa for most of the next six years. Even if he was not a persecutor, he had no sympathy for the Church and its divisions, and responded to a dispute between two candidates by expelling both from Rome.[11]

In 312 A.D., after six years of uneasy truce,[12] the self-styled Emperor Constantine took an army across the Alps from Gaul to depose the self-styled Emperor Maxentius. His rival eschewed the safety of the Roman walls, gave battle at the Milvian Bridge on October 28, and was driven with a great part of his host into the Tiber. Now the absolute ruler of western Europe and North Africa, the conqueror made a treaty with Licinius, who became the official Emperor of the west on the death of Severus, but perceived that this meant nothing and was vying now with Maximinus Daia for dominion in the east. A condition of the pact between Licinius and Constantine was that Christians in the east should have the freedom to observe their own religion; it is therefore no surprise that when Licinius overthrew Maximinus, many churchmen saw in this the hand of God.[13]

Constantine they saw not only as an appointed saviour but as a conscientious friend. On the eve of his battle against Maxentius, he received a sign from heaven which persuaded him that one God would suffice. So at least Lactantius wrote a short time after the treaty with Licinius, and so Eusebius later heard from Constantine on oath.[14] The

[11] See Barnes (1981), pp. 38-9. Corcoran (1996), pp. 144-5 asserts (probably enough--see n. 41) that Maxentius restored the church's property only in or after 310, although he rescinded the persecution in 306. He considers Maxentius to be the "tyrannical Emperor" of Optatus I.17, though I have argued in my note that other views are tenable.

[12] On these events, my account of which is intended to be brief and uncontroversial, see Barnes (1981) pp. 28-43. The interlude in which Maximian, father of Maxentius, returned to rule with his son, may be relevant to Optatus I.17, as may the usurpation of Domitus Alexander in Africa (308-9).

[13] See Lactantius, *Mort.* 46-49, transcribing a monotheistic prayer which Licinius distributed to his troops on the eve of battle against Maximinus, together with the accord conventionally styled the "Edict of Milan", and announces toleration for the Christians throughout the imperial provinces. I incline, with Lane Fox (1986) to believe that Maximinus is the tyrant overthrown by the hand of God in Constantine *Orat.* 22.

[14] See Lactantius, *Mort.* 44; Eusebius, *VC* I.27-32; Baynes (1929/31) pp. 60-65; Barnes (1981) p. 43 and p. 306 nn. 146-9.

accounts of the vision differ, but there is no doubt that the Emperor was baptized, that he made many laws which Christians found exemplary, and that he waged both war and peace as the protector of the Church. None the less it has often been maintained that he was not sincerely Christian, or not fully, or not at once. His baptism took place only on his deathbed, which if not a sign of weak belief is at least a sign that he knew himself to be capable of sinning against his faith.[15] He never let the Gospel interfere with his ambitions, and his wars against Maxentius and Licinius, undertaken in the name of Christianity, made no pretence to the clemency that adorned the panegyrics on his earlier campaigns.[16] History, it is true, can show examples of intense religiosity combined with the pursuit of worldly interests; but monarchs of this kind will often propagate their faith with a ruthless zeal that many critics do not find in Constantine. There is, however, a difference between the situation of Constantine and that of Charles V or Philip II: thanks to Constantine himself, they were ruling Christian peoples, whereas Constantine could advance the growth of Christianity only with the consent of his pagan subjects, who probably remained a great majority in his realm.[17]

Whatever his motives, Constantine desired the Church to regard him as a Christian and intended to be its ruler; but after he entered Rome he was obliged to make a choice between two concepts of the church. When he made a grant to the church of Carthage, in the person of Caecilian whom he believed to be its Bishop,[18] he was soon informed that the African metropolis had not one but two episcopates. Caecilian, his predecessor Mensurius and one of the other bishops who ordained him, were all accused of having collaborated with the imperial persecutors by a party from the neighbouring territory of Numidia.[19] This party had installed a rival bishop, Majorinus, whose successor

---

[15] On the baptism see now Fowden (1994).

[16] I intend to write elsewhere on the changes in the depiction of Constantine in the *Panegyrici Latini*. On his clemency see VI (VII) 5.3 and 10.4.

[17] *Codex Theodosianus* II.8.1; Barnes (1981) pp. 51-2. On the paganism of the Empire after Constantine's capture of Rome see Burckhardt (1949) pp. 325-63; Alfoldi (1948) pp. 25-81.

[18] Eusebius, *HE* X.6.1-5. Corcoran (1996), p. 153 concludes that Constantine "was probably already taking a view on the Donatist controversy".

[19] Optatus I.18 and Appendix 1 supplies the main evidence, together with Augustine, *Crescs.* III.30.

Donatus gave his name to the church which was to set up rival bishops in all the major towns of Africa, Numidia and the neighbouring provinces.[20] All who maintained communion with Caecilian they denounced as *traditores* ("handers-over"), since the usual demand that had been made of the clergy by their persecutors was the surrender of sacred books. Constantine, like any Roman Emperor, wanted nothing so much as unity, and had the matter debated first at Rome in 313; then, when he found that the Donatists would not accept the verdict of this session, he transferred the case to a general council, held at Arles in Gaul in 314.[21]

Every official judgment under Constantine was in favour of Caecilian, or at least was so regarded by the Emperor. It could scarcely have been otherwise, for his aim, like that of most of his predecessors over the last half-century, was to make the whole of his realm subscribe to the customs of its capital. A programme of Romanization had almost certainly provided one of the motives for Diocletian's edicts against the Christians, as it had for the first imperial persecution under Decius in 251.[22] Another pagan Emperor, Aurelian, had decreed in 271 that the Roman bishops should be the arbiter in episcopal appointments to the distant see of Antioch;[23] it is not a matter for wonder, then, that Constantine should wish disputes in the western city of Carthage to be decided at the heart of the Roman Empire, and that his own appointees should uphold the Papal verdict against every new appeal.

Constantine, of course, could not appoint himself as president in a matter that was reckoned to pertain to the church alone. Nor could statecraft be the only ground for the rejection of the Donatists. Once it became apparent that these appellants would not accept the verdict of the pontiff or the Emperor, the supporters of Caecilian, who called themselves the catholics, began to write their own histories to show that it was the Donatists themselves who had been the first collaborators, and the first to make a petition to a secular tribunal.[24] The first of these

---

[20] On the persistence of Donatism see Frend (1952a), pp. 169ff.

[21] See Appendix 4, though Optatus himself appears to be ignorant of the Council at I.23. For Constantine's letter summoning Chrestus of Syracuse see Eusebius, *HE* X.5.21-4.

[22] See now Corcoran (1996) on this motive in Diocletianic edicts. A fine discussion of Decius' motives is offered by Benson (1897), pp. 60-64.

[23] Eusebius, *HE* VII.30.17. On this episode see Millar (1971).

[24] See Optatus I.22ff, with Appendix 5

controversialists was Eusebius and the greatest was Augustine; but the former had only limited information, while the latter borrowed much of his from a senior African bishop. It is chiefly on the researches of Optatus, even now, that any attempt to explain the outbreak of the schism must rely.

II. *Optatus of Milevis and his Archives*

Optatus came from the small town of Milevis, and bore one of the honorific names so typical of his countrymen. All that is really known about his person might be reduced to a shorter paragraph than the one that appears in the *Dictionary of Christian Biography*:[25]

"OPTATUS. Saint and martyr (?), bishops of Milevis or Mileum (Milah), a small town of Numidia 25m. N.W. of Cirta, a vigorous opponent of the Donatists. He says of himself that he wrote about sixty years or more after the persecution of Diocletian, i.e., c. A.D. 363. St Jerome speaks of him in general terms as having written during the reigns of Valentinian and Valens, A.D. 365-378. But in the second book of his treatises, Siricius is mentioned as Bishops of Rome, "qui est noster socius". As Siricius did not succeed Damasus until 384, these words may have been inserted, as Baronius suggests, by the transcribers of his book, or he may have oulived the period mentioned by St Jerome and himself inserted them at a later time. The date of his death, however, is unknown".

Because Jerome speaks of six books rather than seven, the article goes on to say that the seventh is "of dubious authenticity". Jerome's statement that Optatus wrote his history under Valens has given rise to speculation that it passed through two editions. We are not forced to believe anything said by Jerome, who was as versatile in error as in

---

[25] Parker (1887), using Jerome, *De Viris Illustribus* 90. It is generall agreed that *Contra Parmenianum*, used by Parker as the title of the whole work, is merely Jerome's description of its origin. The Latin title used by Hurter (1870) is *De Schismate Donatistarum*, but I have followed Labrousse (1995-6) and others in entitling my translation *Against the Donatists*.

eloquence,[26] but support for this hypothesis can be drawn from the work itself. First, although Optatus often looks forward from an early book to a later one, he nowhere makes any reference to a seventh; secondly he introduces the Donatist Macrobius as though he were in possession of his Roman see, yet only a little later gives the names of two successors;[27] thirdly, it is strange that an author writing in the pontificate of Siricius - that is, after 384 - should allude to the persecution of 303 as an event of sixty, rather than eighty years before his time.[28] Interpolation at least may be excluded: no party stood to gain by the insertion of Siricius' name in the list of Roman primates, for the election of Siricius himself was undisputed, and catholic posterity had no interest in imposing a later date on this account of the early stages of the Donatist controversy. Nor will interpolation explain the fact that both the Donatists and the catholics appealed to a different version of the text at the Carthaginian conference of 403.[29]

On the other hand, it must be admitted that no manuscript now extant seems to represent an earlier edition, though there are many inconsistencies that testify to the carelessness of scribes.[30] The arguments and Biblical citations of Optatus in the seventh book are of a piece with the rest of his work, he mentions no new circumstances, and he writes no acerbic preface of the kind that customarily accompanies Augustine's repetitious interventions in the struggle. A number of the arguments adduced for an original date before 384 are futile: for instance, that he must have written before the death in 376 of Bishops Photinus of Sirmium, whom he calls a contemporary,[31] or that since Parmenianus wrote soon after being recalled to his see by Julian

---

[26] On the unreliability of Jerome cf. Barnes (1985) pp. 4-12.

[27] Both passages occur in II.4 Monceaux (1912) points out that the references to Macrobius' successors entail a date after 378. The evidence mentioned in the next few sentences is summarized by Mazucco (1993) pp. 35-7.

[28] See Optatus I.15 and II.4 with notes. As an example of the vagueness possible to ancient authors one might cite *Inventio Sanctae Crucis* I. 201, where the age of Christianity is estimated at 200 (rather than 300) years. On the vacillations of Arnobius, another African, see Simmons (1995), pp. 54-76.

[29] See Optatus I.19 and notes (on the ordination of Caecilian).

[30] Thus at II.4 the Petropolitanus includes Siricius while omitting the successors of Macrobius.

[31] Optatus IV.5

in 362, Optatus must have answered him at once.[32] Jerome is clearly
ignorant of something, since he must have written after all seven books
had been made current. Nothing can be proved, then, but the hypothesis
of two editions fits a number of facts that would otherwise go
unexplained.

Optatus therefore wrote the surviving version of his work in or after
384 A.D. In the first quarter of the fifth century he was seen as an
authority by both parties to the schism. An authority was needed, since
the origins of the crisis, which may have begun as early as 305 A.D,
were obscured by loss of records, by the difficulty of authenticating
documents and by the wilful nescience of partisans on either side. The
story told by Optatus (adding the first appendix to his narrative in Book
I) is as follows. Before the persecution of Diocletian (303-5) - or
perhaps before the renewal of persecution, if this occurred[33] - Caecilian,
then a deacon to Mensurius, Bishops of Carthage, incurred the animosity
of a rich woman named Lucilla, because he had objected to her
extravagant veneration of a martyr (I.16). Under pretence of giving
monies for distribution to the poor, she bribed the Numidian clergy to
conspire against Caecilian (Appendix 1; Optatus I.19). The charge of
collaboration that they wished to bring against him was more true of the
conspirators, but they took (or had already taken[34]) their own
precautions against exposure, producing the so-called Protocol of Cirta
(I.14), and did not make any open allegations against Caecilian until he
was elected to the bishopric on the death of Mensurius in 311 (I.19).

Unable at this time to gain a hearing in their own region, they
appealed in 313 to Constantine, now master of Rome and an open friend
of Christianity (I.22). As he did not wish to intervene in an
ecclesiastical matter, he referred it first to a council of Roman and
Gaulish bishops under the presidency of Miltiades, Bishop of Rome
(I.23). Caecilian was acquitted, but was detained by Constantine for a

---

[32] Cf. the *Parm.* and *Bapt.* of Augustine, frequently cited in this volume. On Parmenianus see Frend (1952a) pp, 192-207, and on Augustine, *ibid.* pp. 227-43.

[33] See notes on I.17 concerning the brief restoration of Maximian and the usurpation of Domitius Alexander. This would give date of, say, 307 for the inception of Lucilla's campaign, which otherwise would appear to have fermented for a long time with no result.

[34] If there were any evidence to allow this, I should like to date the Protocol to c. 308, since another conspiracy of Purpurius and Secundus coincides with the machinations of Lucilla in Appendix 1.

longer period, while Donatus returned to Carthage, against the wishes of the Emperor, and fomented new sedition (I.26). The Donatists advanced a groundless charge of collaboration against Felix of Abthugni, who had assisted at Caecilian's ordination. This may be the same Felix whose defiance of a tyrant in the days of the pagan Empire had brought about the absence of Mensurius from Carthage, and had thus facilitated the conspiracy of Lucilla's dissidents against Caecilian (I.17). The innocence of Felix of Abthugni was established by an African inquiry in 315 (Appendix 2).

This account, however, is manifestly incomplete. It does not, for example, tell us what we hear elsewhere, that Mensurius himself had been accused of collaboration, and was already on bad terms with those who had more respect for martyrs than for bishops.[35] It does not allude to the story that Caecilian, at the instance of Mensurius, had intercepted supplies of food intended for "confessors" (Christian prisoners),[36] who had had therefore starved to death. It does not give any plausible explanation of the interval between the plot of Cirta and its outcome,[37] for the conspirators can hardly have planned to wait until a Christian took the throne. It omits the Council of Arles, perhaps deliberately,[38] and the paragraph on Felix of Abthugni is so obscure that we suspect the train of events was barely visible at the time when Optatus wrote. He seems (unlike Augustine) to have no evidence that Caecilian was pronounced innocent by anyone but Miltiades;[39] and in a passage that brought some comfort to the Donatists and embarrassment to Augustine, he indicates that even Constantine remained uncertain after the council of 314.[40] The appendix shows that the influence of the sovereign was more strenuously and more willingly exerted than Optatus cares to notice, and the grant that he made to Caecilian before the Roman synod is ignored. Eusebius, by contrast, transcribes the letter announcing this

---

[35] Augustine, *Brev.* III.25 records that he was reputed to have handed over scriptures.

[36] *Passio Abitinensium* 15. Tilley (1996) p. 26 n.4 argues that this account was written before Caecilian became Bishop.

[37] See Optatus I.14 and notes for the date, which appears to be some time in 305. But see n. 35 above.

[38] Because (a) it suggests that Constantine was not entirely persuaded of the innocence of Caecilian; (b) it removes the centre of authority from Rome.

[39] See Augustine, *Brev.* III.37 and *Cresc.* III.82.

[40] See Optatus I.26 and notes.

donation, because, seeing Constantine as the image and vicegerent of the Creator, he is not afraid to show him building the church into his Empire.[41] If we ask why Constantine showed such immediate favour to the catholics, the obvious reply for us would be that Optatus' hero found the party which favoured bishops over martyrs more submissive to the pontifical (and secular) authority of Rome.

Historians crave dates as well as episodes, but where Optatus offers these, he is almost always wrong. He may be our only witness to a return of Christian freedom under Maxentius, but we cannot say for certain what event he means to allude to between 306 and 312[42] This reprieve is thought by some to have led to the election of Silvanus, which in turn seems to coincide with the year in which Lucilla bribed the Numidian bishops to conspire against Caecilian; if that is so, Optatus' date for the protocol of Cirta is unlikely to be accurate, being recognised in any case as the least probable of three.[43] Another event that only he recalls is the composition of a pamphlet, *De Tyranno Imperatore*, by Felix, one of the deacons of Mensurius.[44] This for many scholars marks the outbreak of the crisis, but any year from 306 to 311 can be proposed with equal likelihood.

If Optatus cannot tell us how the schism originated, can he adjudicate between modern theories as to the cause of its persistence? It seems that the most vigorous opponents of Caecilian came from the province of Numidia, whose fanatical Christianity had provoked an equally violent persecution.[45] Moreover it would seem that one at least, Silvanus of Cirta, had been raised to his bishopric by the lower populace against the wishes of the citizen body.[46] From this it has been concluded that the Donatists were inspired, or at least sustained, by their resentment of the imperial dominion, and especially their antipathy to Carthage, which in its heyday as a "Punic" (that is, Phoenician) settlement had oppressed

[41] Eusebius, *H.* X.6.1-5; for the monarchism of Eusebius see his *Triacontericus* etc.

[42] See Optatus I.18, where the remission seems to follow Felix's pamphlet and to lead almost at once to the ordination of Caecilian. If that is so, the peace may not have been extended by Maxentius before 310. Cf Eusebius, *Hist. Eccl.* VIII.14.1 and my note to Optatus I.18.

[43] At least by Lancel (1979). Augustine, Epistle 43.12-17 connects the protocol with the enmity of Lucilla, who also sponsored the election of Silvanus.

[44] See Optatus I.17 and notes.

[45] See Frend (1952a), pp. 25-49.

[46] See Appendix 1, with Diesner (1961) and Schindler (1983).

the natives brutally, and had now enhanced its natural hegemony by becoming voluntarily a colony of Rome.[47] The fact that both the church and the state abroad upheld the catholics gives substance to the theory that the struggle was not only between the persons but between an indigenous people and its conquerors: the province and the capital the country and the town.[48]

There is much in Optatus' history that seems to tell in favour of this view. It is he who records the election of Silvanus, his appendices that expose the poor Latinity of Caecilian's accusers; he is the one who informs us that the Donatists, often slighted as Numidians in Africa, were also known in Rome by the pejorative name of Hillmen or Montenses.[49] Nevertheless, some caution must be exercised whenever we find ourselves embracing as our own hypothesis the judgment which an ancient source is patently inviting us to draw. It is no surprise that the catholics, relying as they did upon the authority of the government, should represent their adversaries not only as barbarians,[50] but as natural outsiders with an inveterate disposition to rebellion. Since Roman provincial government aimed first at peace, it was always in the interests of the catholics to belittle the support enjoyed by the Donatists in Carthage; yet Donatists continued to appoint their candidates to the see of Carthage, to regard them as their leaders, and to bring about impressive demonstrations in their favour. It may be true that much of their support was drawn from the lower ranks of society; but poverty may be advanced as a motive for insurrection in any people even of Roman or Punic origin. Nothing is said in ancient sources, and nothing need be said now, about the hereditary impatience of the native folk, the Berbers, or the ruthlessness inspired by their worship of the anthropophagous Saturn.[51] Nor is it true that Donatists were always the oppressed: in Optatus' time they boasted authors who were as learned

---

[47] See Teutsch (1962), pp. 101-107.
[48] See Frend (1952a), Brisson (1958), and for criticism Mandouze (1960).
[49] See Optatus II.4; Jerome, *Alt.* etc.
[50] At I.18 Optatus insists that the only adversaries of Caecilian were Numidians; at III.3 he says that the possessions of the catholic church are denied to *barbarae gentes*.
[51] See Frend (1952a), pp. 32-47.

and as eloquent as any that the catholics could provide,[52] and at the outbreak of the schism they would seem to have had enough faith in the Empire to make a series of appeals. Once the failure of these had made them rebels, they would naturally align themselves with dissidents who, like the robber-bands called circumcellions, were more concerned to rectify injustices in Africa than to tamper with a judgment overseas.[53]

Although the imperial edicts of the late fourth century stigmatized the Donatists as heretics, Optatus is prepared to distinguish heresy from schism. He is perhaps the first African to do so;[54] but it is easy enough for him to accept the sacraments of the Donatists when he does not admit that the ministry is any proof of virtue in the minister.[55] He aggravates the offence of his opponents to a nicety by arguing from the precedents in Scripture that apostasy itself is not so impious as schism.[56] The tendency to sin being universal and its effects being often secret, no Christian has the right to judge another, and to act as the Donatists do is to pre-empt the work of Christ on the final day. The Church is a field that bears both wheat and tares, a net containing every kind of fish.[57] This reasoning, which was soon to be applied with greater force against both Donatists and Pelagians by Augustine, had already been used by a Donatist, Tyconius,[58] in a fruitless remonstration with the rigour of his own conventicle. It was by the strength of precedent, however, that the rigorists prevailed.

Optatus either fails to note the witnesses on the Donatist side or claims them as his own. He has no right, for example, to Tertullian of

---

[52] Parmenianus himself being one; the eminent scholar Tyconius was cited as an ally of the catholic case in Augustine's *Contra Parmenianum*, and his rules of interpretation are treated with great respect in the latter's *De Doctrina Christiana*.

[53] See Frend (1952b), with Grasmuck (1954) and Kriegbaum (1990) on differing attitudes to the role of the state in ecclesiastical affairs. Optatus III.4 refers to the uncontrolled atrocities of the circumcellions.

[54] Thus Cyprian's Epistle 73 makes no distinction between Novatianists, who merely supported an anti-Pope, and Marcionites, who denied the Trinity and the Incarnation.

[55] See note 78.

[56] See Book VII.1ff. This paradoxical argument may betoken a hardening of opinion as he embarked on a second edition

[57] See III.7 and IV.9, though the parables are used far more explicitly by Augustine and Jerome (*Alt.* 22). Both parables occur in Matthew 13, and dispute over their application is already attested by Hippolytus of Rome in his attack on the laxity of Bishops Callistus, *Refutatio* IX.12.22-23

[58] On Tyconius see Batiffol (1920), Vol I, pp. 109ff.

Carthage, who was not afraid of schism and did not forgive apostasy.[59] And he quotes the name, but not the words of a Carthaginian bishop, widely admired in both the eastern and western provinces, whose high view of his own bishopric appeared to put the Donatists beyond all danger of refutation in their native Africa. Cyprian - Pope Cyprian, as some called him[60] - had opposed the Roman schism of Novatian, who contended that the elected Pope Cornelius had erred by pardoning Christians who had lapsed under persecution. In his struggle against subversive factions in his own city, he insisted that no charismatic authority should be accorded to a martyr without the guidance of the official clergy.[61] By itself this gave a better argument to the orthodox than the Donatists, but the latter could profess to be true successors of the saint in the austerity of their ecclesiastical discipline, and above all in their doctrine of the sacraments, which entailed that there could be no valid baptism that was not performed by a duly-appointed minister of God. Cyprian had maintained, against Bishop Stephen of Rome, that recipients of schismatic baptism ought to be rebaptized when they sought communion with catholics;[62] and the fact that the Donatists rebaptized those catholics who joined them, whereas the catholics did not repeat any baptism administered in the proper form, was cited by some Donatists as a proof that they had a better claim to be the one church of Christ.

. The practice of rebaptism was defended by the Donatist Bishop of Carthage, Parmenianus, who was also to provoke two long polemics from Augustine.[63] Using Biblical images already adduced by Cyprian, Parmenianus argued that because the church is one - the second Paradise, the ark to save the nations, the eternal kingdom signified by

[59] Tertullian is cited at I.9, but his *De Pudicitia* 10 seems to me to announce a physical secession from ordinary congregations.

[60] See Epistle 30, where the Roman clergy address him with the title Papa, and Benson (1897), pp. 29-31.

[61] See Cyprian, Epistle 52; Benson (1897), pp. 118-171.

[62] See Epistle 73 and Puller (1893), pp. 51-86, where it is noted that a clear decision against the position of Cyprian may not have been taken as early as the Council of Nicaea in 325, which is often thought to have vindicated Stephen of Rome.

[63] Augustine, *Bapt.* VI-VII is our source for the decisions of the Carthaginian council under Cyprian, which approved the rebaptism of schismatics, though not the excommunication of those who held the contrary opinion.

Israel - it can only have one rite of initiation.[64] Whereas the catholic inference was that baptism is valid whether administered by a catholic, a Novatianist or a Donatist, that of Parmenianus was that only one of these churches had the power to confer the sacrament, and he tried of course to demonstrate that this one was his own. In reply Optatus does not doubt the applicability of verses from the Old Testament to ecclesiastical discipline; on the contrary, he not only expounds each passage in his own favour, but presses other texts against the Donatists with an ingenuity seldom imitated in his own day, and perhaps unmatched before the Reformation. Augustine himself cannot condone the equation of Donatus with the apostate depicted by Ezekiel as the fallen king of Tyre.[65]

Augustine was to develop a theology of baptism that was well beyond the training or capacity of the Bishop of Milevis. It requires no common genius to argue, first, that the Church as a school of charity must bear with its sinful brethren; next that baptism, though it is the infallible gift of God, has no benign effects outside this school of charity; and finally that the Donatists are thus unwitting creditors of this universal charity, whom the church must now constrain, with all the force at its disposal, to accept the blessings promised at the font.[66] The arguments of Optatus, by comparison, are both threadbare and redundant, though it is a point of interest to theology that he shares the Latin doctrine of an inherent sinfulness in human beings, which at once explains the necessity of sinning and excuses the church's toleration of it.[67] He builds (perhaps unwittingly) on Cyprian's principle that catholicity is the keystone of the church;[68] and, if he lacks Augustine's subtlety in wedding

---

[64] See Optatus I.5ff and II.1ff.

[65] See Optatus III.3 and Augustine, *Cath.* 42. It may be observed that Augustine, by resisting typological applications of such phrases as "lying water" and "oil of the sinner" to the visible sacraments reinforces the tradition of construing the Bible allegorically (i.e. with generic and moral rather than with particular and historical denotation).

[66] On Augustine's contribution to the theology of a global catholic church see Batiffol (1920), Vol I, pp. 127-276.

[67] I.8 at least has been taken to imply this, and II.20 asserts that no-one can be perfect. Since, however, Optatus states at VII.1 that Seth did not inherit Adam's sin, he had not yet arrived at Augustine's notion of a biological transmission of sin from Adam to all his posterity.

[68] On Optatus' relation to Cyprian see Eno (1973) and (1993). Cyprian's notion of catholicity assumes the primacy of Peter, but not a local perpetuation of that primacy in Rome.

ecclesiology with theology, he does, by his distinction between the members and the gifts of the church, anticipate Augustine's cardinal premiss that we can have a church without ministers, but not a church without Christ.[69]

Optatus' definition of Christian unity sets him apart from other Africans, whether catholic or Donatist, in that it indicates the primacy of Rome. The man who forgets the Council of Arles is able to supply the names of all the bishops who sat at the Roman session with Miltiades, as though it would be superfluous to recount any more proceedings after this.[70] A certain *principalitas*, indeed, had been accorded to the Roman see in the second century by Irenaeus,[71] but Cyprian of Africa had refused to bow to the verdict of Pope Stephen in the third. Tertullian stood with Cyprian,[72] and if Augustine never denied the primacy of Rome, he never affirmed it in the works of his maturity.[73] Optatus represents the views of catholic bishops in the half-century after the death of Constantine, when they found that his son Constantius favoured heretics while his grandson Julian turned to paganism.[74] Naturally they came to feel that the best defence of orthodoxy was a strong episcopate. In 343 the western council of Sardica declared that this implied a sovereign Papacy, and the privileges of the Apostolic see in the western provinces were confirmed in 378 by the Emperor Gratian on behalf of Pope Damasus.[75] The latter was succeeded by Siricius, who preferred, like his contemporary Optatus, to base the Roman claim to primacy on that which Christ accords in

---

[69] Cf Augustine, *Cresc.* II.13.

[70] See Optatus I.23-5.

[71] See Irenaeus, *AH* III.2. Molland (1950) and Abramowski (1977) deny that Irenaeus intended to assert the Papal primacy. Since Irenaeus does not distinguish presbyters from bishops, he does not appear to hold a doctrine of "apostolical succession" through episcopal ordination, and may be adducing Rome as the exemplar, not the norm, of catholicity.

[72] See n. 58. He remained, like Cyprian, a proponent of catholicity; thus the attack on Praxeas, *Adversus Praxean* 1, for turning the Bishop of Rome against the Montanists, presumes that this Bishop's office gives him authority over other congregations. He was not a true schismatic, since he ordained no rival clergy, and Rankin (1995) is therefore right to argue that he never left the church.

[73] I do not think that the Roman Catholic historian Batiffol (1920), Vol I, pp. 184-209 succeeds in explaining why Augustine abandons the Romanizing interpretation of the Petrine texts in his prose writings against the Donatists.

[74] See Optatus II.16 and notes.

[75] See Puller (1893), pp. 177-82.

Matthew's Gospel to St Peter.[76] Optatus did not live to see the estrangement that ensued between Rome and the catholic church in Africa.[77] With his reading of the "Petrine texts", his principle that only bishops have the right to speak and his insistence that the sacraments work by virtue of their ministry,[78] he endorses a political elevation of the clergy which would finally emancipate them from both king and people; borrowing the same word, *operarius*, to designate both ministers of the sacraments and officers of martial law,[79] he presents the reign of Constans, son of Constantine as a happy partnership of church and state.

The writings of Optatus thus shed light on, and may even have contributed to, one important process in church history. He is also to be valued as a rare, although a highly tendentious, witness to the actions of Macarius and Ursacius, the military commanders who were charged by the Emperor Constans with the futile task of bringing peace to Africa.[80] The utility of his work for the historian, however, lies primarily in the appendices, the materials collected there being all the more reliable because they belie the narrative which the editor has constructed, as other evidence contradicts his dating. The Donatists compiled their martyrologies, Eusebius preserved a few of Constantine's less interesting directives, and Augustine quotes some records of sectarian proceedings;[81] but had tradition been less kind to Optatus, almost all the offical records would be lost.

The Appendix is a collection of ten documents, which do not seem to have been edited by Optatus. If he had, he could not have failed to see that Appendix 5 comes from the aftermath of the Council of Arles in 314 and not from the preparation for the Roman hearing of the previous year. Had he been the compiler of the archive, he would no doubt have included the epistle from the Donatists to Constantine which

---

[76] See Puller (1893), p. 183.

[77] See Munier (1972/3) and Puller (1893), p. 185ff.

[78] See Matthew 16.18-19; Optatus II.4 and VII.4 in this volume.

[79] See especially I.6 (*operarii* of unity) and V.5 (*operarius* of baptism). Each is justified by a divine commission.

[80] See Book III, with Frend (1952a), pp. 168-207. Optatus apears to have written at the inception of, and perhaps with a hope of preventing, the Donatists' triumphant interlude under Optatus and Gildo (Frend, *ibid.*, pp. 208-226).

[81] See Eusebius, *HE* X.5; Augustine, *Brev.* and *Cresc.* III.

is cited in the first book of his own history, and also the proceedings of the Numidian bishops, the "protocol of Cirta", to which he alludes at I.14. Augustine quotes the Protocol at greater length, together with the exact words of the judgment which Constantine pronounced in 313.[82]

Also omitted are the records which the Donatists themselves brought to the Carthaginian conference of 403, and the letters from the Emperor to Miltiades and Chrestus of Syracuse which are preserved for us in the tenth book of Eusebius' *Ecclesiastical History*.[83] Almost all the documents in the archive were written by Constantine or his officers to persons holding authority in Africa and Numidia, or else within these provinces and under the supervision of the local magistrates. The exception is the letter from the bishops at Arles (Appendix 4), copies of which will have been brought back to Africa by the catholics who put their names to it. Caecilian himself may have had a copy of the letter (Appendix 6) which declared that he was still to be detained for a further hearing after Arles. Appendix 2 implies that when the records of a trial were made available it was through the secretaries (*exceptores*) who had been present, though it is not clear that they had any other office than their own houses, or any regular duty to keep these records or pass them on. Some of the imperial letters may have been retained in the houses of provincial governors.[84] Our archivist would therefore seem to have been an African of the catholic party, who had access to public records in his own country, but did not hold any commerce with the Donatists or take pains to gather evidence overseas.

The archivist has tried to arrange the documents according to the sequence of events described. The order is as follows:

1. Proceedings under Zenophilus, held in 320, but referring to events in the persecution of 303. These "prove" that the opponents of Caecilian gave both money and books to the persecutors, buying their own promotions to ecclesiastical office and compounding these enormities with robbery of the poor.

---

[82] *Cresc.* III.30 and *Brev.* III.82.

[83] *HE.* X.5. Yet Chrestus does not appear in Appendix 4.

[84] To judge at least by hints in Appendix 2. One may gather from Corcoran (1996), pp. 31-3 that the imperial archives are better understood than those of the provinces.

2. Proceedings held in 314 or 315 to establish that the charges against Felix of Abthugni were fictitious.
3. A letter of Constantine to the *vicarius* Aelafius, announcing the forthcoming Council of Arles to ratify the verdict pronounced in 313 at Rome. This, with its unknown addressee and open declaration of the writer's intent to make the whole world catholic, is the document most likely to be spurious.
4. The letter of the bishops at the Council of Arles, which began on August 1, 314 A.D. This, since it does not allude to Caecilian, and offers only a qualified acknowledgment of the Roman primacy, cannot be a forgery, or at least not by Optatus.
5. A favourable letter from Constantine to the catholic bishops of Africa in the aftermath of the Council. This is misquoted and inaccurately dated at Optatus I.23.
6. A letter from Constantine to the Donatist bishops, still in Gaul, announcing a further hearing for their charges against Caecilian. It is clearly not a catholic fabrication.
7. A letter from Constantine to Domitus Celsus, *vicarius* of Africa from April 28, 315 A.D. to Jan 11, 316 A.D. This may be earlier than its predecessor, since Constantine expresses an intention to visit Africa, which he seems to have renounced in Appendix 6.
8. A letter of April 28, 315 A.D. from two magistrates to Domitius Celsus, announcing the departure of the Donatists from Arles. This letter must have been written before Appendices 6 and 7, which indicate that the journey was delayed.
9. A letter from Constantine to the catholic bishops of Africa, written in 321 A.D. and reaffirming his hostility to the Donatists.
10. A letter of the same tenor, written in 330 A.D. by Constantine to the catholic bishops of Numidia. By promising a new basilica to the catholics, it indicates that the Emperor lacked either the power or the will to wrest the existing church of Cirta from the schismatics.

Most of these materials belong to the early years of Constantinian rule in Africa and Italy, and show that the Emperor's zeal for the propagation of Christianity was combined with a prudent charity toward the pagan officers whom he charged with the execution of his projects.[85] The Roman world had never heard of a King who forced his subjects to observe his own religion, and the magistrates would have had no inclination to adopt the passing foible of a sovereign who, in any case, was only one of two. Nevertheless this monarch who addresses godly pagans as his coreligionists asks them to extend his special protection to the Christians, and in particular to the catholics who already formed an empire within the Empire. These archives show how quickly, and with what aims, the royal neophyte became the moderator of a universal church.

III. Note on this Translation and Commentary

The appendices to Optatus have been edited, together with other documents of the crisis, by Routh (1846) Von Soden (1913) and most recently by Maier (1987).[86] When I began the translation of Optatus the latest text was that of Ziwsa, published in 1893. I have now had the opportunity to collate this with the edition of Labrousse. The translations of Labrousse and Maier, printed on facing pages to the Latin text, have been more useful to me than the older English rendering by Vassall-Phillips (1913). I know of no full commentary on Optatus in any language, though I have made use of Labrousse's notes, together with those in Hurter's small edition of 1870. The title of the work is called in some editions *Contra Parmenianum* ("against Parmenianus"), though only because it is so described by Jerome, who is more interested in the contents than the name. For this translation, the customary title, *Against the Donatists*, has seemed most serviceable.

The style of my translation is always leaden, sometimes prolix and generally obscure when it attempts to be elevated. If it were otherwise, it would not do justice to the original, the style of which is as poor as is compatible with correct Latinity. That is Optatus' fault, but it is not his fault that his text contains many local names which have not passed into a recognized English form. I have used what I understand to be the nominative case of these, and where the site is known I have supplied

---

[85] See especially the end of Appendix 7 (to Celsus).

[86] Lancel (1988) prefers the text of Ziwsa to that of Van Soden, which is borrowed by Maier for his commentary.

the modern name in the notes and index. Where there is a regular English form, I have adopted it. The localities are depicted on the accompanying map.

Square brackets indicate matter that is absent from some manuscripts, or supplied by modern conjectures; occasionally I have clarified the syntax by the addition of words in ordinary brackets. Bold type is used for excerpts from contemporary documents and letters, italics for titles of books, whether modern or ancient, and for quotations from the scriptures. Readers should be warned that the allusions to the Old Testament will often find no echo in modern versions. Optatus, like most Christians in the western Roman Empire, relied upon the so-called *Vetus Latina*, which was a rendering, not of the Hebrew, but of the Septuagint, the Greek Old Testament used by Hellenized Jews and Gentile Christians. It was his young contemporary Jerome who prepared the Latin translation from the Hebrew, which subsequently became the Vulgate of the Roman Church.

Where my notes to the work and its appendices supply the prosopography and chronography required for the understanding of events, I owe almost everything to previous scholars, to whose research Mazzucco's bibliography (1993) was an indispensable guide. Where I have tried to elucidate the theological argument, I have drawn on my own researches, and I hope that the result will not be found devoid of interest by historians. The catholic church grew up around its sacraments, and the history of its theological statements is in many cases the history of the formulae and practices that were needed to defend them. Optatus is occasionally the only one who tells us what these were in the late fourth century,[87] and he offers in addition an exemplary illustration of the manner in which the Bible, and especially the Old Testament, could be used in their defence. If it is ever true, as some maintain, that what is said is as much a part of history as what is done, it is true *a fortiori* of ecclesiastical history. Conciliar definition, the cement of unity within the church, would have been impossible without a persuasive reading of the scriptures; and in the refutation of sectarians by typology Optatus was a model for Jerome's dialogue against the Luciferians, as my notes to Book II indicate. Above all, as will be

---

[87] See e.g. his reference to the *mitra* at II.19 and to the functions of the *curator*, the use of the term *basilica* and the burning of books under persecution in Appendix I.

evident from my notes throughout the volume, he was the mentor of Augustine, whose polemics against the Donatists (and especially his principle of inexorable charity, described above) contain his most important contribution to the mediaeval theory of the church.

OPTATUS:

First Book against the Donatists

1. All we who are Christians,[1] dearest brethren, are commended to Almighty God by a single faith, part of which is to believe that Our Lord, the Son of God, will come as judge of the age; being the one who has already come and in his own human nature[2] was born through Mary the Virgin; suffered, died, was buried and rose again; and, before he ascended to the heaven whence he had descended, bequeathed to all of us Christians [his own] peace through the Apostles.[3] Lest he should seem to have sent this only upon the Apostles, he spoke thus: What I say to one of you, I say to all.[4] Then he said I give my peace to you, I leave my peace to you.[5] Therefore peace has been given to all Christians, which patently is a thing of God's, as he calls it "mine". When, moreover, he says I give to you, he wishes it not only to be his own, but also that of all who believe in him.

---

[1] The following statement has almost the form of a creed, stressing the humanity and future reign of Christ. as the *Symbolum Nicaenum* (ancestor of our Nicene Creed) had done in 325. The credal belief in the Holy Spirit had not yet been fixed by the Council of Constantinople (381). The reference to the virginity of Mary, possibly important for the doctrine of Christ's inherent sinlessness, is not found in the Nicene Creed, but had been part of others, and was reaffirmed at Constantinople: see Kelly (1972), 100-130 on the "Old Roman Creed".

[2] Literally, "his own man". It was a principle of orthodoxy that the human and divine in Christ could be separated only in thought, and that all his acts as man were also acts as God.

[3] If we follow the MS reading *storiam* (defended by Ziwsa with a reference to Commodianus, *Carmen Apologeticum* 151), we might render, "he bequeathed his history to all of us and his peace through the apostles". Here I have taken *suam* from the *apparatus criticus*. Other conjectures are *victricem pacem* ("he bequeathed his victorious peace"); and *victor iam* in Turner (1925-6) p. 288: "now victorious he bequeathed his peace".

[4] Mark 13.37, though in a different context. As will become apparent, Optatus treats the Bible as a reservoir of texts whose application is determined more by his context than by theirs.

[5] John 14.27; at John 20.21-3 this peace is associated with the gift of the Spirit, often regarded as the bond of unity in the Church (1Cor 12.7-13 etc.). Optatus' citation of this is unparalleled, but most resembles the so-called "Blasphemy of Sirmium" of 357, a statement which attempted (illegitimately, in the later judgment of the orthodox) to reconcile the catholics with other groups who did not accept the full divinity of Christ

2. If this peace had remained sound and unblemished as it was given, and had not been disturbed by the authors of schism, today there would be no dissension between us and our brothers, nor would they be making the inconsolable laments to God which Isaiah the prophet tells of,[6] nor would they be incurring the names and actions of false prophets, nor would they be building up a tumbledown and whitewashed wall, nor would they be ruining those whose minds, though less astute, are yet merely simple; nor would they be holding forth veils of ruin by laying hands improperly on every head; nor would they be blaspheming God or rebaptizing the faithful; nor would we be weeping for the deceived or murdered souls of the innocent, which God has already wept for, saying through the prophet Ezekiel: *Woe to those who make a veil over every head and every age to ruin souls. The souls of my people have been ruined, and they have cursed me among my people, so that they may murder souls that ought not to have died by giving my people empty and seductive tidings.*[7] And yet these wrongs have been committed by those who are our brethren.

3. But, in case anyone should say that I am rash to call people of this kind brethren, we cannot bereave them of Isaiah's prophecies. Although even they do not deny, and everyone is aware, that they feel hatred toward us and curse us, declining to be called our brethren, we nevertheless cannot depart from the fear of God, since the Holy Spirit exhorts us through the prophet Isaiah, saying: You who fear the word of the Lord, hear the word of the Lord: *those who feel hatred toward you and curse you, declining to be called your brethren, say to them nevertheless, "You are our brethren".*[8] They are therefore undoubtedly brethren, though not good ones. So let no-one be surprised to hear me call those people brethren who cannot fail to be brethren. We and they, indeed, share one spiritual birth, but our actions are contrary. For it is also true that Ham, who impiously ridiculed his father's nakedness, was

---

[6] Cited below in chapter 3. The "whitewashed wall" recalls the abusive epithets of Jesus (Matt 23.27) and Paul (Acts 23.3), as well as the practice of whitewashing shrines (cf Jerome, *Contra Vigilantium* 8).

[7] Ezekiel 13.18; the Latin differs greatly from Jerome's later Vulgate, since it follows the Greek translation or Septuagint (see introduction). Optatus here strangely omits a reference to fragments of bread; but cf the extended version at IV.6.

[8] Isaiah 66.5. The same unsolicited charity is extended to the Donatists, with the same text, by Augustine at *Post Gesta* 58.

the brother of innocent men, and incurred the yoke of slavery for his own fault, so that one brother was indentured to another.[9] Therefore this name of brother is not lost even when sin intervenes. But in another place I shall speak of the crimes of those brethren who, sitting over against us, slander us and assail us with scandal, who conspire with that thief who steals from God and make common cause with adulterers, that is with heretics,[10] praising their own sins while they contrive accusations against us, the catholics.[11]

4. All of them indeed clamour in various places with baleful cries, [to which I shall respond severally as occasion warrants]; but we have had difficulty in finding one with whom we can converse by writing and in the present manner. I mean Parmenianus our brother[12] - if, that is, he allows himself to be spoken of by us or by that name. And since they refuse to form an episcopal college with us,[13] let them not be colleagues if they do not wish it; however, as I said above, they are brethren. My brother Parmenianus, then, rather than speak windy and naked words like the others, has not only said but even set out in writing whatever views he was able to form.[14] Since truth compels us to respond to these

<hr>

[9] Genesis 9.22-5. Ham was the son of Noah, a type of Christ in Hilary, *Myst.* 12-14, and the ark was a Biblical type of the Church. Augustine, *Cath.* 9 and 33, reports that certain Donatists had argued, on the basis of Genesis 6.14, that the true Church (i.e. their own) was so sealed that the efficacy of the baptismal water could not escape from it..

[10] The equation of heresy with adultery is an obvious development of Biblical imagery (e.g. Ezekiel 17), and here alludes specifically to Song of Songs 6.8 (see below, n.33).

[11] The term is used in the sense explained by Eusebius, *Contra Marcellum* I.1, "extending throughout the whole world". The eighth decree of the Nicene Council (325) distinguishes the Catholic Church from the Katharoi, or Novatians, Roman schismatics. The term is ridiculed by a Donatist writer at *Passio Donati* 12, but Augustine, *Brev.* III.3 records that at a council of 411 the Donatists had claimed it for themselves.

[12] Successor to Donatus as Bishop of Carthage, banished in 358 but recalled by Julian in 362 (Augustine, *Parm.* I.19; *Retractationes* II.17).

[13] This may refer to general intercourse rather than to any proposal for a formal council. None the less synods to resolve disputed points were frequent among Christians, especially in Africa from the third century on. In the west the Gaulish Council of Arles (314) was preceded perhaps by that of Eliberis/Elvira, and certainly by many in Africa, as can be seen from Benson (1897). As Augustine's *Parm.* reveals, Parmenianus, writing c. 372, rejected the conciliatory arguments of his fellow-Donatist Tyconius. On the proceedings of Donatist Councils see Augustine, *Cresc.* III.22-28, IV.5 etc.

[14] The work (perhaps ironically styled a *scriptura*) which Optatus answers here appears to have been written in five books, perhaps before 366. See Maier (1987), p. 42, n. 12.

words, there will be a certain debate at a distance between us, whereby the desires of others will also be satisfied. For many have often expressed the wish that there should be a conflict between certain champions of each side in order to draw out the truth. This can indeed happen; but since they deny access and forbid approaches, avoiding conference and refusing parley, let you and me, brother Parmenianus, debate on the principle that, seeing I have neither spurned nor despised your writings which you wished to be in the hands and mouths of many, but have listened patiently to whatever you said, you too will listen to my humble answers.

5. For I know, and you do not deny, and everyone of sense perceives, that you have written at such length with no other motive than to administer a shameful beating to the catholic church with your writings. But, as is apparent, you have one thing in mind and your speech says something else. In sum I do not see that everything you say tells against the catholic church: rather, you say much in favour of the catholic church, though you are not a catholic, so that it would not even have been necessary for us to answer your writings, were it not that, among other things that (as we shall show) have nothing to do with us, you said that we had requested military force against you.[15] So poor is your instruction that you asserted what you had not seen and had heard from false reports, despite what we have read in the Epistle of the Apostle Peter: *do not judge your brethren on the strength of opinion.*[16] However, in other parts of your writing you have said some things that count for us and against you, such as the analogies of the flood and circumcision; some that count both for us and for you, like the things that you have said in praise of baptism - except for this one thing, that you have treated the flesh of Christ ineptly; the reason why it counts for you is that, although you are outside, it was none the less from us that you went forth.[17] For this counts for both sides, that you have proved heretics to be excluded from the catholic sacraments - if, that is, you did not associate yourselves with them, when you are patently schismatic. Certain things count for us alone, like your remarks on the unity of the

---

[15] See Optatus III for these events..
[16] Not attested in any Epistle attributed to Peter (cf 1Peter 3.8, 2Peter 1.10). Ziwsa suggests James 4.11. Optatus does, however, cite non-canonical sayings; cf p. 161 n. 74.
[17] Allusion to 1John 2.19.

church, and certain things against you through ignorance, because you are a foreigner, like your reproaches against collaborators and schismatics. Even what you said about the oil and sacrifice of the sinner, that too counts against you. And by this you have said nothing against us, except for your ignorant statement that we requested miltary force; that this statement of yours is a calumny I shall show by irresistible proofs. Take away this calumny, and you are ours.

For what counts more for us, what is more on our side, than your statement, in an analogy with baptism, that the flood happened only once?[18] And when you said that a single circumcision was sufficient for the salvation of the Jewish people, you spoke for us as though you were of our party.[19] For this is the claim that we make by defending the unity of baptism in the Triune name,[20] and does not count for you, who brazenly and illegally repeat the baptism of which these two are figures. And yet you do not deny that what is commanded to be done once should not be repeated. But you, after subtly praising that which is worthy of every expression of praise, have cleverly insinuated a reference to yourselves, as though, being allowed but once, it were allowed to you and forbidden to others. If it is not allowed to collaborators,[21] it should not have been allowed to you, whose leaders we show to have been collaborators. If it is not allowed to schismatics, it should equally not have been allowed to you, among whom is found the origin of the schism. If it is not allowed to sinners, we also convict you of being sinners by divine testimony. And nevertheless, since the fact of being once allowed depends not on the choice of a man but on

---

[18] The analogy between the ark and the Church is followed by a reference to baptism at 1Peter 3.20-1. Cf Tertullian, *Bapt.* 8; Ambrose, *Myst.* 24. For Donatist use of the phrase *unum baptisma* cf. Augustine, *Cresc.* IV.6; *De Unico Baptismo* 10 indicates that Petilian argued that sacrilegious ministers cannot confer the sacrament. Cyprian, the hero of the Donatists, argues in Epistle 73 for rebaptism of Novatianists and Marcionites on the ground that their own baptism, being outside the Church, cannot be the one baptism of Ephesians 4.5.

[19] The analogy between circumcision and baptism is implied by Paul, Gal 5.6 and 5.24, with Romans 6.1ff. Justin, *Trypho* 29 treats circumcision as an unspiritual precursor of baptism.

[20] The usual form, following Matthew 28.19: "baptizing in the name of Father, Son and Holy Ghost". Cf Tertullian, *Bapt.* 6, and the eighth decree of Arles (Appendix 4).

[21] I have used this term throughout to render *traditor*, which signifies one who hands over sacred texts to be burnt.

the fact of being once allowed, therefore we do not correct it after you, since both among us and among you the sacrament is one. The full explanation of this sacrament will be given in the fifth book.

6. Many things indeed you have written brother Parmenianus; yet I do not think that I should answer your several points in the order that you have stated them. For in the first place you offer praises and analogies of baptism, and, except for the flesh of Christ, which you treated badly, the rest is well said.[22] That what you have said counts rather for us will be shown in the proper place. Now in the second place you have excluded heretics, saying that the church is one; but where it is you would not acknowledge. In the third place you have accused collaborators, without specific references or names. In the fourth you have savaged the agents of unity. In the fifth (if I may pass over trifles) you have spoken of the oil and sacrifice of the sinner.

7. But it seems to me best in the first place to indicate the provenance,[23] the identities and the names of the collaborators and schismatics, so that your statements about them may identify their true authors and their own specific culprits. Then I ought to say what and where is the one church that there is, since beside the one there is no other. Thirdly, that military force was not requested by us, and that the crimes alleged against the architects of unity do not pertain to us. In the fourth place, who is the sinner whose sacrifice God rejects, or whose oil is to be shunned. Fifthly about baptism, sixthly about your rash presumption and your errors.

8. But before I say something about particular matters, I shall briefly demonstrate that you have written ineptly about the flesh of Christ. For you have said that that sinful flesh of Christ, when submerged in the flood of the Jordan, was cleansed from universal impurity.[24] You would be right to say this if the flesh of Christ, when baptized, sufficed for all, so that no-one need be baptized for himself. If it were so, the whole

---

[22] Looking ahead to I.8.

[23] Literally "cities". The chief of these, as will appear, was Cirta in Numidia, a province adjoining Africa, but less "Romanised".

[24] Or possibly "from all sins". The later Augustinian view of personal baptism held that it cleanses us from inherited guilt by virtue of Christ's baptism. The Donatists may have thought that Christ was included in Cyprian's statement that when an infant is baptized the sins remitted are not its own but contracted at birth by everyone from Adam (Ep. 59 ad Fidum).

human race would have been there, everything which is born corporeally would have been there. There would be no difference between the faithful and any of the heathen, since there is flesh in everyone; and since there is no-one who does not have flesh, then if, as you have said, the flesh of Christ was submerged in the stream of the Jordan, all flesh would receive this benefit. For the flesh of Christ in Christ is one thing, each person's flesh in himself is another.

What is this opinion of yours that Christ's flesh was sinful? I wish you had said: the flesh of human beings was in the flesh of Christ.[25] Even so you would not have spoken soundly, because everyone who believes is baptized in the name of Christ, not in the flesh of Christ, which belonged peculiarly to him.[26] Add that his flesh, conceived from the Holy Spirit, could not be bathed along with the rest for the remission of sins, as it was seen to have committed no sin.[27] You have added that it was also submerged in the stream of the Jordan. Your use of this word was rather rash, seeing that it ought to have been applied solely to Pharaoh and his people, who sank beneath the weight of his sins like lead, so completely that he remained there.[28] As for the flesh of Christ, you ought not to have said that it was submerged when it descended into the Jordan and then ascended; his flesh is found more holy than the Jordan itself, so that it is more true that it cleansed the water by its descent than that it was cleansed itself.[29]

9. Another point I also cannot pass over. I believe you have acted subtly for the purpose of seducing and deceiving the minds of your audience in that, after the description of circumcision and the flood and after the

---

[25] Tertullian, *De Carne Christi* 16, asserts Christ was born without the "seed of vice" found in other humans. He is thus in the flesh of sin without the sin of the flesh. Augustine (*De Peccatorum Meritis* III.34) says that Christ was born in real but incorrupt flesh; sin is a universal trait of fallen human nature, not an essential characteristic of the nature as God created it.

[26] Cf Origen, *Homilia in Genesim* 3. Augustine (*De Peccatorum Meritis* I, etc.) holds that we inherit Adam's sin by birth, but not the benefits of the Incarnation, which come through the sacraments. For baptism in the name of Christ cf Acts 2.38.

[27] Baptism being primarily for remission of sin (Tertullian, *Bapt.* 7 etc.), Christ's had to be explained in some other way.

[28] Exodus 15.5, though there the army is said to sink like lead.

[29] Cf Ignatius, *Ephesians* 18.2 (c. 112 A.D.), where the birth of Christ from Mary and the Spirit is already emphasised.

praise of baptism, you have (as it were) attempted to revive heretics already dead and buried in oblivion, together with their errors, men of whom it seemed that not only their vices but their very names were unknown in the provinces of Africa. Marcion,[30] Praxeas, Sabellius,[31] Valentinus[32] and others, right up to the Cataphrygians,[33] were overcome in their own times by Victorinus of Petau[34] and the Roman Zephyrinus[35] and the Carthaginian Tertullian[36] and by other champions of the catholic church. Why do you wage war with the dead, who have nothing to do with the affairs of our time? But, since you are a schismatic of today and have no sin that you can prove against the catholics, you have

---

[30] From Pontus in Asia Minor; is alleged to have taught that the world was created by a god who was "just" but not "good", and redeemed by the son of one who was "good", but had nothing to do with matter. See Irenaeus, *AH* I.27.2 and n. 31 below.

[31] Praxeas and Sabellius are both said to have denied the distinction of persons in the Trinity. In the west, they were often called Patripassians, because they made the Father suffer on the Cross. See nn. 35-36 below.

[32] Attacked at length by their contemporary Irenaeus, *AH* I-II, the Valentinians of the second century allegedly taught that the world was caused by the transgression of one element of the Godhead, called Sophia. Although the matter of the world was derived from her, the Valentinians are alleged to have denied that Christ took flesh. See Hippolytus, *Refutatio* VI.35.5-7.

[33] Then the usual name for the movement now called Montanism, described by Eusebius, *HE* V.14-19. It engaged in ecstatic prophecy and introduced new rigours into church discipline (Hippolytus, *Refutatio* VIII.19.2).

[34] According to Jerome, *De Viris Illustribus* 74, this third century author wrote a work *Against all Heresies*. He is now known chiefly by the extant fragments of his *De Apocalypsi.*

[35] Bishop of Rome from 201-217. According to Hippolytus (*Refutatio* IX.6) he was partly responsible for the spread of Sabellianism in Rome, and he may also be the Roman bishop whom Tertullian (*Adv. Prax.* 1) attacks for his refusal to recognise the new prophecy. The letters attributed to him shed no light on the claim made here by Optatus

[36] The first great Latin Christian writer, c. 150-c.225. His works include an *Adversus Marcionem* (our chief source on this heretic), an *Adversus Valentinianos* (based largely on Irenaeus) and an *Adversus Praxean* (our only source on this man). Although he favoured the "new prophecy", estranged himself from the church (*De Pudicitia* 10), attacked bishops (*Adv. Prax.* 1, *De Pudicitia.* 1) and is said by Jerome (*De Viris Illustribus* 53) to have formed his own sect, Tertullian was a pillar of orthodoxy for the Latin Church and is here described as a catholic. For the view that he never left the catholic church see Rankin (1995).

therefore decided to eke out the prolixity of your writing by mentioning so many heretics along with their errors.[37]

10. Now there is another question, why you have mentioned those who do not possess the sacraments which are seen to be common to us and to you. Health demands no medicine; virtue secure in itself does not look outside for reinforcements; truth requires no arguments. It is the sick who seek remedies, the idle and weak who engage reinforcements, the liar who searches for arguments. Meanwhile you have said that heretics cannot possess the gifts of the church, and you have said rightly; for we know that the churches of individual heretics are prostitutes without any legal sacraments, who lack the status of an honest marriage. These Christ rejects as superfluous, he who is the bridegroom of the one church, as he himself declares in the Song of Songs. When he praises one, he condemns the others, since apart from one which is truly catholic, the others are believed to exist by heretics, but do not. This follows from the fact that he affirms in the Song of Songs, as we said above, that there is one dove that is his,[38] the same being his chosen bride, his enclosed garden and his sealed font,[39] so that none of the heretics may have the keys which Peter alone received,[40] nor

---

[37] On Donatist catalogues of heresy see Augustine, *Cresc.* II.4, and cf Cyprian, Epistle 73. As Epiphanius' *Panarion* of 376 and Augustine's compendious attack on all heresies reveal, these assaults on the dead were not confined to schismatics. For a pagan precedent, see Plutarch, *Adversus Colotem* 24.1.

[38] Song of Songs 6.8; cf Epiphanius, *Panarion* LXXX.9, the great fourth-century compendium, where the 80 heresies (including Donatism only under Novatianism) are said to correspond to the eighty concubines of Solomon. Cf also Mark 1.11; Augustine, *Bapt.* I.15 and IV.4; *Cresc.* II.21. Ambrose, *Myst.* 10 and 24 mentions the dove in connexion with the Ark

[39] Song of Songs 4.12 (Septuagint). Cf Augustine, *Cresc.* II.18.

[40] Matthew 16.19. Optatus obviously accepts the Roman equation of Peter with the see of Rome, as does the longer version of Cyprian's *De Unitate Ecclesiae* 4. Passages collected by Benson (1897), pp. 197-9 show that Cyprian was able to deny the affirmation of Roman primacy in Matthew 16.19, and the Donatists, who objected to the "transmarine" tribunal which condemned them,, would have agreed. Even in Augustine, *Cath.* 60, Matthew 16.18 is not referred exclusively to Peter.

the ring by which the font is said to have been sealed; nor (he says) is any of them the occupant of the garden in which God plants his trees.[41]

Your lengthy discourse about these heretics, though it has nothing to do with the present matter, has been sufficient and more. But I wonder why you saw fit to join yourselves to those who are patently schismatics, when you have denied the gifts of God both to these very heretics and to yourselves who are in schism. For you have said, among other things, that schismatics are cut off like branches from the vine, and, being destined for punishment, are reserved like dry wood for the fires of Gehenna.[42] But I see you are as yet ignorant that the schism at Carthage was created by your leaders. Inquire into the origin of these affairs, and you will find that you have pronounced this judgment on your own party, as you have numbered heretics with schismatics. For it was not Caecilian who seceded from Majorinus your grandfather, but Majorinus from Caecilian;[43] nor did Caecilian secede from the see of Peter or Cyprian but Majorinus.[44] It is his see that you occupy, which before that same Majorinus had no existence. And when it is patent and notorious that this is how these things were done, and it is manifestly obvious that you are the heirs of collaborators and schismatics, I am rather surprised, brother Parmenianus, that being a schismatic you have elected to join schismatics with heretics.[45]

Or if that seems right to you and this is your decision, tot up those things which you have said a little earlier. For you declared it to be impossible that one who was soiled could wash with his false baptism, that the unclean could cleanse, that the subverter could restore, that the

---

[41] The Church is imaged as paradise following Irenaeus, *AH* V.20.2; cf. Augustine, *Bapt.* IV.1 and *Cresc.* II.16. Donatists were happy to use this image, as it is found in Cyprian, Epistle 73, which argues for the rebaptism of those baptised by heretics and schismatics.

[42] Combining John 15.6 with Matthew 5.29.

[43] The attack on Caecilian consisted of the claims that (a) he was ordained by a *traditor* (see *Acta Purgationis Felicis*, Appendix 2); and (b) he conspired with Mensurius to cause the deaths of imprisoned confessors by starving them (*Passio Abitinensium* 15). See n. 59 for a further charge against Mensurius.

[44] After the appeal to Rome, described below.

[45] The distinction between heresy and schism was asserted by the Donatists themselves, according to Augustine, *Cresc.* II.4. It was not clearly made by Cyprian of Carthage, whose Epistle 73 assumes that Marcionites and Novatianists are on an equal footing. A schismatic separates himself from the church as an institution, but does not deny its doctrines.

condemned one could bring freedom, that the criminal could bestow pardon, that the damned could grant absolution. All these things could well have applied to the heretics alone: they have falsified the creed,[46] seeing that one speaks of two gods when God is one, another tries to discern the Father in the person of the Son, another steals from the son of God the flesh by which the world has been reconciled to God,[47] and there are others of this kind who are known to be strangers to the catholic sacraments. Hence you should repent of having added schismatics also to this class of men; for you have turned the sword of judgment against yourself, since you think you were aiming at others, and have not considered how great a distinction there is between schismatics and heretics. Hence it is that you also do not know what the holy church is; and thus you have confused everything.

11. The catholic church is made known by simplicity and truth in knowledge, singleness and absolute truth in the sacrament, and unity of minds. A schism, on the other hand, is engendered when the bond of peace is shattered through discordant sentiments, nourished by bitterness, strengthened by rivalry and feuds, so that the impious sons, having deserted their catholic mother, go out and separate themselves, as you have done, and, having been cut off from the root of the mother church by the blade of bitterness, depart in erratic rebellion.[48] Nor are they able to do anything new or anything else, except what they have long since learned from their own mother.

12. Heretics, on the other hand, exiles from the truth who have deserted the sound and truest creed, fallen from the bosom of the church through their impious sentiments, contemptuous of their good birth, have set out to deceive the ignorant and unlearned by claiming to be born of themselves.[49] And whereas they had previously fed on wholesome foods,

---

[46] Translating *symbolum*, the Latin equivalent of the Greek *sumbolon*, which usually denotes an official creed. See nn. 1-5 above; earlier Latin writers such as Tertullian had referred instead to a "rule of faith" (*regula fidei*).

[47] Marcion, Praxeas/Sabellius and Valentinus. See nn. 30-32.

[48] Cf 1John 2.19, John 15.1-6, Hebrews 12.15, Revelation 22.16 etc. The statement that the Church has only one root underpins Cyprian's argument for rebaptism in Epistle 73, so it is likely that Parmenianus also used this image.

[49] Cf 2Timothy 3.6-7 on the seduction of the ignorant. The claim to be born of himself is ascribed to Satan by Prudentius, *Hamartigenia* 171; cf also one reading of Ezekiel 29.3 (LXX).

through the corruption of a bad digestion they vomited forth lethal poisons in their impious disputations to destroy their wretched victims.[50] You therefore see, brother Parmenianus, that heretics, being wholly estranged from the house of truth, are the only ones who have different and false baptisms, by which he who is soiled cannot wash, nor the unclean cleanse, nor the subverter restore, nor the condemned bring freedom, nor the criminal bestow pardon, nor the condemned grant absolution. You have rightly closed the garden to the heretics, you have rightly recalled the keys to Peter, you have rightly taken away the power of cultivation lest those who are patently alien to the garden and paradise of God should cultivate their trees; you have rightly taken away the ring from those who are not allowed to admit to the font. To you schismatics,[51] on the other hand, although you are not in the catholic church, these things cannot be denied, because you have administered with us the true and common sacraments. So, whereas all these things are rightly denied to heretics, why did you think it proper to desire that these be denied to you also also, who are manifestly schismatics? For you stand without. So far as in us lies, our wish was that only heretics should be damned; so far as in you lies, you have desired that we strike you together with them in a single judgment.

13. But now, that we may return to dealing with the several points in the proposed order, hear in the first place, who the collaborators were, and learn more fully who were the authors of the schism. In Africa it is well known that two evils of the worst kind were committed, one in collaboration, the other in schism, but both evils were apparently committed at the same time and by the same people. You should learn, then, brother Parmenianus, what you clearly do not know. For a full sixty years ago and more[52] the storm of persecution spread throughout the whole of Africa, which made martyrs of some, confessors of others, laid low not a few in grievous death, but let those who hid go

---

[50] Cf 1Cor 3.2, 2Peter 2.22 and the frequent comparisons of heretics to serpents (Athanasius, *Festal Letter* 29 etc.).

[51] See n. 45 above.

[52] *ferme sexaginta annos et quod excurrit.* The meaning of *ferme* must be "exactly" here, since *quod excurrit* can only mean "and upwards". It is surprising none the less that Optatus does not suggest a larger figure, since he either wrote or revised his work more than seventy years after the persecution of 303.

unharmed.[53] Why should I recall the laity, who at that time were supported by no office in the church? Why recall the great number of ministers?[54] Why recall the deacons who stood in the third, or the presbyters in the second rank of priesthood? The very foremost, the leaders of all, certain bishops of that time, in order to procure a few minute extensions to this uncertain light at the cost of life eternal, impious gave over the instruments of the divine law. Among them were Donatus of Mascula,[55] Victor of Russicade,[56] Marinus from the Aquae Tibilitanae,[57] Donatus of Calama[58] and the murderer Purpurius of Limata, who, when interrogated about the sons of his own sister, because he was said to have confessed to having ordered their execution in the prison of Milevis, said: "I both killed them and kill, not only them, but also everyone who has acted against me"[59] Also there was Maenalius,[60] who, in order not to be convicted of offering incense by his

---

[53] On the history of the persecution see Frend (1952a); De Ste-Croix (1954); Frend (1965); Barnes (1982), pp. 15-43. My reading of I.17 suggests that Maximian, Diocletian's partner, was as willing an oppressor as Diocletian and Galerius.

[54] Turner (1925-6) p. 289 argues that these ministers will be subdeacons; but cf Book 2 n. 50.

[55] Not the great Donatus: Mascula is the modern Khenchela. In the Acts of this meeting, held at Cirta and recorded in Augustine, *Cresc.* III.30, Donatus gives an ambiguous answer and rests his case with God. The aim of the meeting, according to Augustine, Epistle 43.12-17, was to cover the crimes of those present by incriminating the absent, and to gratify Lucilla, on whom see I.18-19 and Appendix 1.

[56] In the Acts (n.54) he admits to having capitulated to Valentianus. Rus(s)icade is the modern Philippeville.

[57] In the Acts (n.54) he admits to having given chartulas to Pollus. Thibilis is the modern Announa.

[58] In the Acts (n.54) he is said to have collaborated by handing over medicinal codices, a ruse forbidden by Tertullian. Calama is the modern Guelma.

[59] Recorded in the Acts (n.54), where he argues that Secundus too could have purchased his life only by being a traditor. Augustine, *Brev.* III.27, says that Purpurius killed the sons of his sister while they were imprisoned in Milevis. It is possible that Optatus acquired his information in his native town.

[60] See Maier (1987) p. 117, n. 60. Maenalius does not appear in Augustine's version of the Acts, but an account of his obstinacy is given in Appendix 7.

fellow-citizens,[61] shrank from attending a conference of his own people by feigning a disease of the eyes.

14. These and others, whom we shall prove a little further on to have been your leaders, assembled after the persecution in the city of Cirta, since the churches had not yet been restored, at the house of Urbanus Carisius on March 13,[62] as the writings of Nundinarius, then a deacon,[63] testify, and as is witnessed by the antiquity of the documents which we shall be able to produce for those who doubt it. For we have appended to the last part of this book a complete record of these matters as a full confirmation. These bishops, on interrogation by Secundus of Tigisis, confessed their collaboration. Purpurius alleged against Secundus himself that he also stayed a long time with those who remained, and did not flee, yet was released, and had not been released without reason, but rather because he had collaborated. Forthwith all stood and began to murmur, and Secundus, fearing their vehemence, took the advice of the younger Secundus, his brother's son, that he should commit a case like this to God.[64] Those who had remained were consulted: that is, Victor of Garba, Felix from Rotarium and Nabor from Centuriona.[65] These replied that a case like this should be committed to God. And Secundus said: "Be seated, all of you"; then all said: "Thanks be to

---

[61] The burning of incense on an altar was often the only act required of Christians by officials. On its importance in pagan religion see Nicholson (1994), p. 6, citing the 3rd/4th century apologist Arnobius, *Adversus Gentes* VII.26.

[62] Augustine, *Cresc.* III.29 gives the date as March 4 303 and Urbanus Donatius as the proprietor. See Maier (1987), p. 114 and p. 118, nn. 26-8. Augustine, *Brev.* III. 31-2, reports that at the Carthaginian council of 411 the Donatists repudiated the records of these proceedings on the grounds that twelve bishops could not have congregated in one house at a time of persecution. The objection was, however, overruled by the magistrate, and the date of the meeting determined (by Augustine) as March 5 305. Lancel (1979) shows that his dating is precarious, not least because it implies that persecution had abated before Maximian's abdication on May 1 305.

[63] Nundinarius, deacon to the alleged collaborator Silvanus, is frequently asked for information in Appendix 1 and citedby Augustine, *Cath.s* 46 and *Cresc.* III.33, but the writings ascribed to him here are lost.

[64] See the Acts of the meeting at Cirta (n.54). Thiges or Tigisis is the modern Kourbata. See further n. 70 on Secundus.

[65] Their names appear at the end of the Acts (n.54) where they agree that the alleged *traditores* should be left to the judgment of God. Victor of Garba is probably the same Victor who became the first Donatist "Bishop" in Rome: Optatus II.4.

God", and sat. So now you know, brother Parmenianus, who were the manifest collaborators.

15. Then shortly after this, all these people - such as they were, collaborators, sacrificers and murderers - went to Carthage and after the ordination of Caecilian, created a schism by ordaining Majorinus, whose see you occupy. And since it has been demonstrated that your leaders were guilty of collaboration, it follows that these same people were the authors of the schism. So that this fact may be clear and manifest to all, it must be shown from what root the branches of error stretch forth even up to the present day, and from what font this rivulet of foul water, creeping secretly, has diffused right up to our own times. It must be said whence and where this other evil is known to have arisen, what causes conspired, what persons were active, who the authors of this evil were, who nourished it, whose judgments between the parties were sought by the Emperor, what judges sat, where the council took place, what verdicts were uttered.

Our subject is a division; and in Africa, as in the other provinces, there was one church, before it was divided by those who ordained Majorinus, whose hereditary see you occupy. It must be seen, who remained in the root with the whole world, who went out, who occupied another see, who erected altar against altar, who performed an ordination in the face of another valid ordination, who lies under the sentence of the Apostle John: *For they were not of us,* he says, *for if they had been of us, they would have remained with us.*[66] Therefore he who has chosen not to remain at one with his brethren has followed heretics and, like the Antichrist, has gone out.

16. No-one is unaware that this took place at Carthage after the ordination of Caecilian, and indeed through some factious woman or other called Lucilla, who, while the church was still tranquil and the peace had not yet been shattered by the whirlwinds of persecution, was unable to bear the rebuke of the archdeacon Caecilian.[67] She was said

---

[66] At last an explicit quotation of 1John 2.19; cf, above, n. 15. For the Antichrist see 1John 2.22, 2John 1.7. Augustine quotes 1John 2.19 at *Bapt.* III.26, another work against Parmenianus.

[67] See Appendix 1 6 and 20, and Augustine, *Cresc.* III.33, though Optatus adds much information not found elsewhere. Adoration of martyrs is attested, e.g.. by Tertullian, *De Monogamia* 10, though bishops had attempted to restrain it since the time of Cyprian. See

to kiss the bone[68] of some martyr or other - if, that is, he was a martyr - before the spiritual food and drink, and, since she preferred to the saving cup the bone of some dead man, who if he was a martyr had not yet been confirmed as one, she was rebuked, and went away in angry humiliation. As she raged and grieved, a storm of persecution suddenly arose to prevent her submitting to discipline.

17. At the same time a certain deacon called Felix, who was arraigned as a criminal because of a notorious letter about some tyrannical Emperor or other,[69] is said to have taken refuge in fear of danger at the house of Mensurius.[70] When he was asked for, Mensurius publicly refused; a report was sent, and the reply was that, if Mensurius did not

---

his Epistles 22, 25 etc., and the 25th and 60th canons of Eliberis (c. 305). Dolger (1932) and Frend (1969) p. 546 show that Lucilla herself was regarded as a martyr. Augustine, *Cathos* 73, calls her *femina nobilis*, but this may be a sarcasm rather than an indication of her civic status. See further Lockwood (1990).

[68] Or possibly "mouth" (*os*) if the body had not yet decayed.

[69] Since *tyranno* should mean "usurper", the Emperor, *pace* Lancel (1979), is unlikely to be Severus, legitimately appointed as Augustus of the west in 306. Kriegbaum (1986), pp. 135-43 persuasively maintains that he is Maximianus, father of Maxentius, who broke with the latter and claimed the title Augustus in 308, three years after his reluctant abdication as the partner of Diocletian. This agrees with the view of Barnes (1975), though Barnes understands the "tyranny" to consist primarily in persecution. Frend and Clancy (1977) suggest that the tyrant was Maxentius and the charge (perhaps as late as 311) political. They ask against Barnes (a) why Mensurius' protection of Felix was not remembered by his catholic supporters; and (b) how the church of Mensurius had retained its valuables if persecution had persisted from 303 to 308. But we can answer: (a) the probity of Felix was more questionable than that of either Caecilian or Mensurius; and (b) although the council of Secundus presupposes an abatement of the persecution it may have been later than 305, or else Domitius Alexander, who proclaimed himself ruler of Africa after Maximian and Maxentius disagreed, may have renewed the persecution at the instance of Maximian. The date of 308 for the outbreak of the Donatist controversy accords with the assertion of Tyconius (Augustine, Epistle 93.43) that it started forty years before the pacification of Africa by Macarius in 347.

[70] Bishop of Carthage from 303 or earlier to 311. According to Augustine, *Brev.* III.25, the Donatists accused him of having handed over copies of Scripture, or at least of pretending to do so. They appealed to a supposed correspondence with Secundus of Tigisis (cf n. 64 above), in which the latter averred that he himself had not even used deception. When and by whom Mensurius was summoned, and why he could not return, remains uncertain. Frend and Clancy (1977) hold that he was summoned by Maxentius in 311 to answer for his protection of Felix; but, as Kriegbaum (1986) says, the theory that these troubles began with Alexander's usurpation in 308 makes his failure to return more comprehensible.

give up Felix the deacon, he was to be brought to the palace. The congregation was greatly distressed, because the church had a great many ornaments of gold and silver which it could not bury in the ground or carry with it. He entrusted these as if to faithful seniors,[71] making an inventory which he is said to have given to a certain old woman with the proviso that, if he did not return, that woman should give it, when peace was restored to the Christians, to the person whom she found in occupation of the episcopal see. He went off to plead his cause, was ordered to return, but was unable to reach Carthage.

18. The storm of persecution was finished and concluded. When Maxentius, at God's bidding, extended indulgence to Christians,[72] liberty was restored. It is said that in Carthage Botrus and Celestius, craving ordination, took pains to ensure that only local bishops should be sought to perform ordinations in Carthage, the Numidians being absent.[73] Then by the vote of the whole populace, Caecilian was elected and ordained bishop by the hand of Felix of Abthugni.[74] Botrus and Celestius were disappointed of their hopes. When Caecilian took his seat, an account of the gold and silver was handed to him, with witnesses in attendance, just as it had been entrusted by Mensurius. The aforesaid seniors, who had lapped up the prey committed to their avaricious jaws, were called

---

[71] These appear to be persons without ecclesiastical office (not therefore "presbyters") who exercise administrative functions with regard to the congregation. See Rankin (1995), pp. 139-141 for the various theories.

[72] See Maier (1987), p. 114, n.21. If Kriegbaum (n. 58 above) is correct, the indulgence would be later than 308, and would therefore be the act referred to by Eusebius, *Hist. Eccl.* VIII. 14.1. If Optatus is referring to an earlier indulgence, he is the only witness to it. The tradition of a "persecution" of Christians by Maxentius was largely a Constantinian fabrication, though he did banish rival claimants to the Roman see in the hope of peace. See Barnes (1981), pp. 37-9.

[73] There is therefore a reason for the Numidians to object to Caecilian, though the latter is not to blame. The Numidians were persecuted by Florus, perhaps even before the imperial edicts. Their Christianity is supposed by some to have inherited a fanatical quality from the indigenous worship of Saturn: see Frend (1952a). Numidians are singled out for praise by a Donatist writer (Macrobius) in *Passio Maximiani* 2. For the catholics the remoteness of Numidia was a further proof of the marginality of the Donatists. See Augustine, *Cath.* 51 and *Post Gesta* 38; and note the possibility, broached by Alexander (1980), that the catholics invented an obscure see for Donatus.

[74] The attack on Felix (who may or may not be the deacon of I.17: see n. 77) was primarily a means of undermining Caecilian. See Appendix 2 for his acquittal.

together, and, since they were under pressure to return it, withdrew from communion.[75] So also did those who had not succeeded in being ordained by bribery,[76] and Lucilla, who had long been unable to endure discipline. This powerful and factious woman, with all her crew, refused to join in communion. Thus three causes and persons conspired to ensure that malignity worked its effect.

19. The schism of that time, then, was brought forth by the anger of a humiliated woman, nourished by ambition, strengthened by avarice. By these three parties charges were fabricated against Caecilian so that his ordination might be declared improper. A summons to come to Carthage was sent to Secundus of Tigisis. Hither came all the collaborators mentioned above, receiving hospitality from the avaricious, the ambitious and the angry, but not from catholics, by whose petition Caecilian had been ordained. Meanwhile none of the above-named came to the church, where the whole city was gathered with Caecilian. Then Caecilian issued a command: "If there is anything to be proved against me, let an accuser come forth and prove it." At that time nothing could be fabricated against him by all these enemies, but suffered defamation on account of the one who ordained him, who was falsely said by these men to be a collaborator[77]. Once again Caecilian commanded that if Felix, as they believed, had conferred nothing upon him, they themselves should ordain Caecilian as though he were still a deacon.

Then Purpurius, relying on his wonted malice, as though Caecilian too were the son of his sister, spoke as follows: "Let him come forth hither", as though he would lay hands on him to make him bishop and shake his head in repentance.[78] When this was known, the whole church

---

[75] This explains the hostility of the schismatics toward Caecilian. Augustine, Epistle 43.18 seems to imply that the Council was a conspiracy to incriminate Caecilian while exculpating others from the same charge of collaboration.

[76] For accusations of bribery sponsored by Lucilla, see Appendix 1.15ff and notes thereon.

[77] If this Felix is the deacon of I.17 the charges may refer agreement made by himself or Mensurius to compound for his political offence. Appendix 2 throws little light on the substance of the charge.

[78] Or, as Turner (1925-6), wishes to rewrite it, "As if Secundus was going to impose hands on him in his bishopric and break his head with a penance". Cf the Donatist practice of laying hands on lapsed Bishops at I.24, and the note of Hurter (1870), pp. 55 and 64. Kriegbaum (1986) pp. 107-112 suggests that the intention of Purpurius was conciliatory. There had evidently been much animosity before the ordination: Augustine,

FIRST BOOK AGAINST THE DONATISTS 19

held Caecilian back from handing himself over to the brigands. Either he should have been expelled from the see at that time as a criminal or they should have communicated with him as being innocent. The church was filled by the populace, the episcopal see was filled, the altar was in its place, in which previous peaceable bishops - Cyprian, Lucian and others[79] - had made their offerings in the past. Thus it was that some went out and altar was erected against altar and an ordination was performed illicitly, and Majorinus, who had been a reader in the diaconate of Caecilian, a domestic of Lucilla, was ordained Bishop with her approval, and by collaborators who, as we have said above, had confessed their own crimes to each other and had then granted each other indulgence. It is therefore manifest that those who left the church were the ones ordaining, who had been collaborators, and Majorinus, who was ordained.

20. Meanwhile they decided that from the fountain of their own crimes, which their numerous atrocities had turned to overflowing streams, the single charge of collaboration should be diverted against the one who ordained Caecilian; they expected that rumour would not be able to proclaim two similar stories at the same time. So that they might consign their own wrongdoing to silence, they undertook to defame the life of another; and when they themselves could be confuted by the innocent, they made efforts to confute the innocent, sending letters everywhere which had been written at the dictation of bitterness; these we have appended among other actions. While they were still based at Carthage they sent letters before them, so that they might instil false rumours into the ears of all. Rumour spread the lie among the people, and while false charges concerning one were widespread, the extremely real crimes of the above-named persons were concealed in silence. Often crime causes blushes, but at that time there was no-one to prompt the blushes, since, apart from a few catholics, all had sinned and among

---

Brev. III.30, reports a council of uncertain date condemning Caecilian. *Brev.* III.29 says that the Donatists, allegedly citing Optatus, quoted Caecilian as saying, "If those who ordained me were collaborators, let [my accusers] themselves come and ordain me". This disagrees with our text, but does not constitute an admission of irregular ordination.

[79] Cyprian, Bishop of Carthage 248-258, often cited by the Donatists, because of his insistence upon the rebaptism of schismatics. The Lucian of this passage may be his successor or that of Carpophorius, whose name appears in MSS but is bracketed by Ziwsa here. Turner (1925-6) p. 290 rightly argued that this name should be retained.

many an admitted wrong was like the picture of innocence. The outrage of collaboration, which was patently admitted by Donatus of Mascula and the others named above, was not enough; to their collaboration they added the great atrocity of schism.

21. You see therefore, brother Parmenianus, that these two great crimes of collaboration and schism, evil and weighty as they are, belong to your leaders. Acknowledge then, late though it is, that you have assailed your own party, when you were pursuing the other; and even when it is patent that your party are the architects of this other wrong, you still strive to follow them with iniquitous footsteps, so that, what they were the first to do in the name of schism, you also have visibly been doing for a long time and still are. They shattered the peace in their own time, you extinguish unity. Of your parents and of yourselves it can deservedly be said: *if the blind leads the blind, both fall into the ditch.*[80] Rancorous bitterness blinded the eyes of your fathers, emulation has deprived your own of vision. You too are the last who would be able to deny that schism is the worst evil, yet without any qualms you have imitated Dathan and Abiram and Korah,[81] your abandoned masters, nor have you been willing to set before your eyes the fact that this evil is both forbidden by the word of God and severely avenged when committed. Furthermore, the distance between sins is attested either by the remission or by the punishment. To conclude, among other precepts, the divine command has prohibited these three things also: *Thou shalt not kill, thou shalt not follow after strange gods, and at the head of the ordinances: thou shalt not create a schism.*[82] Let us see which of these three ought to be punished and which forgiven. Parricide is the chief offence; and yet, even though Cain was guilty, he was not struck by God but avenged when killed.[83] In the city of Nineveh 120,000 people were sacrilegious, who were seen to follow strange gods; after the wrath of God and the preaching of the prophet Jonah, a brief fast and a prayer

---

[80] Matthew 15.4 par.

[81] See Numbers 16.1ff, and n.69 below. The same three names occur in the Donatist denunciation of the followers of Maximian recorded by Augustine, *Cresc.* III.22.

[82] The first two commandments are from Exodus 20.12ff; the third is inferred from Numbers 16.

[83] Genesis 4.15; it is not clear whether God carried out the promise to Cain that he would be avenged if killed. Optatus uses the word *parricidium* to denote any heinous crime.

earned indulgence.[84] Let us see whether such results accrued to those who dared to cause the original schism among the people of God.

When God had cast the yoke of servitude from the necks of so many thousands of the children of Israel, he had set none but Aaron over them as their holy priest.[85] But when his acolytes, holding thuribles in their desire for a priesthood that was not theirs by right, had seized it by deluding part of the people, they set before the face of the deluded people two hundred and more acolytes, doomed to perish like themselves in imitation of the sacred rites. God, who hates schism, could not look kindly on this. In a sense they had declared war on God, as if there were another god, who would accept another sacrifice. Therefore God was angry with a great anger because of the schism which had occurred, and what he had not done to sacrilegious men and parricides he did to the schismatics. There stood the line of priests and the sacrilegious multitude, doomed to perish there with their forbidden sacrifices; the time of repentance was denied to them and taken away, because the fault was not of such a kind as to merit pardon. Famine was decreed upon the earth: all at once, it opened its throat against the dividers of the people, and yawned greedily to swallow the despisers of God's commands. In the space of a moment, the earth opened to ingest these men, it snatched them away and closed. And lest it seem that they obtained a benefit from the reward of death, as they were not worthy to live, these men were not even allowed to die. Suddenly imprisoned in a Tartarean dungeon,[86] they were buried before they died. And you are surprised that any such severity has been meted out to you, who either create or cultivate a schism, when you see what suffering was earned by the instigators of the original schism. Is it because such punishments have ceased now that you adjudge yourself and your party innocent? God has set forth a form of punishment in particular cases in order that he may have cause to blame the imitators. Immediate punishment overtook the first sins for an example; the second he will reserve for judgment. What are you going to say in answer to this, you who, having

---

[84] See Jonah 3 for the story, and Genesis 5.11
[85] The story is the one told in Numbers 16. The priesthood of Aaron and his sons is established at Exodus 20.7.
[86] Tartarus being the Greek term for the lowest part of the underworld, where the wicked were punished everlastingly.

usurped the name of a church, covertly nourish a schism and brazenly defend it?

22. But, because I hear that some of your company with a zeal for litigation have records of some kind[87], it must be asked which ones should be trusted as according to reason and concurring with truth. Yours, if there are any, will perhaps appear to be stained with lies. The proof of our records is the forensic strife, the debates of parties and the outcome of adjudications and of Constantine's letter. For as to what you say concerning us - "what have Christians to do with kings? Or what have bishops to do with the palace?"[88] - if knowing kings is something to be blamed, the whole opprobrium falls on you. For your ancestors, Lucianus, Dignus, Nasutius, Capito, Fidentius and the rest petitioned Constantine with these prayers, of which a copy follows while he yet know nothing of these matters:[89]

We petition you, Constantine, best of emperors, since you are of upright stock, as your father did not carry on the persecution in company with the other emperors[90] and Gaul was immune from this

---

[87] See Augustine's *Breviculus* for discussion of such records, together with the Donatist martyrologies.

[88] Attributed at Book 3.3 to Donatus himself. The phrasing is reminiscent of John 2.4 and Mark 1.24 ("What have I to do with thee"), and also of Jeremiah 23.28 ("What has grain to do with chaff?"), which Parmenianus cited (Augustine, *Parm.* III.17). He may have recalled Tertullian's *Quid ergo Athenis et Hierosolymis?* ("What has Athens to do with Jerusalem?") at *De Praescriptionibus Haereticorum* 7.

[89] Cf Augustine, Epistles 53.5 and 73.2. These Bishops are known only from their letter and that of Petronius Annianus (Appendix 8). It is clear, however, that the Bishops are asking for a Gallic council, not the one described in I.23 (see further n. 73). The Council of Arles took place in 314, but, as Kriegbaum (1989) p. 279 observes, Optatus seems to have been unaware of it. If the Donatist letter is wrongly dated, it is possible that Caecilian was the first to appeal to Rome.

[90] Barnes (1973) believes that the Donatists' letter follows the Roman session. He argues that that the *facinus* of which Gaul was not guilty is therefore that of complicity with the Donatists (see further n. 79); he argues (a) that the words *immunis est* imply a continuing *facinus*, and (b) that the clause referring to African schisms, beginning with nam ("for"), is introduced to explain the word *facinus*. But (a) it was not clear in 313/4 that persecution was over everywhere; (b) the *nam* clause may be construed as giving the reason for the whole petition, with the reference to the *facinus* merely completing the parenthetic encomium of Constantius. The idiom of both Donatist and official writings at this period is, in any case, hardly pure enough to allow of minute conjectures. For *facinus* as a crime

outrage, seeing that in Africa there are dissensions between us and other bishops: we petition that your piety should make haste to have judges given to us from Gaul.[91] Given by Lucian, Dignus, Nasutius, Capito, Fidentius and the other bishops of Donatus' party.[92]

23. Having read this, Constantine replied with extreme acerbity, in which response he also exposed their prayers when he said: "You are petitioning me for a temporal judgment, when I myself am awaiting the judgment of Christ".[93] None the less judges were given: Maternus from the city of Agrippina, Reticius from the city of Autun, Marinus from Arles.[94] These three Gauls and fifteen others from Italy arrived at the

---

of Emperors cf Lactantius, *Div. Inst.* I.1.4, the crime is clearly that of persecution. On Constantius' lukewarm compliance with the Diocletianic edicts of persecution, see Lactantius, *Mort.* 15.

[91] It is not clear whether these words belong to the original text, as they are missing in some MSS. The Donatists may have thought that Gaulish bishops would be more sympathetic than Italians; certainly such bishops were appointed.

[92] Note that by 313 or 314 the party is already named after Donatus. According to Augustine, *Cresc.* II.2, they preferred the name Donatiani to Donatistae. I see no reason to correct the phrase *ex parte Donati* to *ex parte Maiorini*, following Hurter (1870), p. 62.2, since the letter of Anullinus, cited by Augustine, *Brev.* III.24, may be of earlier date. Kriegbaum (1989) is, however, probably right to maintain that the letter quoted here followed the Roman conference, which would have taken place while Majorinus was still the leader of the Donatists. See n. 88.

[93] See Appendix 5. Other MSS give a form closer to the reading in the Appendix, but this is not necessarily a proof that the reading is better, as they may have been purposely corrected. Optatus fails to observe that Constantine's response was written to the Council at Arles in 314, which Constantine was forced to convene in the light of further dissensions (see Appendix 3). Augustine, *Brev.* III.37, says that Constantine then wrote to Eumalius - *vicarius* in 316: see Barnes (1982), p. 146 - announcing the complete exoneration of Caecilian (the letter is quoted at *Cresc.* III.82). The decisions of the Council, conveyed to Bishop Silvester of Rome in Appendix 4, say nothing about Caecilian, but affirm that those baptized in the name of the Trinity need not be baptized again. Appendix 8 provides for the return of the Donatist petitioners to Africa.

[94] Agrippina is Claudia Agrippina on the Rhine. The letter of Constantine to Miltiades (Eusebius, *HE* X.5) says that there should be ten bishops of each party; here there are nineteen including Militades. According to Augustine, *Brev.* III.38, it was at this council that Donatus of Casae Nigrae, agreed by all at this time to be another person than the great Donatus, was condemned. Augustine's Epistle 43.15-16 implies that the great Donatus was the one condemned, though in his absence; yet the judgment of Miltiades (reported below) surely refers to this Donatus. See n. 73. Eusebius records no acquittal

city of Rome. They convened at the house of Fausta in the Lateran,
when Constantine was consul for the fourth and Licinius for the third
time, on October 2, the sixth day of the week,[95] the session consisting
of Miltiades the Bishop of the city of Rome;[96] Maternus, Reticius and
Marinus, the Gaulish bishops; and Merocles from Milan, Florianus from
Siena, Zoticus from Quintianum, Stennius from Rimini, Felix from
Tuscan Florence, Gaudentius from Pisa, Constantius from Faventia,
Proterius from Capua, Theophilus from Beneventum, Sabinus from
Tarracina, Secundus from Praeneste, Felix from Tres Tabernae,
Maximus from Ostia, Evandrus from Ursinum and Donatianus from
Forum Claudii.[97]

24. With these nineteen bishops in session, the case between Donatus
and Caecilian was brought into the open, and they severally pronounced
the following verdicts[98] against Donatus, that he had confessed that he
had rebaptized and laid hands on lapsed bishops, which is alien to the
custom of the church. The witnesses brought in by Donatus had
confessed that they had nothing to say against Caecilian. Caecilian was
pronounced innocent by the verdicts of all those enumerated above, and
also by the verdict of Miltiades, which judgment closed with these
words:

**Since it is patent that Caecilian has not been accused in respect of
his calling by those who came with Donatus, and it is patent that he**

---

of Caecilian.

[95] Garducci (1982) has reaffirmed her opinion, against Nash (1976), that this was the
former dwelling of Maximian the partner of Diocletian, and that Fausta was his daughter,
now the wife of Constantine. Maier (1987), p. 151 n. 2 observes that Constantine was
consul only for the third time in 313, and that in 315 (the date suggested here) October
2nd was a Sunday. See Augustine, *Post Gesta* 56 for a more accurate statement.

[96] Clearly one of the fifteen mentioned above, and named at 2.3 in the succession of
Roman Bishops. Optatus' account implies his presidency; Augustine, *De Unico Baptismo*
28 confirms this and pours scorn on the Donatist claims that he was a *traditor*. His *Brev.*
III.34-36 alleges that similar claims against Miltiades, together with the Roman deacons
Strato and Cassianus, were dismissed for lack of evidence.

[97] All Italians, or, as Donatists said, *transmarini* (Augustine, *Brev.* III.3 etc.). On their
obscurity see Pietri (1976) p. 163.

[98] The verdicts are presumably those pronounced on both Donatus and Caecilian, though
Optatus seems to forget that he intended to list more than one verdict in the same
sentence.

has not been convicted in any regard by Donatus, I judge that he should continue to be held in good standing by his eccesiastical communion.[99]

25. It is clear enough, then, that so many adverse judgments were inflicted on Donatus and that Caecilian was cleared by such a great tribunal, and yet Donatus thought it proper to appeal. To this appeal the Emperor Constantine's response was as follows: **O what a madman will dare in his rage! Just as if this were a common case of heathen litigation, a bishop thought it proper to appeal!** etc.[100]

26. At this time the same Donatus petititoned for the right to return ..... arrive at Carthage.[101] Then Philumenus, a supporter of his, suggested to the Emperor that Caecilian be detained at Brixia for the sake of peace;

---

[99] On Donatus see n. 90 On the trial of Caecilian see Appendices 3 and 7 and Maier (1987) pp. 151-8. Domitius Celsus, to whom 7 and 8 are addressed after the Council of Arles, was *vicarius* in 315-6; but neither acquits Caecilian. The supremacy accorded to Miltiades here is remarkable, in view of the fact that Constantine's letter to Chrestus of Syracuse (Eusebius, *HE* X.5) does not state that he presided. Caspar (1927) argues that the voice of the Gallic Bishops has been suppressed in the final judgment; Girardet (1989) reviews the various theories of a conflict between the Emperor and the Pope. We cannot be sure that Constantine convened the Roman council, but the presence of Gallic Bishops may, as Girardet thinks, be a sign that he demanded an oecumenical decision. Pietri (1976) observes (pp. 160-7) that Constantine's recourse to Miltiades imitates the policy of the pagan Emperor Aurelian, and that the resistance of the Donatists may have diminished the standing of the Roman See abroad.

[100] Cf Appendix 5, and 1Cor 6.1 for Paul's prohibition of use of the secular courts. The fourteenth canon of Arles (314) imposes heavy penalties for false accusation of Christians, and the sixth canon of Constantinople (381) forbids bishops condemned by the Church from appealing to the Emperor. As Augustine, *Brev.* III.6 etc. reveals, it was a matter of great importance for each party to affirm that the other had been the first to invoke a secular court. The rest of Constantine's letter is not preserved, but if he styled Donatus a bishop, he must have been indulging in an uncharacteristic bout of irony.

[101] There is a lacuna in the text. Labrousse (1995) p. 228 n.1 notes the reading of the Petropolitanus, followed by Grasmuck (1954), which implies that Donatus was not allowed to return. This passage implies that Donatus had appeared before the Emperor; perhaps it is to the intended hearing at Rome that Augustine alludes in Epistle 43.15, where he says that Donatus had promised to appear before the Emperor with Caecilian, but withdrew. See n. 101.

and so it was done.[102] Then two bishops, Eunomius and Olympius, were sent to Africa, so that, in the absence of both, they might ordain one. They arrived and stayed at Carthage forty days, so that they might declare where the catholic church was. This the seditious party of Donatus would not allow to happen, and every day riots were caused by partisan zeal.[103] What we read as the final sentence of the same bishops, Eunomius and Olympius, is a declaration that the catholic church was the one that was spread throughout the whole world, and that the verdict of nineteeen bishops, given long before, could not be annulled. They communicated with Caecilian's clergy and returned. We have a book of the proceedings over these issues, which anyone who wishes may read in the final sections.[104] While these events were taking place, Donatus, of his own accord, was the first to return to Carthage. On hearing this, Caecilian hurried to join his own folk. In this way the parties were renewed for a second time. It is however patent that so many adverse judgments were inflicted on Donatus, and that Caecilian was pronounced innocent by the same number of verdicts.

27. But since in this same case there seemed to be two people's names on trial in the catholic church, that of the one ordained and that of the one ordaining, once the one ordained had been cleared, the one who ordained still needed to be cleared. Then Constantine wrote to the proconsul Aelianus,[105] that he should set aside public business and hold

---

[102] For these events see Augustine, *Cresc.* III.80-3; also *Brev.* III.37f. On Philoumenous see Batiffol (1914), where he is identified with the person of that name at Athanasius, *Apologia* 60; but cf Mandouze (1982), p. 456. The Donatists cited Optatus to show that Constantine condemned Caecilian (Augustine, *Brev.* 38). Augustine argues that Caecilian was not exiled but preferred the peace of the Church to his own prerogative. The Donatists seem also to have appealed to letters of Constantine recalling their own partisans from exile (Augustine, *Brev.* III.40 and *Post Gesta* 54); the latest of these was written in 321 (*Post Gesta* 56).

[103] Augustine, Epistle 43.20 cannot explain why Caecilian failed to arrive at Rome after the Council of Arles, and speaks of a summons to Mediolanum. See Appendix 6. Labrousse (1995) p. 229 n. 2 canvasses the theory that Encolpius and Olympius came to appoint a new Bishop after the deposition of Caecilian.

[104] Unless he means Appendix 2, recording the acquittal of Felix, this item is not in the Appendix.

[105] In fact Aelius Paulinus, though Aelianus is the name used in Appendix 2. See Augustine, *Brev.* III.42 and Maier (1987), p. 173 n.12. Maier (1987), p. 190 n.12 notes that Aelianus is said by Constantine (cited in Augustine, Epistle 88) to have succeeded

a public inquiry into the life of Felix of Abthugni. As enjoined, he held a session. Those brought in were Claudius Saturianus, the curator of the common weal,[106] who at the time of the persecution had been in the city of Felix, and the curator at the present time of debating the case, Callidius Gratianus, and the magistrate Alfius Caecilianus[107] but also Superius the constable was dragged in,[108] and Ingentius the public scribe hung in fear of imminent tortures.[109] All of them gave answers that yielded nothing of the kind that might incriminate the life of Bishop Felix. A book of the proceedings is in our possession, which contains the names of those who were present in the case of Claudius Saturianus the curator and Caecilianus the magistrate and Superius the constable and the scribe Ingentius and Solon the public official of that time.

After their answers, the proconsul mentioned above spoke this part of his verdict:

Felix the pious bishop is manifestly innocent of the burning of the sanctifying instruments, since no-one has been able to prove anything against him to the effect that he handed over or burnt the most venerable scriptures. For the manifest [result of the] interrogation of all those named above is that no sanctifying

---

Verus as *vicarius* of the diocese of Africa, having formerly been proconsul. He suggests that confusion arose because the full name of Verus was Aelius Paulinus Verus. The province of *Africa proconsularis*, centred on Carthage, was governed by a proconsul, who was not responsible to the *vicarius* of the diocese. The latter included in Constantine's time the provinces of Numidia, Tripolitana, Byzacena and the two Mauretanias. For the list of *vicarii* see Barnes (1982), p. 146.

[106] Or Saturninus: see Augustine, Epistle 88.4. On the functions of the *curator rei publicae* (also called *curator civitatis*), see Liebenam (1897), Lucas (1940) and Jones (1964), Vol II pp. 728-9. The post became more important and more frequent under the Empire of the third century, though after the accession of Constantine it was never held in Africa by a man of senatorial rank. He was charged with the regulation of capital and supply in a city, the restoration and erection of public monuments, the manumission of slaves and confiscation of property. Lucas (1940), p. 68 cites Appendix 1 as a unique witness to his function in a time of persecution.

[107] The first name should perhaps be Calibius Junior: see Augustine, *Cresc.* III.81. Alfius Caecilian was a former *duumvir*, one of the two highest civic magistrates: Maier (1987), p. 191.

[108] On the functions of the *stationarius*, who appears to have been the local chief of police, see Maier (1987) p. 63 n. 27.

[109] In Constantine's letter of 315 to Probianus (Aelianus' successor as proconsul) Ingentius is said to have falsified a letter by Caecilian (Augustine, *Cresc.* III.81). See Appendix 1.

**scriptures at all were found to have been either adulterated or
burnt. The content of our proceedings is that Felix the pious bishop
was not present at that time, nor was a conscious accessory, nor
commanded anything of the kind.**

Obloquy, routed and wiped out, retired from that tribunal amid great
acclamation. Opinion had wavered for a long time while truth seemed
hidden in the mists exhaled by bitterness and rancour. But every writing
also has been put on record and is published in the books of the
proceedings and in the letters which were either put on record or read.
28. You see, brother Parmenianus, that you were wrong to inveigh
against the catholics, hurling at them the false name of collaborators;
clearly you have mixed up the names and transferred the deserts. You
have closed your eyes, so as not to perceive that your parents were the
criminals; you have opened them in order to make incriminating attacks
on innocents who did not deserve it. Everything is said for the occasion,
nothing for the truth, so that the most blessed Apostle Paul might say
of you: *Some indeed have turned to vain speaking, aspiring to be
teachers of the law, and not understanding what they say or what they
speak of.*[110] A little earlier we showed that your parents were
collaborators and schismatics; and you, the heir of these same people,
have desired no mercy for schismatics or collaborators. Now, therefore,
by the documents put on record above, all the weapons which you
treacherously wished to cast at others, repulsed by the shield of truth,
have recoiled with a backward impetus on your own parents. All that
you you have been able to say against collaborators and schismatics,
therefore, belongs to you; for it does not belong to us, since we have
remained in the root and are on the side of everyone throughout the
whole world[111].

---

[110] This book appears as Appendix 2, the quotation being taken from the end of 1 Tim 1.6
[111] Cf Augustine's *satis judicat orbis terrarum* ("the world is sufficient judge") at *Parm.*
III.24.

OPTATUS:

Second Book against the Donatists

Since it has been shown who were the collaborators and the origin of the schism has thus been revealed, so that it seems to be almost before our eyes, and we have also shown how distant heresy is from schism: the next thing to show - as we promised to explain in the second place - is what is the one church which Christ calls his dove and his bride. The one church, then, is that whose sanctity is gathered from the sacraments, not weighed by the pride of individuals; and so this is the one that Christ calls his dove and his beloved bride. This cannot exist among any of the heretics and schismatics; it can only exist, therefore, in one place. You, brother Parmenianus, have said that it exists only among you; unless, perhaps, you aspire to a special claim of sanctity for yourselves on the grounds of pride, so that the church exists where you wish or does not exist where you do not wish. So in order that it may be among you in a tiny portion of Africa, in the corner of a little region, is it therefore not to be with us in another part of Africa? Is it not to be in the Spanish provinces, Gaul, Italy, where you are not? If you want it only to be among yourselves, is it not to be in the three provinces of Pannonia, in Dacia, Moesia, Thrace, Achaia, Macedonia and in the whole of Greece, where you are not? So that it can be among you, is it not to be in Pontus, Galatia, Cappadocia, Pamphilia, Phrygia, Cilicia, or in the three provinces of Syria and in the two Armenias and in the whole of Egypt and Mesopotamia, where you are not?[1] And through so many innumerable isles and other provinces, which can scarcely be numbered, where you do not exist, shall it exist? Where then will the name "catholic" have its proper application, when the reason for calling it catholic is its international and universal diffusion?[2]

---

[1] Augustine records a claim that Donatus was recognized as Bishop of Carthage by the (Easterners') Council of Serdica in 343: *Cresc.* III.38. The western bishops had held a separate council on this occasion, seeing the easterners as partisans of the heretic Arius. In their provinciality the Donatists contrast with the Novatianists, who began in Rome but had a Bishop in Constantinople in the late fourth century (Socrates, *HE.* V.21).

[2] Accepting from Ziwsa's *apparatus* the proposed emendation of *rationabilis* to *non nationalis*; though *katholikos* is the Greek equivalent of *rationalis*, the Latin name for a fiscal official.

For if by your own will you thus lock up the church in a small space, if you take away all the nations, where will be the reward which was merited by the Son of God? Where will that be which the Father freely conferred upon him in the second psalm, saying: *I shall give you the nations as your inheritance and the ends of the earth as your possession?*[3] Why do you curtail such a promise, as if to contain the breadth of his kingdom in a sort of prison? Why do you aspire to resist his outstanding piety? Why do you fight against the deserts of the Saviour? Let the Son possess what has been vouchsafed to him, let the Father fulfil his promises. Why do you put down markers and fix boundaries? When the whole earth is promised by the Father to the Saviour, there is nothing in any part of the earth which appears to be excepted from his possession. The whole earth is given with its nations, the whole globe is the sole possession of Christ. This God proves, when he says, *I shall give you the nations as your inheritance and the ends of the earth as your possession.*

And in Psalm 71 this is written about the Saviour himself: *He shall rule from sea to sea, and from the rivers up to the ends of the earth's compass.*[4] When the Father bestows it, he excepts nothing; you, to vouchsafe a letter, try to take away the whole book! And still you strive to persuade people that the church exists among you alone, taking away the deserts of Christ and denying that God promised them. O what ungrateful and stupid presumption you are showing! Christ invites you with the rest into the fellowship of the heavenly kingdom, and exhorts you to be co-heirs,[5] and you set yourselves to defraud him of the inheritance vouchsafed to him by his Father, vouchsafing a part of Africa and denying the whole compass of the earth which has been given to him by his Father.

Why do you want the Holy Spirit to seem a liar, when he recounts the benevolence of God in Psalm 49, saying, *The Lord God of gods has spoken and has called the earth from the rising to the setting of the*

---

[3] Psalm 2.8, recognised as Messianic since 2.7 was quoted at Jesus' baptism (Mark 1.11).
[4] Psalm 71.8, initially of Solomon. Cf Augustine, *Cath.* 22.
[5] Psalm 49.1. Cf Augustine, *Cath.* 49. These quotations from the Psalms are regarded as decisive by Augustine, who doubts the applicability of other Old Testament passages used by Optatus.

sun?[6] The earth is called, therefore, that it may become flesh, and, as we read, so it did, and it owes praises to its Creator. Moreover, he is referred to by the speech and bidding of the Holy Spirit in Psalm 102, when he says, *The name of the Lord is to be praised from the rising to the setting of the sun.*

And again in Psalm 95: *Sing to the Lord a new song.*[7] If this were the only verse that he spoke, you would be able to say that the Holy Spirit addressed his bidding only to you. But in order to show that it was not said only to you but to the church, which is everywhere, he followed this by saying: *Sing to the Lord, all the earth, declare his glory among the nations, his marvellous works to all peoples.* He said, *among the nations*, he did not say, "in the tiny portion of Africa, where you are". *Declare*, he said, *to all peoples*; in saying *all peoples*, he excepted no-one. And you congratulate yourselves on being the only ones separated from all peoples, of whom this was commanded, and you want yourselves alone to be the whole, when you are nowhere in the whole.

The name of the Lord, he says, *is to be praised by the whole earth, from the rising to the setting of the sun.* Can the heathen without the Law either sing to God or praise the name of the Lord, rather than the church alone, which is within the Law? If you say that this exists only among you, you defraud the ears of God. If you alone praise him, the world's whole compass, from the rising to the setting of the sun, will be silent. You have stopped the mouths of all the Christian nations, you have enjoined silence on all the peoples who yearn to praise God at every moment. If, therefore, God, awaits the praises due to him, and the Holy Spirit bids that they resound and the whole earth is ready to render them, lest God should be defrauded, you yourselves must either give praise with all or, since you have refused to join with all, you alone must be silent.

2. Since, therefore, we have proved that the catholic church is the one that is spread throughout the whole compass of the earth, we must describe its trappings and we must see where are the five gifts, which

---

[6] Cf Gal 4.7. Rom 8.17.
[7] Psalm 112.3, the title "Lord" being taken as a reference to Christ, in keeping with the usual belief of the early Church; followed by Psalm 95.1. The quotation continues.

according to you are six.[8] The first of these is the see, to which, unless the Bishop occupies it, the second gift cannot be joined, which is the angel. We must see, who first occupied the see, and where. If you do not know, learn; if you do know, blush. You cannot be supposed to be ignorant; it can only be, therefore, that you know. To sin is to err knowingly; for sometimes one ignores the faults of ignorance. Therefore you cannot deny that you know that the first episcopal see was set up in Rome, which was occupied by Peter the head of all the Apostles (for which reason he was called Cephas) so that in this one see unity might be presrved by all, lest each of the other Apostles should maintain his own; thus anyone who set up another see against this one see would be a schismatic and a sinner.[9]

3. Therefore the one see, which is the first of the gifts, was first occupied by Peter, then Linus succeeded him, Clement succeeded to Linus, Anacletus to Clement,[10] Evaristus to Anacletus, [Alexander] to

---

[8] See Ratzinger (1954), p. 106. The *cathedra* and the *angelus* are two gifts. The keys are mentioned in III.5, the Spirit in III.7, the font in III.8, the *sacerdotium* in III.9. The Donatists would add the *umbilicus* (III.9), identified with the altar. Pincherle (1925), with the support of Marcelli (1990) p. 37 substitutes the *sigillum* of II.8 for the *sacerdotium*, and identifies the *sigillum* with the *anulus* of I.10; but neither passage warrants the application of the term *dos*. Marcelli, pp. 230-4 rightly argues that the font denotes the water, not the baptism, as Optatus distinguishes sacraments from *dotes*; it is not clear that the same argument can be applied to the priesthood. We cannot determine whether Donatists or catholics made the first list of gifts.

[9] The Roman bishopric of Peter is assumed, e.g., in the sixth canon of the (Westerners') Council of Sardica in 343, but Irenaeus, *AH* III.3.2 says only that Peter and Paul committed the bishopric to Linus. On Peter as head of the Apostles see Matthew 16.18-19; for the name Cephas see 1Cor 9.5 etc and for its equation with the word *Kephale* (head) see the Sardican canon and Maccarrone (1976) pp. 220-7. Eno (1973) and (1993) maintains that Optatus follows Cyprian (Epistle 59.4 etc.) in a symbolic use of Rome with no assumption of primacy; I agree with Merdinger (1989) in seeing Optatus as a proponent of this primacy, though I hesitate to follow Ruysschaert (1973) in crediting Optatus with a belief in the material survival of Peter's chair. Many scholars doubt whether all the churches of Rome accepted a "monarchical episcopate" before the mid-third century: see Brent (1995), pp. 398-457.

[10] Irenaeus, *AH* III.2, writing in the later second century, gives the first extant catalogue of Roman church-leaders. In this Linus and Anacletus both precede Clement, though not perhaps as bishops: see Bevenot (1966), p. 104. Optatus is the first Latin writer to use a variant of the name Anencletus, rather than Cletus. In the *Liber Pontificalis* and the Liberian catalogue Clement is between Cletus and Aneclitus. Turner (1917) p.112ff argues that the presence of the Optatan list in Augustine, Epistle 53.2 suggests an African

Evaristus, Sextus [to Alexander], Telesphorus to Sextus, Hyginus to Telesphorus, Anicetus to Hyginus, Pius to Anicetus, Soter to Pius, [Eleutherius] to Soter, Victor [to Eleutherius], Zephyrinus to Victor, Calixtus to Zephyrinus, Urbanus to Calixtus, Pontianus to Urbanus, Anterus to Pontianus, Fabian to Anterus, Cornelius to Fabian, Lucius to Cornelius, Stephen to Lucius, Sextus to Stephen, Dionysius to Sextus, Felix to Dionysius, [Eutychianus] to Felix, [Gaius to Eutychianus], Marcellinus [to Gaius], [Marcellus] to Marcellinus, Eusebius [to Marcellus], Miltiades to Eusebius, Sylvester to Militiades, Marcus to Sylvester, Julius to Marcus, Liberius to Julus, Damasus to Liberius, Siricius to Damasus, and he is our colleague today.[11] With him, the whole world, in a single fellowship of communion maintained by the exchange of official letters, agrees.[12] Tell us the origin of your see, which you wish to claim for yourselves as a sacred church.

4. But you say that you too have a certain party in the city of Rome. It is a branch of your error, springing from a lie, not from the root of truth. Moreover, if Macrobius were to say where he has his see, could he say, in the see of Peter?[13] I do not know if he has even seen it with

catalogue, perhaps derived from the Greek-speaking westerner Hippolytus.

[11] The bracketed names are inserted by Ziwsa in order to make the list conform with others; cf Duchesne (1886), vi-xii. The list at Irenaeus, *AH* III.3.3 (= Eusebius, *HE* V.6) reverses the order of Pius and Anicetus. Irenaeus' contemporary, Eleuther(i)us, who appears in all other lists, is omitted altogether by Optatus, who has Alexander between Soter and Victor. Siricius gives a *terminus post quem* for (this edition of) Optatus' work of 384/5. See my introduction on this point.

[12] The *Liber Pontificalis* says that the *formata* was invented by Pope Sextus (c. 120) and was "a document certifying to the congregation of an existing bishop that he was in good standing with the Roman see" (so Davis (1989) p. 114.) Ziwsa's index accepts this, as do Battifol (1920), Vol I p. 101 n. 3 and Labrousse (1995) p. 247 n. 2. Yet if this were Optatus' meaning I should expect him to dilate a little more upon this material bond of unity, and it may be that *formatae ecclesiae* from Ziwsa's *apparatus* should be read, to speak of the "church formed by intercourse into a single fellowship of communion".

[13] This Macrobius may be the author of the *Passio Maximiani*, which vehemently attacks the orthodox as persecutors. On the failure of Donatists to ordain elsewhere than Rome and Africa see Augustine, *Cresc.* II.46. Although Macrobius is spoken of as if he were a contemporary, the list of Donatists bishops extends to Claudianus in II.4. On his date, giving a *terminus post quem* of 378 for (the present version of) Optatus, see Monceaux (1913), p. 450ff. *Pace* Labrousse (1995), 245 n. 3, the omission in the Petropolitanus of the successors of Macrobius hardly proves that there was a second edition, seeing that the same MS does not omit Siricius from the list of catholic pontiffs.

his eyes, and he has not approached Peter's memorial, acting like a schismatic against the Apostle, who speaks of communicating with the memorials of the saints.[14] See, there are the memorials of the two Apostles. Tell me if he was able to come up to these or made an offering in the place where the memorials of the saints are agreed to be. Therefore your colleague Macrobius can say only that he occupies the place that was once occupied by Encolpius; and if it were possible to interrogate Encolpius himself, he would say that he occupies the place formerly occupied by Boniface of Ballita. Then if it were possible to interrogate the latter, he would say that his is the place formerly occupied by Victor of Garba, sent long ago by your party to a few strays.[15] How is it that your party has not been able to have a citizen as your Bishop in the city of Rome? How is it that all those acknowledged to have succeeded one another in that city are Africans and immigrants? Do you not see the trickery, the factiousness, which is the mother of schism?

Besides, the request that Victor of Garba be sent from here - I will not say as a stone into the font, since he lacked strength to disturb the purity of the catholic multitude, but because certain Africans preferred to tarry in the city, visibly going out from among us here - was a request of these very people, that someone should be sent out from here as their convenor. Victor was therefore sent; there he was a son without a father, a novice without a guide, a disciple without a master, a follower without a predecessor, a tenant without a house, a guest without a host, a shepherd without a flock, a bishop without a people. For one could not call either flock or people the few who had nowhere to convene among forty and more churches. So they marked off a certain cave outside the city with hurdles, to have a meeting-place there

---

[14] Romans 12.13. Cf Augustine, *Cath.* 49, and *Confessions* VI.2. Labrousse (1995) p. 247 n. 2 observes that the Vulgate has *necessitatibus* rather than *memoriis*. On the relics of the *memoriae apostolorum* in Africa, chiefly in Donatist centres, see Frend (1940). On Peter and Paul as founders of the Roman Church see Irenaeus, *AH* III.3.2 and Ignatius, *Romans* 4.3.

[15] Cf Augustine, *De Unico Baptismo* 28, on Donatist attempts to found a party in Rome.

at that time; hence they were called Hillmen.[16] Therefore, since we see that Claudianus succeeded to Lucian, Lucian to Macrobius, Macrobius to Encolpius, Encolpius to Boniface, Boniface to Victor: if Victor were to say what see he occupied, he could point to no-one before him, nor any see except in the midst of plague.[17] For the plague sent disease-stricken men to hell, and hell is where they are acknowledged to have their gates; it was against these gates, as we read, that Peter received the keys of salvation, Christ saying to him, *I shall give you the keys of the kingdom of heaven and the gates of hell shall not overcome them.*[18]

5. Whence, then, would you arrogate the keys of heaven for yourselves, when you fight against the see of Peter with your presumptuous notions and sacrilegious audacity, rejecting the blessedness which is the merited praise of him who has not departed into the assembly of the impious and did not abide in the way of sinners and has not sat in the seat of plague?[19] Your ancestors went into the assembly of the impious, producing a division of the church. They also entered the way of sinners, when they tried to divide Christ, whose very clothes the Jews did not wish to rend, and that despite the Apostle's exclamation, *Is Christ divided?*[20] I wish that, having already entered the evil way, they would acknowledge their sin and return upon themselves, that is they would mend their errors and recall the peace that they have put to flight, which would be to return from their way; for in a way one walks, and does not abide. But, since your parents refused to return, it is patent that they stood in the route of sinners. Their steps had been impelled by madness, but lingering discord held them back and bound them. And, so that they could not go back to better ways, they put fetters of schism on themselves, so that they might stand pertinaciously in their error, making it impossible to go back to the peace which they had deserted.

---

[16] The Montenses appear at Augustine, *Petil.* II.247; *Cath.* 6; Jerome, *Alt.* 28. Epiphanius, *Ancoratus* 13, equates them with the Novatianists (i.e. supporters of the rival to Cornelius in 251), but this, like his allusion to Donatists as Novatianists at *Panarion* 59.13, may be the false hypothesis of a Greek. On the size of the Roman congregation see Eusebius, *HE* VI.43.

[17] Looking ahead to II.6.

[18] Matthew 16.18-19.

[19] Psalm 1.1. Cf Augustine, *Brev.* III.18.

[20] 2Cor 1.13.

Nor did they listen to the Spirit, who says in Psalm 33, *Turn aside from evil and do good; ask after peace and pursue it.*[21] But they abode in the way of their own sins. They even sat in the seat of plague, which, as we said above, sent people to death in their delusion. But while you cultivate the error of your parents, studiously defending it, you have chosen to be heirs of iniquity, when you could, albeit belatedly, have been children of peace. As it is written in the prophet Ezekiel, *Raise your voice over the son of iniquity, lest he should follow the footsteps of his father, since the soul of the father is mine and the soul of the son is mine. The soul that sins will be punished alone.*[22] If you do not like the fact that your parents have sinned, let them alone give a reckoning for their own offence; in this way, you at least could be blessed, and hear praise from the mouth of the prophet, who says in Psalm 1, *Blessed is the man who has not departed into the assembly of the impious and did not abide in the way of sinners, and has not sat in the seat of plague; but his will was in the law of the Lord.* What else is it to have one's will in the law of the Lord but to learn divine precepts with reverence and fulfil them with fear? In this law it is written, *Peace to men of good will on earth;*[23] and in another place, in the prophet Isaiah, *I shall lay the foundations of peace in Zion;*[24] and in another place, *Let us see what the Lord says, since he will speak peace to his own folk;*[25] and in another place, *The Son of God has come, and his place is made in peace;*[26] and in another place, *Let the mountains receive peace for the people and the hills righteousness.*[27] And in the Gospel, *My peace I give to you, my peace I bequeath to you;*[28] and Paul says, He who sows peace will also reap peace; and in all his letters, *Let peace abound to*

---

[21] Psalm 33.18.
[22] Ezekiel 18.4 and 18.20.
[23] Luke 2.14. On Christianity as a law see James 1.25 etc.
[24] Isaiah 60.17.
[25] Psalm 84.9. Quoted by Donatists (Augustine, *Cresc.* IV.18).
[26] Psalm 75.3.
[27] Psalm 71.3. Cf Augustine, *Cresc.* III.72.
[28] John 14.27

you in the name of the Father and of the Son and of the Holy Spirit;[29]
and in Psalm 33: *Ask for peace and you will obtain it.*[30]
Peace has withdrawn, put to flight by your fathers; you ought to have
sought for it, as God commands, yet you would neither seek it for
yourselves nor accept it freely when offered. For who has heard of you
in all the provinces of your birth?[31] And who of those that have heard
of you does not marvel at your error, who does not condemn you for
your outrage? Therefore, as it is manifest and clearer than light itself
that we have so many peoples on our side and so many provinces are
with us, and you now see that your position is in part of a single
province and that your errors have separated you from the church, it is
vain for you to claim this name of church, along with thes gifts, for
yourselves alone. These gifts are rather among us than among you,
being patently so intertwined and indivisible that one can be seen to be
inseparable from another. For they are nominally plural, but they are
joined by their one purpose in the body, like the fingers in the hand,
which we see to be distinguished by their several intervals. Hence he
who holds one necessarily holds all, since none can be separated from
its peers. Add to this that we possess not only one but all as our
property.
6. Therefore of the aforesaid gifts the see is, as we said, the first, and
we have proved that it is ours through Peter. This draws with it the
angel,[32] unless perhaps, claiming it as your own, you have it locked in
your purses. Send him, if you can, let him exclude the seven angels,
who are among our colleagues in Asia. John the Apostle wrote to these
churches, but you are proved to have no dealings in communion with
these churches. Where will you find an angel, who could move the font

---

[29] 2Cor 9.6; Romans 1.7 and 1Cor 1.3, though conflation with 2Cor 13.13 is required to
introduce the Holy Spirit.

[30] Psalm 33.10.

[31] The phrase *tot provincias* ("so many provinces") seems to be ironic, even if it includes
all those enumerated in Appendix 3. Jerome, *Alt.* 15 also argues that Christianity cannot
be confined to a single province (in this case, Sardinia). Jerome seems to have made
frequent use of Optatus' arguments against the Luciferians, who believed that almost all
bishops were tainted with the Arian heresy See further nn. 16, 51, 56 and 91.

[32] The term derives from the addresses to the angels of each of the seven churches of Asia
in Revelation 2.1 etc.

in your presence[33] or be numbered among the other gifts of the church? Whatever is outside the seven churches, is foreign. Or if you have one from there, you communicate through one with the other angels, and through the angels with the aforesaid churches, and through the very churches with us. If that is so, you have lost your case.

7. Already, you see, it is impossible that all these gifts should be among you; for you cannot, on your own, claim the Spirit of God for yourselves, or confine that which is understood but not seen. For thus it is written in the Gospel, *For God is a Spirit*[34] and *he blows where he will, and you hear his voice and know not whence he comes and whither he goes.*[35] Allow God to go where he will, and let him have freedom to come where he will, as he can be heard but not seen. And yet, in your zeal for recrimination, you have chosen to blaspheme freely, so that you said, "For in that church what Spirit can there be but the one who brings forth children of Gehenna?".[36] You have vomited a reproach from your breast and have thought fit to add a testimony from the Gospel, where we read, *Woe to you, hypocrites, who compass sea and land so that you may make one proselyte, and when you have found him, make him twice as much a child of Gehenna as you are.*[37] If this reproach had to be made, (which cannot be) I wish that someone else from your number had made it, baseless though it is! I am, however, very surprised that you should have said this; you would make a charge falsely against someone else, which, if you considered your own ordination, could make you blush? For you have cited the Gospel reading, *Woe to you, hypocrites, who compass sea and land so that you may make one proselyte*, that is, that you may change someone's adherence. What party you adhere to, I do not know, yet I think that it was not seasonable for

[33] Augustine, *Post Gesta* 20, treats the angels as personifications of the churches. Turner (1925-6) p. 294 notes that Optatus is a rare Latin witness to the longer text of John 5.4, which says that a pool acquired salutiferous properties when stirred by an angel. Tertullian, *De Baptismo* 6 mentions the angel at baptism.
[34] John 4.4. It is not clear whether Optatus treats this and the following as a single quotation; both passages appear to be invoked as proof of the divinity of the Holy Spirit.
[35] John 3.8, which can be related to baptism by way of John 3.5.
[36] Cf the following quotation and language cited by Augustine, *Cresc.* III.22, used by the Donatist majority against the followers of the schismatic Donatist Maximian.
[37] Matthew 23.5. Donatists applied this to the orthodox: *Passio Donati* 6. Augustine, *Cath.* 8, deprecates the arbitrary application of this text.

you to say this, as you may well repent of this saying. Have we
traversed any lands? Have we arrived at foreign ports? Have we brought
over any Spaniard or Gaul, or ordained an immigrant over those who
knew no better?[38]

8. For it is patent that the font is one of the gifts, from which heretics
can neither drink nor give others to drink, since they are the only ones
who, lacking the whole seal, that is the catholic sacrament, cannot
unlock the true font.......[39] For when it is written in the Song of Songs,
your navel is as a lathe-turned bowl,[40] you have tried to assert that the
navel is the altar. If the navel is a member of the body, it cannot be one
of the gifts, because it is a member; if it is one of the trappings, it is not
part of the body.[41]

9. Now it appears that there can be only five gifts, and these gifts, as
they belong to the catholic church, which is in all the aforesaid
provinces, can also not be lacking among us here in Africa. Understand,
albeit belatedly, that you are the impious sons, you are the boughs
broken off the tree, you are the branches cut from the vine, you are the
stream severed from the font. For the stream cannot be a source, when
it is small and not born of itself, nor can the tree be severed from the
bough, when the tree rejoices in the foundations of its own roots and the
bough, if it has been cut off, dries up. Do you now see, brother
Parmenianus, do you now divine, do you now understand that you have
been fighting against yourself with your arguments, since it has been
proved that we are in the holy catholic church, in which is also the
sacrament of the Trinity, and that through the see of Peter, which is
ours - through that the other gifts are also among us? Even the
priesthood, which you seem to have reckoned void in us as an excuse
for your error and bitterness, as you rebaptize after us but after

---

[38] The first and second of the rhetorical questions look back to II.3-4; the meaning of the
third is unclear.

[39] I follow Ziwsa and others in indicating a lacuna.

[40] Song of Songs 7.2. The interpretation of the navel as an altar may be related to the
notion of the Delphic oracle as the navel of the world (Pausanias X.16.3 etc.). Marcelli
(1990), pp. 232-3 argues that Optatus rejects this *dos* because Donatists equate it with the
eucharist, a sacrament, not a gift.

[41] The distinction between gifts and members may rely on 1Cor 12.5-13, where Christians
are baptized "in" one Spirit, who bestows many gifts, and "into" one body with many
members.

colleagues of your own who are taken in error you do not do this.[42] For you have said that, if a priest is in sin, the gifts can work on their own.[43]

Therefore, since we have explained what heresy is, what schism is and what the holy church is, the attributes of this church also have been set forth, and the fact that the catholic church is this one that is spread throughout the whole compass of the earth, of which we among others are limbs, and whose gifts are in her everywhere. Also we have proved in the first book that the slur of collaboration does not belong to us, and that this crime has been condemned by us as well.

10. Now I would have you answer me this, why you have chosen to speak only of the gifts of the church and been silent about its sacred limbs and inner life, which beyond doubt are in its sacraments and in the names of the Trinity. With this concurs the faith and profession of believers, which is perfected amid angelic acts, when heavenly and spiritual seeds are mingled, begetting a new nature in the regenerate from a sacred shoot, so that, in this accord of faith with the Trinity, the one who was born to the world may be reborn spiritually to God.[44] Thus God becomes the father of human beings, and the church their holy mother.[45]

I understand the reason for your failure to mention all these things: it is to prevent the principle of baptism from being recognised in them all. No minister of this, being a man, would claim for himself what you do. And thus you have chosen to address yourself solely to the gifts of the church, which, as though they were grasped in the hand or locked in a chest, you have denied to catholics and vainly tried to claim as your

---

[42] See Augustine, *Cresc.* III.16-18 on the reconciliation with the followers of Maximian; *ibid.* II.13-14 on the catholic refusal to recognise Donatist bishops who accepted Donatist baptism.

[43] According to Augustine, *Petil.* I.6, Petilian maintained that only one with a good conscience could be baptized, and that if one were unwittingly baptized by an evil minister, God would perform the work; Cresconius (*Cresc.* III.12 etc.) argued that *bona fama* would stand proxy for good character. Both held that those baptized by catholics, must be rebaptized as Donatists.

[44] Cf Justin, *1Apol* 61.3 for rebirth; Tertullian, *De Baptismo* 6 for the angel, etc.

[45] For church as mother see Gal 4.19ff; Methodius, *Symposium* VIII.6, where the seed also appears. *Passio Donati* 14 shows that Donatists felt themselves entitled to the same metaphor.

prerogative. When regeneration is in question, when the renewal of the human being is in question, you make no mention of the faith of believers or of their profession. While you choose to speak only of the gifts, all these things without which that spiritual birth cannot be effected, you have consigned to silence, and, though it is the gifts that belong to the bride, not the bride to the gifts, you have set out the gifts, as though they were seen to bring forth of themselves, and not the inner life, which is seen to reside more in the sacraments than in the trappings.

11. Nor do I omit the fact that with your mouth, and in our own sense, you have declared the church to be paradise (which is undoubtedly true), the garden in which God plants his trees.[46] And yet you deny God his riches, by confining his garden in a small space, when you claim all things undeservedly for yourselves alone. Now God's plantings are various seeds through various precepts. The righteous, the continent, the merciful and the virgins are spiritual seeds;[47] of these God plants trees in paradise; vouchsafe to God that his garden may be spread far and wide. Why do you deny him the Christian peoples of the east and north, even of all the western provinces and innumerable islands, against which you alone, a handful, are in rebellion, and with whom you have no dealings in communion?

12. Now your lie can also be condemned in the place where you perform daily sacrifices.[48] For who would doubt that you cannot omit this legal obligation in the mystery of the sacraments? You say that you make an offering to God for the church, which is one. This itself is part of a lie, to call that one of which you have made two. And you say that you make an offering to God for the one church, which is spread

---

[46] Cf I.10..

[47] The image of the seed derives from the parable of the sower (Matthew 13.3-23 par); Cyprian's *De Habitu Virginum* infers that martyrs reap a hundredfold, virgins sixtyfold and the righteous thirtyfold. There being no true martyrs in Optatus' day, the continent are substituted. The four virtues may be equated (cf Ambrose, *De Paradiso* 11-19) with the four rivers of Paradise, to which Optatus also alludes in enumerating the three points of the compass not occupied by his opponents.

[48] For the term "sacrifice" cf 1Cor 5.7. Despite its use in Book 3, the word is no doubt meant to be pejorative here, as pagan sacrifices had been abolished and God rejected those of Jews (Hosea 6.6 etc.). Hanson (1985) notes that sacrificial imagery is rarely used of the eucharist before the late fourth century.

throughout the whole compass of the earth. What if God were to say to each of you, "Why do you offer for the whole, when you are not in the whole?" If we displease you, what has the city of Antioch done to you, or the province of Arabia, whose inhabitants, as we can prove, you rebaptize when they come to you?

13. In one thing alone, brother Parmenianus, we cannot be ungrateful to you, that even though you are a stranger to it, you have chosen to praise our church, that is the catholic one which fills the whole compass of the earth, by enumerating its gifts. It is true you have erred in the number, and in saying that your own is the closed garden and the sealed font and the one bride. This we say of ours, for you have spoken of a strange one. Whatever you have been able to say of the praises of the church, we too have said the same before. With you we also condemn collaborators, namely those whom, if you recall, we exposed in the first book. And when we hold communion with the whole world and all the provinces with us, you have chosen to compare the two churches as though Africa alone has Christian peoples, where, through your fault, two parties are seen to have been created. And having forgotten that Christ declared his bride to be one, you have stated that in Africa there are not two parties, but two churches. Surely there is one, which deserved to be identified by the mouth of Christ, who says, *One is my dove, my bride is one.*[49]

14. And you, forgetting this saying, have spoken in these words to cast a slur on the catholics: "For neither can that be called a church, which feeds on bloody morsels and battens on the blood and flesh of the saints". The church has certain limbs of its own, the bishops, presbyters, deacons, ministers[50] and the host of the faithful. Tell me, to what class of people in our church can this imputation of yours be ascribed; above all, name some minister, point out some deacon by his own name, show that this was done by some presbyter, prove that bishops committed this, explain how one of our number lay in wait for anyone. Which of us has persecuted anyone? Whom can you either say or prove to have been persecuted by us? Since unity displeases you, if you deem this a crime,

---

[49] See Song of Songs 6.8.
[50] Though Hippolytus' *Apostolic Tradition* attests subdeacons and readers (pp. 21-2 Dix and Chadwick), it is likely that the term *minister* here comprehends the three previous orders, as when it recurs in this chapter. In chapter 24, the term has disappeared.

denounce us for having communicated with the Thessalonians, the Corinthians, the Galatians, the seven churches which are in Asia.[51] If it seems to you wrong or if you think it felony to have communicated with the memorials of the Apostles and all the saints, we not merely do not deny having done so, but glory in it.

15. But, so that I may show that it is your party which, to use your words, has fed on bloody morsels and battened on the blood and flesh of Christians, I must now rehearse your raging madness from its own beginnings, I must uncover your impiety, I must demonstrate your stupidity. The first task in this is to expose your shameful happiness and criminal rejoicing when it was agreed that you should be allowed to return to practise your original error in freedom. Reckon the times, examine the course of events, consider the different judgments and several persons. Call to mind Constantine the Christian Emperor, what service he displayed toward God, what wishes he had,[52] so that, all schisms having been put aside and all dissension having died throughout the world, the holy mother church rejoiced to see her own sons at one. He had restored, in one communion, wives to their husbands, sons to their parents, brothers to brothers. These are things in which God witnesses to his joy, when he says, Behold how good and how pleasant it is for brethren to dwell in unity.[53] But when one peace had joined the peoples of Africa with the orientals and others across the sea, and unity itself, with the restoration of all the limbs, had consolidated the body of the church, this grieved the devil, who is always annoyed by the peace of the brethren.[54] At that time, under a Christian Emperor, his idols

---

[51] The first three are addressees of Pauline letters, the last are the seven Churches of Revelation 2-3. Cf Augustine, *Cresc.* II.46 and *Cath.* 31. For the paradigmatic importance of these churches cf Victorinus of Petau, *De Apocalypsi*, where, on Rev 1.16, he likens the seven churches to Paul's seven addressees and, in chapter 3, distinguishes seven categories of saint. The Donatists will have noted that all these churches are reprimanded by the apostolic authors. Jerome, *Alt.* 24 and Augustine, *Post Gesta* 4 make this last fact a catholic argument, as showing that Christ was willing to plead with sinners.

[52] Constantine, Emperor of the whole west from 312-337, and the first who openly favoured Christianity. For his constant support of catholics against Donatists see Appendices 3-10.

[53] Psalm 132.1. Catholic and Donatist writers cited this Psalm against one another: see Augustine, *Petil.* II.238-9.

[54] Cf 1Peter 4.8. Donatists ascribed catholic measures against them to the devil: *Passio Donati, Passio Isaac et Maximiani* etc.

were deserted and he was like a prisoner hiding in his temples. At that time your leaders and chiefs had been banished as they deserved, there were no schisms in the church, and the pagans were not allowed to perform their sacrilegious rites.[55] Peace, which God loves, dwelt among all Christian peoples; the devil mourned in temples, you in foreign lands.

16. Then, as everyone knows, there followed another Emperor, who, conceiving evil designs with you, from being servant of God became a tool of the enemy, and declared himself an apostate by his edicts.[56] You brought a petition to him, that you might be able to return; these prayers, if you deny making them, we can read. Nor did the one whom you asked offer a difficulty; to fulfil his own design, he bade them go, as he knew that they were going to disturb the peace with their madness. Blush, if you have any shame; freedom was restored to you by the same voice that commanded the idols' temples to be opened.

17. It was almost at the same instant that your madness returned to Africa and the devil was released from his imprisonment.[57] And you do not blush that you and the enemy have common joys at the same time! You came as madmen, you came in anger, mutilating the limbs of the church, subtle in deceit, ruthless in slaughter, goading the sons of peace into war. You drove many into exile from their sees, when, with hired bands, you broke into the churches; many of your number, in many places which it would take too long to tell by name, committed bloody murders so atrocious that an account of these deeds was submitted by the judges of that era.[58] But the judgment of God intervened and

[55] A passage which supports the (otherwise unverified) statement of Eusebius, *VC* II.45, that Constantine abolished pagan sacrifice. For Gratian's later banishment of Donatists see the 5th-century *Codex Theodosianus* XVI.6.2.

[56] See Maier (1987), pp. 42-3 on Julian's edict of recall at the beginning of 362 A.D; cf Augustine, *Petil.* II.224. Julian (361-3) restored rights to those who had been deprived of them by his Christian predecessors: these included pagans, Jews, Donatists and Athanasius (cf Jerome, *Alt.* 19, with the same intention of discrediting an "orthodox" party). See Smith (1995), pp. 5-9.

[57] See Revelation 20 and the Letter of the Churches of Vienne and Lyons (Eusebius, *HE* V.1.5) on binding the devil.

[58] We are unfortunately dependent on Optatus for a circumstantial account of the Donatist atrocities. Cf Augustine, *Cresc.* III.48-9 and 66 for similar claims to possess authentic records. Donatists had archives of their own (*ibid.* 80) and denied the authenticity of those adduced by catholics (*ibid.* 88).

overtook you, causing the death of that profane and sacrilegious emperor who had commanded your return, the man who, at your instance, had either sent or was proposing to send a persecution.

18. In the aforementioned places a massacre of catholics was carried on. Remember in the individual places how you operated. Was not Felix of Zaba one of your number, and Januarius of Flumen Piscium, and others, who ran together at the greatest speed upon the fortress of Lemellef?[59] Being present there, when they saw that the church was closed against their importunity, they ordered their comrades to scale the roofs, tear off the coverings and throw down the tiles. Their bidding was fulfilled without delay; and when the catholic deacons defended the altar, many were covered in blood from tiles, and two were killed, Primus son of Januarius and Donatus, son of Ninus, while your fellow-bishops, named above, were present and urging on; so that without doubt it was said of you, *Their feet are swift in shedding blood.*[60] Primosus the catholic bishop of the aforesaid place made a complaint about this affair in your assembly at the city of Theneste[61], and you listened hypocritically to his complaints. See, you are the ones who did what you described: "That is no church, which feeds on bloody morsels", and "The sending of a military force is one thing, the ordaining of bishops another". What you have said to discredit us was done by others, not by us; what you say ought not to have happened was done by you.

You have also recalled the saying of the blessed Paul, *The church should be without scar or stain.*[62] With your own bishops present and issuing commands, catholic deacons were killed upon the altar; and a like thing happened at Carpi. Do these not seem to you indelible stains? In the cities of Mauretania there were tumults of the people at your entry, infants who had been at the point of birth died in their mothers'

---

[59] See the index to Ziwsa (1893) p. 235 for defence of the form Lemellefense against the MS Lefellense. Zaba is the name of towns in Mauretania Sitifensis and Numidia; the former is more likely as Flumen Pisicum and Lemellefense were also in Mauretania Sitifensis.

[60] Psalm 13.3 Septuagint. Used by the Donatists against Maximian's followers: Augustine, *Cresc.* III.22.

[61] Also given in the forms Tevestina and Thebestina, this is another city in Numidia, the richest soil of Donatism.

[62] Ephesians 5.27. Violence against bishops incurs a special penalty, since they are anointed with oil in ordination.

wombs. Does this not seem to you a scar that cannot be healed or smoothed away by any remedies? What offence of this kind did we commit? We await the revenge of God. And you discredit Macarius,[63] though, if he did anything harsh for the sake of unity, it may well appear trivial enough, when you for the sake of dissension have done so many evil, harsh, bloody and hostile deeds.

Why should I remember Tipasa, the city of Mauretania Caesarea, where the onset of the Numidians Urbanus of Formae and Felix of Idicre, two men of filth inflamed with bitterness, rushed to disturb the minds of people who were quiet and at peace?[64] By the partisan madness of some officials, Athenius the chief magistrate being present with soldiers, the large catholic community was expelled from its own homes amid panic and bloodshed. Men were mutilated, married women were dragged, infants were slain, foetuses were torn out.[65] See, it is your church, led by its bishops, that has fed on bloody morsels. After this you have added another thing: "Let the greed of the vultures gobble what it will, yet the number of the doves is greater".[66] Where is the tenacious memory which the common saying attributes to the liar? You have forgotten that a little before you said that the church was called the one dove of Christ in the Song of Songs. If there is one church among you, there is one dove; if there is one dove, why have you chosen to say "the number of doves is greater"?

19. And an enormous outrage was committed, which seems trivial to you, when you aforesaid bishops violated everything sacrosanct. They ordered that the eucharist be poured out for the dogs - not escaping a sign of divine judgment, for the same dogs, inflamed with madness, treated their very masters like strangers and enemies, mutilating them with avenging teeth as though they were thieves, guilty as they were of

---

[63] Whose deeds are considered later in Book 3.

[64] Unauthorized preaching in another bishopric was regarded as a great offence in the fourth century, and the Donatists who were willing to agitate other provinces can hardly blame Rome for its intervention.

[65] Combining standard charges against persecutors with standard libels against heretics. Cf Origen, *Contra Celsum* VI.27; Lactantius, *Mort.* 38.1; Constantine, *Oratio ad Sanctos* 25 etc.

[66] Perhaps alluding to Matthew 10.16 and 24.28.

the sacred body. And they also threw the phial for chrismation[67] through the window, in order to break it, and though the throwing enhanced the fall, there was no lack of an angelic hand to take away the phial by spiritual stealth; having been thrown out, it could not feel its fall, and through God's protection it settled unharmed amid the rocks.

And these things might not have happened, if you had kept in memory the injunctions of Christ, who says, *Do not give what is holy to the dogs, and do not throw your pearls before pigs, lest they should trample them under their feet and turning round attack you.*[68] How could the agents of unity have done this sort of thing, from which you are at fruitless pains to cast discredit upon us catholics? When they returned from this scene, Urbanus of Formae and Felix of Idicre found mothers whom they had turned from a chaste condition[69] into that of women. See, brother Parmenianus, what sort of men you are hiding. And when you should have been blushing for your own side, you accuse innocent catholics! Meanwhile among the crimes and outrageous wrongs of the aforesaid Felix, he did not hesitate to commit nefarious rape on a girl whom he had captured, on whom he himself had placed the headband,[70] and who had shortly before called him father.[71] And, as though he would become holier through sin, he hastened quickly to Tysedis, and thus made bold to rob Donatus, a bishop seventy years of age and an innocent man, of the title, office and honour of his bishopric.[72] He came as a schismatic against a catholic bishop, as a

---

[67] On the chrismation (anointing with oil) which followed and confirmed baptism in the western church, see Hippolytus, *Apostolic Tradition*, pp.38-9 Dix and Chadwick.

[68] Augustine, *Enarratio in Psalmum* 75.16 says that a *castimonialis* is a virgin dedicated to God, who would sin gravely in breaking her vow. Optatus is the first Christian writer to use this term, though Tilley (1996) p. 18 n.24 records *castimonialae* in the Donatist *Passio Maximae* etc.

[69] Matthew 7.6. Optatus may also be thinking of Christ's answer to the Syrophoenician woman at Mark 7.27.

[70] A symbol of dedication to virginity, though Tertullian, *De Virginibus Velandis* 14, contrasts the matronal *mitra* with the veil. The term *mitra* recurs in Isidore of Seville, *De Eccl. Off.* II.17.11, and Jerome, Epistle 130 confirms that in the fourth century the veiling was a public ceremony. Cf Optatus VI.4 and Tilley (1996) p. 18 n.24.

[71] Cyprian, *De Habitu Virginum* exhorts the virgin to remain what "her father's hands" have made her; hence the statement here that the girl called Felix father.

[72] Not the great Donatus. The name (meaning "endowed") was among the commonest in Africa, as was Optatus ("wished for").

criminal against an innocent, as a sacrilegious man against a priest of God, an unchaste man against a chaste one, as one who was yet no bishop against a bishop. Yet, secure in your decision and connivance, armed with your laws and decrees, he hurled on the head of the innocent the soldier-bands which had aggravated his sins a little while before, and he made bold to pronounce a verdict with that tongue which seemed unready even for doing penance. See, brother Parmenianus, what sort of men you are defending, see for what sort of men you said that the gifts have long been working.

20. Tell us yourselves, as you wish people to think you holy and innocent, where is that sanctity which you freely arrogate to yourselves? The Apostle John does not dare to profess this when he says, *If we say that we have no sin, we deceive ourselves and truth is not in us.*[73] The one who said this wisely reserved himself for the grace of God. For it is characteristic of a Christian person to desire what is good and make progress in the good that he wills; but it is not given to a human being to be perfect, so that, after the completion of a person's allotted period, it remains for God to give some assistance to him in his weakness; for he alone is perfection and Christ alone is the perfect Son of God. All the rest of us are half-perfect, for to will is ours and to make progress,[74] but to be perfect belongs to God. Hence the most blessed Apostle Paul says, *it is not of him that wills or of him that makes progress but of him that belongs to the grace of God.*[75]

For even Christ our Saviour did not give perfect sanctity, but promised it; he says indeed, *You shall be holy, because I am holy.*[76] Therefore he alone is perfect and holy. What he says is not, You are holy; what he said is, *You shall be holy.* How does it come about, then, that in your pride you claim this perfect sanctity for yourselves? Possibly in order to make it apparent that you are deceiving yourselves

---

[73] 1John 1.8; cf Augustine, *Cresc.* IV.33ff.

[74] Augustine would have thought this a careless statement, as it says nothing of God's assistance in the regeneration of the will (Phil 2.13 etc.). The impotence of the human will, and the consequent impossibility of perfection, were not so heavily stressed by Augustine against the Donatists as they were against the Pelagians; but at *De Doctrina Christiana* III.46 he accuses the Donatists scholar Tyconius of ascribing too much to human volition.

[75] Romans 9.16. On original sin see Book VII, nn. 18. 19 and 23.

[76] Leviticus 11.48, quoted at Matthew 5.48.

and truth is not in you. You have refused to be of John's school. For when you delude others, you promise that you will give indulgence for their sins, and, though your intent is to condone sins, you profess your innocence and give remission of sins as though you yourselves had no sin. This is no presumption but a deception, not truth but a lie. Yes, for within a few minutes of imposing hands and conferring transgressions, you turn to the altar and cannot omit the Lord's Prayer, *Our Father which art in heaven, forgive us our debts and our sins.*[77] What are you called when you confess your own sins, if you are holy when you forgive those of others? So it happens both that you deceive yourselves and that truth is not in you.

But it is apparent that your own nurse, pride, dictates this to you, as Christ himself bears witness in the Gospel. Yes, for, even if he has not spoken your names, he has none the less shown your character through a parable; for thus it is written, *Jesus spoke this parable on account of those who think themselves holy and despise others.* The facts themselves show that this was said of you, since you exalt yourselves as though you were holy and display manifest and open contempt for us. *Two,* he says, *went up to the Temple to pray, one a Pharisee and the other a publican.*[78] The Pharisee was swollen, proud, puffed up, such a one as we see you to be, not prostrating his body or bowing his neck, but saying with a haughty aspect and a swelling breast, *I give you thanks, God, that I have done no sin.* This is to say to God, I have nothing in me that you can forgive. O reckless folly, O pride worthy of punishment and damnation! God is prepared to forgive, and the criminal hastens to refuse forgiveness. The humble publican, knowing his own humanity, asked in this way, saying, *Be merciful, Lord, to me a sinner.* Thus [humility] deserved acquittal,[79] thus pride in the Pharisee, your master, went down from the temple under condemnation. Sins with

---

[77] Matthew 6.9 and 12, with Luke 11.4. Optatus fails to see that the form "you shall be" is a disguised imperative.

[78] Luke 18.9. The quotation continues. Again the charge of Pharisaism is retorted upon the Donatists.

[79] Ziwsa notes that the word *humilitas* is omitted in some MSS. If it is left out, the publican is the subject of the sentence. *Justificari* ("to be acquitted") had become the technical term for the remission of sins in God's sight through Christ's sacrifice.

humility are found to be better than innocence with pride.[80]
Furthermore, when you are not free from the heinous sins of
collaboration and schism, you congratulate yourselves on being proud
as well.

21. Now, since we have proved that you ought to blush for your joys,
and your folly has been exposed in so many places, it remains to say a
little of your profound impiety. For who can recount all the things that
either happen or have happened because of you? It is patent that you
have managed everything with a certain malignity, so that under deeds
of one kind you contrive to do other kinds, with the result that, when
a presbyter or bishop is cast down, the people is thereby taken captive.
When could a crowd of people stand firm, having seen its director
destroyed by you? It is no different from the feasting of the wolves
when the shepherd has been killed by some misfortune.[81] You have
given exorcism to the faithful and have washed walls without reason,[82]
so that by iniquity of this kind you may snatch away the minds of the
simpler folk. By these plots of yours the minds of some have been cut
off, and, having hidden the light of cunning under a cloud of simplicity,
you have laid the wretches low by sending arrows of deceit before you
from the quiver of your breasts.

It was therefore of you that the Holy Spirit foretold through the
prophet David, *For see the sinners have stretched their bows, they have
prepared arrows in their quiver, to shoot in the dim moonlight those
who are upright of heart.*[83] What less than this have you done with your
designs? The innocent have been shot, the faithful disarmed, the priests
have been robbed of the honour of their name. O what unheard-of
impiety, to preserve amidst the tortures of penitence those whom you
have cut off! In comparison with your deeds the inhumanity of bandits
seems more moderate. The victims of your murder are still alive; the
bandit gives the compensation of death to those whom he has cut off.

---

[80] The pride of contumacious clergy was stigmatised by the Council of Carthage in 348
under Gratus, which approved the mission of Paulus and Macarius and forbade rebaptism
of those baptized in the name of the Trinity. Cf Augustine, *Cresc.* II.38.

[81] Cf John 10.10-13; the *Passio Donati* again shows that the Donatists could turn the
image to their own purpose.

[82] A reference to baptism, which was regarded as the exorcism of a congenital daemon:
see Tertullian, *De Anima* 39; Hippolytus, *Apostolic Tradition*, pp. 33-8 Dix and Chadwick.

[83] Psalm 10.3. The quotation continues.

Those whom you have been able to deceive have been ambushed by the poverty of their own faculties. For those who had been ordained in the name of God had of course been rendered perfect by his work. And you fight as enemies against the work of God, destroying the work of God with the levers of your malice!

Thus it is apparent that you are the ones of whom it was said in Psalm 10, *For what you have made perfect they have destroyed*. Your impiety has made you proud, but justice accuses you, watching from heaven; and people make the mistake of praising you as you practise evil, so that it is of you that the Holy Spirit said in Psalm 9, [*While the impious man is proud, the poor man is consumed; they are taken in the plots that they conceive*],[84] since the sinner is praised in the desires of his soul, and he who does evil is blessed. What is more evil than to exorcise the Holy Spirit,[85] to break the altars, to cast the eucharist to beasts? And so that your people may send you into error, they praise you and call you happy, speak well of you, swear by your names and are seen to respect your persons instead of God.

22. It is customary for people to name God in order to prove their faith on oath. But when oaths are sworn through you, there is silence among your party concerning God and Christ.[86] If the divine sanction has migrated from heaven to you, now that oaths are sworn through you, none of you nor any of your party should be idle: refuse to die, command the clouds, send rain if you can, so that it may become more usual to swear by you and there may be silence about God. For even in former times, what more than your people could the devil do to promote the building of temples and the fashioning of idols? He could do nothing else than silence talk of God, while humans in their error were speaking only of the devil.

23. O what a mixture of sacrilege with impiety, when you freely listen to people swearing by you and do not let the voice of God come to your

---

[84] Psalm 9.23-4; but the words must be supplied.

[85] The Holy Spirit having been received at baptism (Mark 1.11; 1Cor 2.12ff), the rebaptism exorcises this, and not a demon. Hence it is the most heinous sin: Matthew 12.32 par.

[86] Contrast Augustine, *Cresc.* II.13 on the regularity of Donatist ordination; but the Donatists themselves refer to the cult of Donatus in a letter quoted by Augustine, *ibid.* III.62.

ears, when he says in Psalm 104, *You shall not touch my anointed ones, or lay a hand on my prophets.*[87] Not only do the books of Kings attest the anointing of kings and priests, but David in Psalm 132 speaks as follows, *Like the ointment on the head, which runs down on to the beard of Aaron.*[88] Yet you, on the contrary, try to despise God's precepts with the same vigour that those who fear God show when they try to fulfil his commands. Teach us where you are commanded to shave the heads of priests, when there are so many instances on the other side to show that it should not be done. Saul, before he sinned, deserved anointing, but after his anointing committed no small offence. When God saw this, wishing to show by example that the oil was not to be touched, he declared his repentance. For we read that God spoke thus, *I repent of having anointed Saul as king.*[89]

And of course God was able to take away the oil that he had given. But since he wished to teach us that even in a sinner the oil should not be touched, the very one who had given it expressed repentance. Therefore if God, for the sake of teaching you, was unable, because unwilling, to take away what he himself had given, who are you that you take away what you have not given? And you who should have prepared your ears to listen have instead prepared a dagger for transgression. And when you were able to be sons of God, you have chosen to be sons of men, and in order to take a bite from other people's honours, you have turned your teeeth into arrows and weapons, you have sharpened your tongues into swords, you have fuflilled what is written of you in Psalm 56: *Sons of men, their teeth are arrows and their tongue is a sharp sword.*[90]

24. Therefore you have sharpened your tongues into swords, which you have wielded to kill not bodies but honours, you have cut off not limbs but names. What profit is it for men to live when you have killed their honours? They are sound of limb, yet carry the remains of their stolen dignity. For you have extended your hands and spread deadly veils over every head, so that, while there are, as I said above, four types of head in the church, of the bishops, of the presbyters, of the deacons and of

[87] Psalm 104.15. Quoted by Donatists: Augustine, *Petil.* II.44.
[88] Psalm 132.2; 131.1 is quoted above on the benefits of unity.
[89] 1Samuel 15.11.
[90] Psalm 56.5. Cf Augustine, *Petil.* II.33.

the faithful,[91] you have chosen not to spare a single one, you have ruined human souls. These acts of yours God bewails in his prophet Ezekiel, when he says, *Woe to those who make a veil - that is who lay a hand - over every head and over every age for the ruin of souls.*[92] You have found boys; you have wounded them with a penance, so that none could be ordained;[93] acknowledge that you have ruined their souls. You have found faithful people of long standing; you have made them repent; acknowledge that you have ruined their souls. You have found deacons, presbyters, bishops; you have made them laics; acknowledge that you have ruined their souls.

25. The one on whom you have now tried to lay your hand had been your fellow and comrade; you ran the same course. Grant that he has sinned, when he patently has not sinned; he was fallen, as you judge; if you have read the Apostle, you should inquire to whom you stand, he to whom he falls. If you are a servant, acknowledge your master and understand that it is not to you that he was fallen, who a little before had run his course with you. Why do you invade the power of another, why are you so rash as to step up to God's tribunal? And when you yourself are a criminal, you dare to pass sentence on another, yet you have read, *He who stands, stands to his own master, and he who is fallen is fallen to his master.*[94] His master, however, has the power to raise him; *who are you, to judge another's servant?*

You should have learned from God's boy David that you ought not to have touched the oil conferred on a priest by God.[95] He was anointed by Samuel in such a way as to take as little as possible from the previous gift to Saul. Then when a single cave contained them, either by God's order or by the contrivance of events, Saul, who had sinned, had come into the power of the boy David. Without seeing he was seen, in as much as it often happens that one who has come from fuller light

---

[91] See above, n.50.

[92] Ezekiel 13.18.

[93] This may have some reference to the penance imposed on Caecilian at I.19. Jerome, *Alt.* 5 says that by making "Arian" bishops do penance the Luciferians were reducing them to lay status, and denying the work of the Holy Spirit no less than if they had rebaptized them. (Yet catholics did not recognise Donatist bishops, who were rivals to their own).

[94] Romans 14.4.

[95] On David's anointing see 1Samuel 16.13. The frigid dramatization bespeaks a training in Latin schools of rhetoric.

cannot see another next to him in the darkness of an enclosed space.[96]
Countless hosts were following their established king, but the king
himself had come into the power of another. David had in his hands the
moment of victory; he was able to cut off his careless and unsuspecting
adversary with no pains, and without involving many in bloodshed and
strife, to reduce the cost of war to a murder. Both his retainers and the
moment urged him on, opportunity was exhorting him to victory. He
had already begun to draw the blade, already his hand had its weapon
ready against the throat of his enemy, but he withstood them because his
memory was replete with divine commands, he contradicted the retainers
who were urging him and the moment, as though he were saying this,
"Pointlessly you goad me, Victory, vainly, Opportunity, you beckon me
on to triumphs". He wished to defeat his enemy, but the first duty is to
observe the divine precepts of the Lord. *I shall not lay my hand*, said
he, *on the Lord's anointed.*[97] He restrained his hand together with the
sword; and, fearing the oil, he saved his enemy, completing his
obedience when he avenged his death.[98]

You neither fear God nor acknowledge your brethren, you sharpen the
razors of your tongues on the whetstone of bitterness, and trampling the
divine precepts you have rushed on those in charge of the wretched, so
that, having cut off the leaders, you can drag their blind and unlearned
people into captivity. You crave the honours of innocent priests; hence
such is the inbred hunger in your folly that you make your maws a
gaping sepulchre. For every sepulchre one burial suffices, then it is
closed; for your maw the burials of honours have not been nearly
enough, and they still gape as you seek to devour someone, so that it is
deservedly said of you, *Their maw is a gaping sepulchre.*[99] For you even
assume the right to curse, when it is written, *Bless and curse not.*[100] If
anyone has done anything against your will, you aim your terrors, you
hold out curses, and because some people can deserve more evil than
good, whatever has been done according to God's judgment or the

---

[96] Perhaps an allegory with reference to John 1.5f and 3.19, where darkness and light
symbolize revelation and ignorance.
[97] 1Samuel 24.7.
[98] At 2Kings 1.14-15 David executes the assistant of Saul's suicide.
[99] Isaiah 5.11; Psalm 13.3; Romans 3.13.
[100] Romans 12.14

sinner's desert you vindicate with your acrimonious curses, since it is deservedly said of you, *Their mouth is full of cursing and acrimony.*[101]

You glory in the fact that it has been possible for certain people to die by your curses. Surely we are not allowed to kill. Or do you think yourselves innocent because you used no blade? Then let the poisoner also adjudge himself innocent, if only blades can do murder. Let a person not be conscious of guilt when he has killed another by stealing his food; let a person think himself innocent who had suffocated one who wished to live by inhibiting his breathing. There are many ways of killing, but there is one name for death. When you protest with oaths that a person has been killed by your curses, what does it matter whether you smite with the sword or strike with your tongue? You are undoubtedly a murderer, if one who lived is dead because of you. For anyone of this kind among you, it is vain to profess himself a Christian or a priest of God, when it is written [in Solomon], *God does not cause death nor take pleasure in the destruction of the living.*[102]

I do not believe that you can have forgotten what you did in certain places, when you wantonly killed those who preached the law of God, that is his prophets, against the bidding of God, who says, *And do not lay your hand upon my prophets.*[103] Deuterius, Parthenius, Donatus and Getulicus, the bishops of God, you cut off with the sword of the tongue, pouring out the blood not of the body but of their honour. They lived on after this as human beings, but as priests who held God's honours they were killed by you. It is notorious and proven that in the time of persecution certain lax bishops lapsed from the confession of God's name and offered incense;[104] nevertheless, none of those who escaped laid hands on the lapsed or ordered the piercing of their knees. And you do today, in the aftermath of unity, what no-one did in the aftermath of the offerings. As it is written, You shall not touch my anointed ones or lay a hand on my prophets. God protects his oil, because, if sin comes

---

[101] Psalm 13.3; Romans 3.13.

[102] Wisdom 1.13. The words "in Solomon" are omitted in some MSS. The African code of 419 numbers Wisdom among the books of Solomon, though Augustine (*De Doctrina Christiana* I.12) accepts that the attribution is merely conventional.

[103] Psalm 104.15 again. The bishops are otherwise unknown.

[104] An unusual confession: Augustine, *Cresc.* III, *De Unico Baptismo* etc. regularly maintains that the facts are unknown.

from man, the oil is none the less from God. You shall not touch, he
says, my anointed ones; and so - lest when striking at a person's sin, the
oil, which is from God, should also be smitten - God has reserved his
own property for his own judgment. Yet you rush on another's property
everywhere, corrupting the felicity of all. For what greater infelicity is
there than for priests of God to live on, without being what they were?
26. Married women, boys as well and virgins, compelled by you in the
absence of any sin, their innocence and modesty intact, have learned
under your tuition to do penance. Is there any less infelicity here? You
have trampled on sex, you have molested age; truly it was said of you
in Psalm 13, *Contrition and infelicity are in their ways, and the way of
peace they have not known; there is no fear of God before their eyes.*[105]
You have demanded that the folk do penance; nor was it enacted by
anyone, but exacted by you. Nor were there equal intervals of time, but
in all your enactments you showed respect of persons, ordering one to
do penance for a whole year, another for a month, anther for barely a
full day. If consent to unity is the sin that you wish it to be, if the fault
is similar, where is there not equal penance for the same guilt? There
is no doubt that the people that believes is called Israel, the single
communities daughters of Israel,[106] that is, those who have seen God
with their minds or believed in God. And yet you have compelled these
folk to bend the knee and bow their necks and, joining their heads in a
row, to make a mass of penitents. These are the folk God grieves for,
saying through the prophet Ezekiel, *Woe to the daughters of Israel, who
make pillows, that is, instruments of the neck, that they may put them
under the elbows and under the hand.*[107] Clearly that means under your
elbows and hands and when you stretch veils of penitence over the
heads of these men and women. The nature of your impiety and folly
has been shown, and your pride demonstrated; your stupidity was also
to be revealed, but this I shall demonstrate in the sixth book.

---

[105] Psalm 13.3 again.
[106] In the Old Testament, "daughters of Israel", as in the following citation, means Israelite
women; the singular "virgin daughter of Israel" is a periphrasis for Israel or Jerusalem.
[107] Ezekiel 13.18 again.

OPTATUS:

Third Book against the Donatists

1. In my judgment, I have said enough in the second book about the church, which is the spouse of Christ, and about its gifts and its inheritance from the Saviour. The next tasks are, first to show the errors of the schismatics; then, what was causing unity to emerge; thirdly, who brought it about that a military force was sent. It is indeed true that the agents of unity took many harsh measures, but why do you impute these to Leontius, Macarius or Taurinus?[1] Impute them to your ancestors, who, as it is written in the prophet, *have themselves eaten sour grapes, that your teeth may be troubled.*[2] First {it should be imputed} to those who divided the people of God and formed unneccessary churches, then to Donatus of Carthage, who was the next to provoke an attempt to bring about unity; thirdly to Donatus of Bagaia, who gathered a demented crowd, in fear of whose violence Macarius summoned the aid of an armed force to guard himself and his orders.[3] Then armour bearers came with quivers, every city was filled with shouting people; on the proclamation of unity, you all fled. No-one was told, "Deny God"; no-one was told, "Burn the Scripture"; no-one was told, either, "Lay incense" or "Destroy the churches"; now these are the events that engender martyrdoms.[4] It was unity that was proclaimed; there were

---

[1] All appear below in the role of *comites*. The *comites*, or imperial companions, were an order established by Constantine; see further Jones (1964), Vol I, pp. 104-5. In Africa, a military *comes* would replace the usual *vicarius* only in times of great disorder; the distinction between the *comes* and the *vicarius* is not always clearly maintained by ancient writers.

[2] See Ezekiel 18.2 and Jeremiah 31.29, neither of which implies that God himself approves the saying.

[3] On this powerful figure, the "other Donatus", see Frend (1952a) pp. 178-9 and Maier (1987), p. 257 n. 6. His revolt provoked the ruthless measures of Macarius, and Bagaia remained a centre of unrest as late as 394, when a Council of 310 Donatists condemned the followers of Maximian, who had refused to accept the reconciliation of Primianus to the Donatist Church. See Augustine, *Cresc.* IV.5ff etc.

[4] Alluding to the pagan persecutions. Although the text implies that laying incense and destroying churches were presented as alternatives to the same people, one was a private order to the Christian and the other to the (normally pagan) magistrate. The second canon of the Council of Carthage under Gratus (348), by stipulating that only the church could

only exhortations that God and his Christ should be prayed to on equal terms by the whole people gathered in one. At first there was no intimidation; no-one had seen a rod, no-one had seen a place of detention; as I said above, there were only exhortations. You were all afraid, you fled, you quailed, so that what is written in Psalm 52 was certainly said of you: *They quailed in fear where no fear was.*[5] Therefore all the bishops fled with their clergy, and some died; those who were stronger were caught and banished to far places.

2. And yet of all these measures none was taken at our wish, none in consultation with us, none with our cognizance, none with our collaboration; but all the proceedings, bitterly deplored by God in his sorrow, were in retribution for your second translation of the {baptismal} water from its ancient fishpool to yourselves, in defiance of the interdict.[6] But I do not know if it came with that fish, which is understood as Christ, which in the recitation of the patriarchal narratives is said to have been caught in the Tigris, whose gall-bladder and liver Tobias took to guard the woman Sara and to bring light to the blindness of Tobias; by the insides of the same fish the demon Asmodeus was driven away from the girl Sara, who is understood as the church, and blindness was expelled from Tobias.[7] This is the fish, which in baptism is introduced into the waves of the font, so that what was water may also be called a fishpool because of the fish. The name of this fish according to its Greek appellation IKHTHUS contains a host of holy names in its individual letters, being in Latin *Jesus Christ Son of God*

---

recognise a martyr, rendered it impossible for a Donatist to acquire that dignity. Cf also Augustine, *Cresc.* IV.55-62; the Scriptural justification for the catholic view can be found at 2Peter 2.20.

[5] Psalm 52.6.

[6] Alluding, it would seem, to Isaiah 22.9, quoted below. The baptismal font is already called the *piscina* by Tertullian, *Bapt.* 5; cf Ambrose, *De Mysteriis* 22. The term invites comparison, useful to catholics, with the image of the Church as a net containing both good and bad fish, at Matthew 13.47-9.

[7] See Tobit 6.9 and 6.19, though Labrousse (1996), p. 12 n. 1 suspects confusion with the Sarah who was the wife of Abraham. Before Jerome's translation of the Hebrew Torah, the books now called the Apocrypha were sometimes treated as canonical (two appear in Athanasius' list in *Festal Letter* 39).

Saviour.[8] This fishpool, which in the whole catholic church throughout the world abounded with saving waters for the life of the human race, you translated to serve your own will, and you dissolved the single baptism, by which walls are made to guard human beings, and you made, as it were, other walls, but no good building.[9]

You were unable to construct without destroying. And what sort of building can it be, which is constructed from a ruin? This is the thing that God bewails and weeps for through Isaiah the prophet when he says that *the daughter of his own kind is sorrowful.*[10] To be of God's kind is to be of no kind, since he exists of himself and remains for eternity. It is a like case with the water, which we say is not created.[11] It is with regard to the injury done to this water that God speaks of his tears, which you have caused, and which, as he testifies, cannot be dried by any consolation. He says to you through Isaiah the prophet, *Let me go, I shall weep bitterly, no-one will be able to console me in the sorrow of the daughter of my own kind.* In this place our innocence is defended, since God in his sorrow declares his anger against you, revealing also the cause and showing his reason.

After this, he does not say "in Zion", but in one of its valleys it is performed;[12] not in that Mount Zion which a small stream separates from the walls of Jerusalem in Syria Palestina. On top of this there is a plateau, not very large, in which there were seven synagogues where the Jewish people could gather to learn the Law given by Moses; but no litigation was heard there, nor did anyone pronounce judgment there, nor was any sentence delivered there by any judge, since it was a place

---

[8] *Iesous Khristos theou huios soter*: "Jesus Christ, Son of God, Saviour".Cf *Oracula Sibyllina* VIII.217, Constantine, *Oratio ad Sanctos* 18, Tertullian, *Bapt.* 1. On the Christian iconography of the fish see Morey (1910) and Labrousse (1996) p. 12 n. 3.

[9] Foreshadowing the symbolism of Ezekiel 13, quoted below.

[10] A loose citation of Isaiah 22.4, which shows how Optatus construed the phrase *in contritione filiae generis mei.*

[11] Relying on Isaiah 22.9-10 (below), Optatus seems to identify the water with that of Genesis 1.2; cf. Tertullian, *Bapt.* 5 and Ambrose, *De Mysteriis* 9. He may regard it as an embodiment of the Spirit, identified with baptismal oil in Book IV.

[12] Optatus seems to be thinking of Isaiah 22.5, where in a particular valley the prophet sees "a day of destruction, perishing and trampling, with error from the Lord of hosts".

of teaching, not of controversy after teaching.[13] If any case was
necessary, it took place within the walls of Jerusalem. Hence it is
written in the prophet Isaiah, From Zion shall emerge a Law and the
Word of God from Jerusalem.[14] It was not, therefore, on that Mount
Zion that Isaiah saw the valley, but on the holy mountain, which is the
church, which raises its head through all the Roman world under
heaven. On this mount the Son of God rejoices in the first Psalm in
being appointed as king by God his Father, saying, *Since he has
appointed me as king over Zion his holy mountain*,[15] that is, over the
church, whose king and bridgroom and head he is - not on that
mountain where there are no portals that God loves, but on the
mountain of the church, which bears a spiritual name.[16]

Through the portals of this church enter in the innocent, the just, the
compassionate, the continent and the virgins; these are the portals which
the Holy Spirit speaks of through David in Psalm 86, when he says, *Its
foundations are on the holy mountains; God loves the portals of Zion.*[17]
(He is speaking) not of that physical mountain, where now there are no
portals and since the victories of the Emperor Vespasian, the traces of
the ancient ruins are barely visible.[18] Therefore the spiritual Zion is the
church, in which Christ is appointed as king by God the Father, the
church which exists throughout the whole world, in which there is one
catholic church. For the most holy prophet David bears witness in

---

[13] See Labrousse (1996) p. 14 n. 1 But Schurer (1979), Vol II, p. 445 n. 80 says that only
Christian sources give this information (cf Epiphanius, *De Mensuris* 14 and the Bordeaux
pilgrim's *Itinerarium*, which states that only one remains). Jewish sources allege as many
as 480. See Schurer (1979), p. 447-54 on the order of service.
[14] Isaiah 2.5.
[15] Psalm 2.6, already quoted as messianic at at Mark 1.15 par. Donatists quoted the whole
Psalm to show that God wished his people to be free of secular rulers: Augustine, *Petil*
II.202.
[16] For the contrast between the physical and the spiritual Zion cf Hebrews 12.18-24, and
Gal 4.26 for the heavenly Jerusalem as the church. Optatus' reference to portals
anticipates the following citation from Psalm 86.
[17] Psalm 86.1.
[18] Or rather Titus, son of Vespasian, who completed the conquest of Jerusalem in 70 A.D.
The event brought about an irrevocable divorce between Christianity and Judaism because
(a) Christians had fled the city before the siege began; and (b) the fall of the Temple
seemed to confirm the abolition of the Law and the supersession of animal sacrifice by
that of Christ. See Mark 13 Revelation 22; Eusebius, *HE* III.5.2 etc.

another place too that Zion is the church, saying, *Zion, praise your God, who has strengthened the bolts of your portals, and pronounced blessings on your sons in you.*[19] In the several provinces of the whole world we understand the several valleys of the mountain, and when Isaiah's vision is not located in the whole mountain but in one valley, this is merely Africa, in which alone, when the existing temples to God were enough, your leaders wanted to found others; here alone walls were thrown down, and the water of the sacred fishpool was transferred, and you set up novelty against antiquity and human water was consecrated against divine water.

For all this God addresses his questions and reproaches to the valley of Zion, saying, *Why have you done this? Thus, since you have gone up into needless temples, every city is full of cries, your people are wounded, not wounded with the sword, and dead in you, not dead in war. From least to greatest, your leaders' wits are wandering as they wander through the mountains, they are turned to flight, and those who are caught are straitly bound and your stronger men are driven far away. Let me go; I shall weep bitterly; no-one will be able to comfort me in the sorrow of the daughter of my own kind, and the Elamites shall come with their quivers* - in the Latin tongue Elamites means the regiments of the camps[20] - and he follows this up, saying, *your sanctuaries shall be brought into public view, and the secrets of the house of Israel shall be laid bare.*[21] This was done in Africa, and why all this was done, God has declared when he blames you, saying, *Since you have transferred the water of the ancient fishpool to your own city, and have cast down the walls of Jerusalem, so that you make make another rampart; and you have placed the water between the two ramparts and have refused to look on the ancient fishpool, or on him who created it in the beginning.*

3. You see now, brother Parmenianus, that everything recoils on you, whose leaders sowed the cause of all these events, then on Donatus of

---

[19] Psalm 147.1-2, not ascribed to David in its title.

[20] Jerome's *Onomasticon* (45.19) construes Elam as *dei populus*; if the *populus* is taken to be the "hosts of the Lord" (as in Jahweh Sabaoth), this may generate an interpretation like that of Optatus, which appears to have no other parallel.

[21] Isaiah 22.4-8. confused with 21.2. See Labrousse (1996) p. 19 n. 2. Isaiah 22.9-10 follows shortly.

Carthage, whose poison is seen to have disturbed the work of unity. In this work I shall show that our agents did not do anything at our desire or through their own malice, but at the provocation and instance of causes and persons, set up irresponsibly by Donatus of Carthage, as he was striving to appear a great man. For whom has he deceived but you, because you are an immigrant and false stories could be told to you? Or who can deny a matter to which the whole of Carthage is the principal witness,[22] namely that the Emperor Constans did not initially send Paulus and Macarius to bring about unity,[23] but with alms to relieve the poor, so that they might breathe, be clothed, eat and rejoice throughout the several churches? When they came to Donatus, your father, and told him why they had come, he, inflamed by his wonted folly, broke out into these words: "What has the church to do with the Emperor?"[24]

And from the fount of his irresponsibility he poured many curses, just as he once did to Gregory,[25] whom he had no scruple in writing to as follows: **Gregory, stain of the Senate and disgrace to the prefecture,** and other things of the kind; the prefect wrote back to Donatus with patience worthy of a bishop. The copies of these letters are recited everywhere by the mouths of many. Even then he was contemplating an injury to rulers and kings in defiance of the precepts of the Apostle Paul, though, had he been listening to the Apostle, he would have prayed for them daily. For the teaching of the blessed Apostle Paul is as follows: *Pray for kings and rulers, that we may live a quiet and peaceful life with them.*[26] For the commonwealth is not in the church,

---

[22] Cf the preamble to the acts of the Council of Carthage under Gratus (348), though it is not said there that Paulus and Macarius ever had any other aim than the imposition of martial law. Macarius took stern measures to pacify the Donatist resistance, and catholics were later styled "Macarians" by their indignant adversaries: see Augustine, *Petil* II.208.

[23] Constans was the son of Constantine the Great, and ruler of the west from 337 to 350. Because he supported Athanasius, an intransigent defender of the Nicene creed of 325, Constans was regarded as a champion of orthodoxy, in contrast to his more conciliatory brother Constantius, who ruled the east.

[24] On the antecedents of this phrase, see I.22 and notes, with Augustine, *Brev.* III.10.

[25] On the prefecture of Gregory (336-7) see Maier (1987) 253-4, esp. 253 n. 4. The praetorian prefecture was the summit of an equestrian career, but after Diocletian the functions were only administrative and fiscal. In Constantine's empire, different prefects were assigned to different areas, Gregory being a prefect of Africa when it was temporarily divided from Italy.

[26] 1Tim 2.2.

but the church in the commonwealth, that is in the Roman Empire, which Christ calls Lebanon in the Song of Songs, when he says, *Come, my choice bride, come from Lebanon,*[27] that is from the Roman Empire, where there are holy priesthoods and modesty and virginity, which do not exist among barbarous peoples, and, if they did, could not be held safe.[28]

Paul is right to teach that we should pray for kings and rulers, even if the Emperor were the sort who lived in a heathen manner; how much more when he is a Christian, how much more when he fears God, how much more when he is pious, how much more when he is merciful, as the event itself proves! For he had sent ornaments to the house of God, he had sent alms to the poor, and nothing to Donatus. Why then did he lose his wits? Why was he angry, why did he reject what had been sent? And when they who had been sent told him that they were going through the several provinces and would give to those who wanted to receive, he said that he had sent letters everywhere to prevent what had been brought from being distributed anywhere to the poor.

Oh, what a way to take care for the wretched, to look after the poor, to come to the sinner's aid - so God cries, saying, *I am he who has made the poor and the rich,*[29] not because he was unable to give to the poor as well, but, if he gave to both, the sinner would not be able to find any means to aid himself. It is written indeed, *Just as water extinguishes fire, so alms extinguish sin.*[30] Surely both are in God's presence, both the one who gives and the one who opposes the gift. What if God should now say to Donatus, "Bishop, what would you have Constans be? If an innocent man, why did you refuse to receive from the innocent? If a sinner, why did you not allow him to give, when I made the poor for his sake?" Under this interrogation, how will he turn out? Why did he take pains in his irresponsible folly to stand in the way of so many of the poor? He had come to believe that he held the

---

[27] Song of Songs 4.8.

[28] Lebanon is identified with Assyria at Ezekiel 31.3; Tertullian, *Adv. Marcionem* IV.11 takes it as symbol of idolatry, which a Christian can easily equate with the Roman Empire. The professed contempt of Optatus for barbarians contrasts with the praise accorded to such peoples in apologists such as Justin; now that the Empire supports the catholic church, it is coterminous with Christendom. But cf Augustine, *Cresc.* III.71.

[29] Proverbs 22.2.

[30] Ezekiel 3.33.

principal place in Carthage; and since there is no-one higher than the Emperor save God himself who made the Emperor, when Donatus raised himself above the Emperor, he had already, as it were, exceeded human limits, so that he almost deemed himself God rather than man, because of his lack of reverence for the one whom humans feared next after God.

Hence through Ezekiel the Holy Spirit reproaches the Prince of Tyre, that is the prince of Carthage, when he speaks through his prophet in these words: *Son of man, say against the Prince of Tyre, Thus says the Lord God: Because your heart is lifted up and you have said, I am God.*[31] The first proof that Tyre is Carthage is given by Isaiah, in whom we read, *A vision about Tyre*, then follows, *Wail, ships of Carthage.*[32] Then secular literature also asserts that Tyre is Carthage;[33] and if there is another city which is called by this name, no such deed has been observed in any other as is well known to have been committed in Carthage. *Speak*, says God, *against the Prince of Tyre.* He did not say that he was to speak against some temporal king, nor to many, but to one, that is Bishop Donatus. For it was not right for the prophet Ezekiel, whom I have lately named, to compare to anyone but a prince the bishop who, as I have said, was claiming for himself the principal place in Carthage, who lifted up his heart, who seemed to himself superior to the human race, and who wanted to have everybody, even his associates, under him. He would never accept any of the offerings, though this involved faith, and Christ his God, as well as the complaints of many whom he injured in his very association with them, by doing something or other in secret and afterwards perfunctorily mingling with

---

[31] Ezekiel 28.2. As usual, Optatus applies the verse to a historical figure (though not a contemporary of the prophet himself), in contrast to, e.g. Origen, who interprets him as the devil (*De Principiis* I.5.4-5). He ignores the fact that there was a catholic Bishop in Carthage, and that Donatists were regularly derided as Numidians. If catholics invented a Numidian see for Donatus, as Alexander (1980) argues, he knows nothing of it.

[32] Isaiah 23.1. Labrousse (1996) p. 26 n. 1 observes that the Vulgate does not speak of Carthage; the Septuagint, however, has done Optatus' work for him by translating the Tyrians as *Karchedonioi*, and this may have been reproduced in the Latin version known to Optatus. Augustine, however, doubts the applicability of the verse at *Cath.s* 42.

[33] Because the Carthaginians are called *Tyrii* by Virgil at *Aeneid* I.574 etc. Sidon was in fact the mother city of Carthage; but *Tyrii*, like *Poeni*, can refer to all Phoenicians.

the rest. In this way his heart was elated, so that he seemed to himself no longer a human being but God.

In the people's mouths, indeed, he was rarely called Bishop, but Donatus of Carthage.[34] And he fully deserved to be named and reproached as the prince of Tyre, that is of Carthage, because he was first of bishops, as though he himself were more than the rest; and since he wished to have no human traits, he lifted up his heart, not like the heart of a human being, but like the heart of God, as he craved to be something more than other humans. God's speech to him follows on, *You have said, I am God.* Thus, although he did not use this expression, he either did or suffered all that fulfils the sense of this expression. He raised up his heart, so that he judged no human comparable with himself, and he seemed higher to himself because of his inflated thoughts, since whatever is above humanity is virtually God. Then, whereas bishops ought to serve God, he exacted so much for himself from his bishops that they all revered him with no less fear than God; that is to say, since he thought himself God, and since humans should swear by God alone, he suffered humans to swear by himself in the same way as by God.[35] If anyone had made this error, he ought to have prevented it; as he did not prevent him, he thought himself God.

Moreover, whereas, before his proud behaviour, all who believed in Christ used to be called Christians, he had the audacity to divide the people with God, so that those who followed him were no longer called Christians but Donatists;[36] and if any ever came to him from any province of Africa, he did not ask, them anything, according to the usual human custom, about the rains, the state of peace, or the produce of the year,[37] but these were his words to every individual who came: "How does my party stand among you?" - as if he had already divided the people with God, so that he could already speak without fear of his own party. For from his time up to the present day, if ever some case

---

[34] Cf Augustine, *Cresc.* III.38 on the title given to Donatus by the (easterners') Council of Serdica in 343.

[35] See Book 2.25 (p. 55 above).

[36] Though, according to Augustine, they preferred the name *Donatiani* or *pars Donati*; see Labrousse (1996) p. 30 n. 1.

[37] Comments on the inquisitiveness of ancient towndwellers can be found, for example, in Caesar, *De Bello Gallico* IV.5.

about church matters is carried on before a public court, the individuals questioned have spoken in such a way, according to the Acts, as to say that they were of Donatus' party;[38] about Christ they were silent. And what shall I say of the clergy, when, as I have already mentioned in the first book, we read prayers addressed long ago to Constantine and signed in the following manner with the names of the bishops: **Given by Capito, Dignus and other bishops of Donatus' party?** And their petitions, if you please, were against bishops, who, since they were not of Donatus' party, dwelt in the catholic party of Christ. And, as he was not a bishop amongst his fellow-bishops, and did not want to be a human among humans, it is patent that he raised up his heart and thought himself God.

Brother Parmenianus, you know well the names of those men of yours who performed ordinations, and you are not ignorant as to where they were, and we too have taught you who addressed petitions or to whom, and from what sort of person they asked the right to return and were able to return with you. Now, seeing that they read before the judges of Africa the very prayers that they had made, in which was written, **Given by bishops of Donatus' party**, what are they going to say in that impending divine judgment, when in this age they have in another way confessed that they are not of the church of Christ and have freely declared that they were of Donatus' party, though Christ's own words are written in the Gospel: *He who has confessed me before human beings, I shall confess him in the presence of my Father?*[39] These people have confessed Donatus, not Christ.

And in case this proof-text, which manifestly relates to the man himself, should seem a small one, there is a further testimony in the conclusion of the reproach cited above, where God has said that he would not die on land;[40] and everyone knows that this is what took place.[41] He lived in the house of God and he was in the heart of the sea;

---

[38] Cf the letter to Constantine at I.22.

[39] Conflating Mark 10.32 and Luke 12.8.Cf the letter to Constantine at I.22, which Optatus proceeds to quote.

[40] Cf Ezekiel 9.3.

[41] For the practice of drowning Donatists see *Passio Isaac et Maximiani* 12-14; *Passio Marculi* 12

everywhere we read the sea as the present age,[42] while he was not only in charity with certain Christians, but because of his knowledge of secular literature was also in the heart of the sea, that is, was in love with the age and because of his knowledge seemed to himself wise. But this wisdom of his God had rendered vain, when he says, *Surely you are not wiser than Daniel?*[43] How well deserved was this belittlement of his wisdom, which in his eyes made him wiser than Daniel in rejecting the gifts of kings, when he refused to accept what was seen to have been sent by a Christian Emperor! And he seemed to himself a new Daniel, or Daniel's superior in wisdom, because Daniel himself, when obliged to accept gifts from King Belshazzar, that is a ring, a brooch and other things, is reported to have said, *May your gifts remain with you, King.*[44] And this response of his was wise, involving no insult to the king and not condemning but deferring what he offered, not in the way that Donatus heaped every insult that he could upon Constans and rejected what had been sent by him for the poor.

But the sainted Daniel was found to be wise in refusing to accept the rewards offered on that day; for what was being asked of him was still in heaven, and it would have been foolish to accept a sort of wage from that king for what was not yet in his power. For that reason, he would not at the time accept the rewards that were offered on that day. Then when God showed him what he could declare to the aforesaid king, he brought it back to Belshazzar, and what he had previously seemed to reject he now freely accepted.[45] Deservedly God reproaches the prince of Tyre, Donatus, when he says, *Surely you are not wiser than Daniel?* But oh, how far is the presumption of Donatus from the character of Daniel! For what Belshazzar gave, he gave to Daniel, not the poor; what Constans the Christian Emperor sent at that time he had sent for the poor, not Donatus. Hence he says, *The wise have not taught you their wisdom,*[46] since you have refused to learn from Solomon, this saying of

---

[42] See Revelation 17. 15, 21.1; Augustine, *Petil* II.235 etc.
[43] Ezekiel 28.3.
[44] Daniel 5.17. For the argument from Daniel that kings are to be respected, cf Augustine, *Petil* II.243-4.
[45] Daniel 5.29.
[46] Daniel 2.27.

his, *Hide bread in the heart of the poor and he will pray for you.*[47]
After all, he also refused to learn from Daniel himself this advice which
he gave to Nebuchadnezzar as to how he could make satisfaction when
he had offended God. *And you, King,* he said, *listen to my advice and
let it please you: redeem your sins with alms, and your injustices by
compassion on the poor.*[48] Daniel urges a sinful and sacrilegious king to
give alms; Donatus, who deserved reproach, opposed the merciful
intention of the Christian Emperor Constans. The reason for reproaching
him is that the wise did not teach him their wisdom, since he did not
allow what the Emperor had sent to be given through him. Hence it is
patent that Donatus was the fount of evil causes.[49]

4. And so whatever harsh measures may have been taken to bring about
unity, you see, brother Parmenianus, who ought to bear the blame for
it. You say that we catholics requested military force; if that is the case,
why did no-one at that time see an armed military force in the
proconsular province? Paulus and Macarius were coming to relieve the
poor in every place and exhort individuals to unity; and when they came
near the city of Bagaia, then (as I said above) the other Donatus, bishop
of that city, desiring to raise an impediment to unity and an obstacle to
the arrival of the aforesaid persons, sent heralds through the
neighbouring places and all the market-towns, calling the disaffected
circumcellions by name with an invitation to assembly at an appointed
place.[50] And the assembly solicited at that time consisted of the same
people whose insanity a little while before was seen by those very
bishops to have been impiously inflamed. For when, before the
establishment of unity, people of this kind were roving from place to

---

[47] Ecclesiasticus 29.15.
[48] Daniel 4.24.
[49] Mocking the Donatist claim to possess the one true font.
[50] Roving bands who courted death while destroying property. According to Augustine the
name *circumcelliones* was derived from the phrase *circum cellas vagare* (*Contra
Gaudentium* 1.32), while Isidore of Seville, *Etymologiae* VIII.(5).53 says that it signifies
rusticity (*agrestes*). Frend (1952b) speculates that the cells were those of martyrs. The
circumcellions may have called themselves *agonistici*: see Thornton (1986). Catholic
authors, and the legislation in their favour, represent the circumcellions as a fanatical party
stirred up by the Donatists, who then failed to control them. Schindler (1983) contends
that they were the party of the common people (*plebs*), and Frend (1952b) notes that they
were derided by the scholarly Donatist Tyconius.

place, when Axido and Fasir were being called leaders of the saints by these same maniacs,[51] no-one could be secure in his own possessions; the records of debts had lost their force, no creditor at that time had the freedom to enforce payment, all were terrified by the letters of those who boasted that they had been leaders of the saints; and if there was any delay in obeying their behests, a raging multitude suddenly flew to their aid, and, as terror went before them, besieged the creditors with dangers, so that those who should have had suitors on account of their loans were forced into grovelling prayers through fear of death. Each one hastened to write off even his greatest debts, and reckoned it a gain if he escaped injury at their hands. Even the safest journeys could not take place, because masters, thrown out of their vehicles, ran in servile fashion before their own retainers, who were sitting in their masters' place. By the verdict and bidding of those men the conditions of master and slave were transposed.

And when they showed spleen against the bishops of your party, the latter are said to have written to Taurinus, then the count[52] that men of this kind could not be corrected within the church, and required that they receive chastisement from the aforesaid count. Then Taurinus, in response to their letters, ordered an armed military force to proceed through all the market-towns, where the madness of the circumcellions was wont to rove. In the locus Octaviensis[53] hosts were killed and many decapitated, whose bodies could be numbered up to this day among the defaced altars and tables. When the burial of some of this number had commenced, Clarus the presbyter in the locus Subbulensis was compelled by his bishop to undo the burial.[54] This revealed that what had happened had been ordered to happen, since it was forbidden even to give them burial in the house of God.

After this the multitude of these men had increased. Thus Donatus of Bagaia found the means to lead a raging mob against Macarius. To this class had belonged those who, in their false desire for martyrdom, used

[51] Mandouze (1982) p. 132 can add nothing on these figures.
[52] On Taurinus see Augustine, *Petil* III.29 (where the Donatist initiative in making the appeal is emphasised again) and Mandouze (1982) p. 1100. Nothing else is known of him
[53] A place in Numidia or Byzacena. Ckarus is otherwise unknown.
[54] A place in Mauretania Caesarea.

to bring assailants on themselves for their own destruction.[55] From this source also came those those who used to cast their vile souls headlong from the peaks of the highest mountains.[56] See from what sort of resources that other bishop Donatus had made up his cohorts! Fear of this alarmed those who were carrying the money-boxes that they solicited on behalf of the poor, and to meet so great an emergency they devised the plan of requesting an armed military force from Count Silvester,[57] not for the purpose of doing violence to anyone, but in order to resist the force deployed by the aforementioned Donatus. These were the conditions that brought about the appearance of an armed military force. See now who should or can be held responsible for what had happened.

They had there an innumerable mob of those they had summoned, and it is agreed that sufficient supplies of grain had been prepared; they made, as it were, public barns from the church, awaiting the arrival of those on whom they would be able to vent their madness; and they would have done whatever their insanity had dictated but for the resistance of the armed military force. For when assessors, as is the custom, were sent on ahead of the soldiers, they were not received suitably, in accordance with the words of the Apostle, who says: *to whom honour is due, honour; to whom tax, tax; to whom tribute, tribute; owe nothing to anyone.*[58] Those who had been sent were beaten, along with their horses, sent by those whose names you have broadcast with the flail of recrimination. They themselves were the inventors of their own injuries, and taught what sufferings might be theirs by the injuries that they themselves had previously contrived. The harassed soldiers returned to their ranks, and what two or theree had suffered was a grief to all. All were aroused, and even their captains were powerless

---

[55] Cf the voluntary martyrdom of Euplius in Musurillo (1972), pp. 310-320.

[56] This act is attested in pagans (*Anthologia Palatina* VII.471); cf Augustine, *Cath.* 50. On the growing unwillingness of the Church to approve of self-inflicted martyrdom under the Christian Empire, see Thornton (1986). On Optatus' argument that Macarius' acts were not a persecution, see Cecconi (1990).

[57] Little else is known of Silvester, on whom see Mandouze (1982) p. 1083. The assessors sent by him were *metatores*, whose business, according to Hurter (1870), p. 145 n. 1 was to spy out places for soldiers' accommodation and encampment. The word remained uncommon: see Labrousse (1996), p. 44 n. 1.

[58] Romans 13.7.

to restrain the enraged soldiers. Thus was committed the deed that you have recalled as a way of denigrating unity. This and your other troubles have their own causes and the agents whom I have shown to be culpable. This indeed we did not see, but, like you, have it on hearsay. If hearsay makes criminals, we have you on our side, for hearsay treats you in like fashion; if hearsay has nothing to do with the fact, we ought not to incur the blame for what others did on your provocation.

You proceed to complain that under Leontius and under Ursacius a host of people were injured,[59] and some killed under Paulus and Macarius, and that their successors proscribed I know not how many, as occasion arose. What has this to do with us, how does it reflect on the catholic church? Whatever you allege, you did, as you would not freely accept the peace proposed to you from God, preferring your legacy of schism to the precepts laid down by the Saviour. You have challenged the agents of unity; impugn unity itself, if you can! For I surmise that you will not deny that unity is the greatest good. What has the character of the agents to do with us, when it is patent that their actions were a good thing?[60] For wine is trampled and pressed by the sinful agents, and so from this a sacrifice to God is offered; and oil too is made by base people, and some of evil lives and unclean speech, and yet it performs its simple duties of giving flavour, light and even holy chrism.

5. You say that the agents of unity were evil; perhaps that was according to the will of God, who sometimes chooses what he himself could have forbidden. For some evils happen for the worse, some evils happen for the better. A robber does an evil for the worse, a judge does an evil for the better, when he avenges the sin of the robber.[61] For this is the voice of God: *Thou shalt not kill*;[62] and this is the same God's voice: *if a man is found sleeping with a woman who has a husband, you shall kill both.*[63] One God and two contending voices. Moreover, when

---

[59] Cf *Passio Donati* 2. Augustine, *Petil* II.209 implies that Ursacius died violently, and rebuts Petilian's claim that this reveals the judgment of God. On Leontius see Mandouze (1982) p. 362, and on Ursacius *ibid.*, p. 1235.

[60] The same argument is the basis of Augustine's case for the validity of baptisms and ordinations performed by sinful ministers. See Brisson (1958), pp. 164-178.

[61] Cf Augustine, *De Civitate Dei* XIX. 5-6 on the evil involved in judicial punishment.

[62] Exodus 20.13; Deuteronomy 5.17.

[63] Deuteronomy 22.22; though it was miscegenation, rather than adultery, that offended Phineas.

Phineas, son of a priest, found an adulterer with an adulteress, he raised
his hand with his sword, and stood uncertain between the two voices of
God. On this side was heard: *Thou shalt not kill*; on the other was
heard: *You shall kill both*[64] If he struck, he would sin; if he did not
strike, he would fail in duty. He chose the better sin, to strike the blow.
And perhaps there had not been lacking some who wished to condemn
the avenger of this crime as if he were a murderer; but God, so as to
show that some evils are done for the better, spoke saying: *Phineas has
appeased my anger.*[65] And God was pleased by the murder because it
avenged fornication. What if God now is also pleased by what you
claim to have suffered, you who have refused to enjoy the unity which
pleased God, along with the whole world and the memorials of the
Apostles?[66]

6. Against my will, I am forced at this point to mention those whom I
would not, those whom you set among the martyrs, through whom the
people of your communion swear, as if this were the one true religion.
These indeed I would willingly pass over in silence, but the cause of
truth does not tolerate our silence, and the very names provoke rabid
spleen to bark mindlessly against unity, and some in their contempt for
unity hold that it should be accused and shunned, because Marculus and
Donatus are said to be slain and dead.[67] As if no-one ever deserved to
die for the vindication of God! No-one ought to have been harmed by
the agents of unity; but neither should bishops have despised the divine
commands whose bidding is: *Seek peace and pursue it.* And again: how
good and pleasant for brethren to dwell in unity.[68] And again: blessed
are the peacemakers, for they shall be called the sons of God.[69] If some
would not readily hear this nor devoutly do it, whatever they may
possibly have suffered, if it be an evil to be killed, they are the cause
of their own evil.

---

[64] Numbers 25.7 with rhetorical embellishment.

[65] Numbers 25.11. In fact he is called son of Eleazar, son of Aaron the priest.

[66] Romans 14.14; cf Book 1 n.

[67] See *Passio Marculi* at Maier (1987), pp. 277-91, and Labrousse (1996) p. 49 n. 2 on
his cult. As Maier (1987), p. 257 n. 6 says, there will have been a lost *Passio* for Donatus
of Bagaia.

[68] Psalm 33.15 and 132.1 again.

[69] Matthew 5.9. The Donatists found the catholic application of this verse hypocritical; cf
Augustine, *Petil* II.153.

7. But Macarius, according to you, seems open to a challenge, since you hold that he might have done this without the will of God. On this charge you have longstanding criminals: accuse first Moses, the lawgiver himself, who, when he descended from Mount Sinai, almost before the tables of the law had been put forward, in which it was written, *Thou shalt not kill*, ordered the killing of three thousand people in a single moment.[70] Defer Macarius' case for a little, and first call into judegment Phineas, the priest's son, whom I mentioned a little earlier: that is, if you can find some other judge than God. For what you accuse in his person has been praised by God, because it was done in zeal for God. Subdue meanwhile the cries that spleen dictates against Macarius. Go back to the prophet Elijah, who, in obedience to the will of God, killed 450 in the river Chison.[71]

But perhaps you would say that those people were killed deservedly, your own without desert. Vengeance never follows, unless the cause has preceded it. Moses, as we have said, took vengeance, Elijah took vengeance, Phineas took vengeance; and you will not have it that Macarius took vengeance. If those who are said to have been killed had done nothing, let Macarius be a criminal in this, that he acted alone, without our knowledge but on your provocation.[72] Why should we incur resentment when the deeds are those of others? And the cause is in you, because it is said to have taken place for your sake, as you were outside - yet you still seem to be outside.

It was not in us, who dwell within and have never departed from the root. But, since we have listed the names of the aforementioned men, let us see why Moses ordered the killing of three thousand people, why Phineas killed two and why Elijah killed 450, why Macarius killed two, whose names, as I said above, you have broadcast with the flail of recrimination.[73]

---

[70] Exodus 32.13f and Numbers 25.9. The first figure should be 23,000, a reading suggested by a marginal note in Ziwsa's apparatus. The correct number occurs at VII.6.

[71] 1Kings 18.40.

[72] Cf Augustine, *Cresc.* III.45.

[73] Perhaps an ironic allusion to the winnowing prophesied at Matthew 3.12 and 13.30. The latter asserts that judgment within the church will be deferred to the final day, and is therefore frequently quoted by Augustine against the Donatist use of Jeremiah 28.23 (*Contra Parmenianum* III.17 etc.).

It is patent that they took vengeance on those who had despised the divine command. For the voice of God is: *Thou shalt not make thyself a graven thing, and Thou shalt not commit adultery is the voice of the same God.*[74] The same God said *Thou shalt not sacrifice to idols,* and *Thou shalt not create a schism,*[75]. *Seek peace and pursue it* is the precept of the same God[76]. In the time of Moses the people of Israel worshipped the head of a calf, which a sacrilegious flame forged for them; therefore three thousand people deserved to be killed, because it was seen that the voice of God had been despised. Phineas struck two adulterers with a single blow: he deserved to be praised by God, because he killed despisers of the divine precepts. And the 450 whom we read that Elijah killed, were killed for this reason, that against God's bidding, on account of their being false seers, they had despised the precepts of God.

And those whose names you use to incriminate Macarius are not far from being false seers; because God said that you were going to be false seers, as I am about to prove forthwith. And when they would not consider peace, lest they should dwell at one with their brethren, they pertinaciously withstood the precepts and the will of God. Therefore you see that Moses and Phineas and Elijah and Macarius acted in like fashion, beacuse all of them vindicated the precepts of the one God. But I see that at this point you distinguish times, making the times before the Gospel one thing, those after it another; in the latter you can say, as it is written, that Peter already put away the sword with which he had cut off the ear of the high priest's slave, and that Peter could have made a show of devotion in killing this slave.[77] But Christ had come to suffer, not to be defended, and if Peter had fulfilled his own design, the passion of Christ would have seemed to be an avenging of the slave, not a liberation of the people.

8. For Macarius did not draw out the sword that Peter had put away in its sheath: God proves this, when he says to the valley of Zion,

---

[74] Exodus 20.4; Deuteronomy 5.8. Then Exodus 20.14; Deuteronomy 5.17.
[75] A free quotation of Exodus 20.5 or Deuteronomy 5.9, followed perhaps by an even freer reference to 1Cor 1.10.
[76] Psalm 33.15, as above.
[77] Matthew 26.51 par.

Wounded in thee, not wounded with the sword.[78] Otherwise, prove that
anyone was struck by the sword at that time. He says next: *Dead in
thee, not dead in war.* For this reason you should consider whether it be
not rash to call those people martyrs who experience none of the
Christians' wars. For nothing was done or heard of the sort that is
usually heard and done in a Christians' war, which is called persecution,
and was carried on by two beasts of the four that Daniel saw rising
from the sea.[79]

The first was like the lion: this was the persecution under Decius and
Valerian.[80] The second was like the bear: another persecution which
took place under Diocletian and Maximian,[81] at which time there were
also impious judges waging war againt the Christian name. Among
them, a little more than sixty years ago, was Anulinus in the proconsular
province, and Florus in Numidia.[82] Everyone knows what their artful
cruelty contrived: raging war was declared against the Christians, the
devil held triumphs in the temples of the daemons, the altars smoked
with unholy odours, and because people could not approach the
sacrilegious ceremonies, they were everywhere compelled to lay incense.
Every place was a temple for enormity, old men close to death were
defiled, infancy in its ignorance was polluted, little ones were taken
from their mothers for an atrocious purpose, parents were compelled to

---

[78] Isaiah 22.2.

[79] See Daniel 7.3ff. The beasts of Daniel were commonly identified with the great Empires
that preceded Rome (see Daniel 7.19-26), but Optatus is no doubt reading through the lens
of Revelation, which cryptically describes the history of the Roman Emperors (cf
Victorinus of Petau, *De Apocalypsi* XIII).

[80] The persecution begun by Decius (249-251) was first repealed, then renewed, by
Valerian in 257. Confiscation of Christian property and execution of leaders began after
Christians refused to comply with the edict of universal sacrifice. See Eusebius, *HE* VI.39
and VII.10, with Lactantius, *Mort.* 4-5.

[81] See introduction. The name Maximian probably refers here to Diocletian's western
partner since 285, and there is thus no hint that Optatus follows Eusebius and Lactantius
in casting the blame on the eastern Caesar Galerius.

[82] Africa, which included the cities of Carthage and Utica, was governed by a proconsul,
whereas the region to the south and west, Numidia, was governed by a diocesan *vicarius*.
The documents concerning Annulinus can be found at Maier (1987) pp. 140-6. On Florus,
who was notorious for his savagery and may have anticipated the edict, see Frend (1952a).

commit bloodless parricide,[83] some were compelled to overthrow temples of the living God, some to deny Christ, some to burn the divine laws, some to lay incense.

That any of these things was done by Macarius even you will not be able to pretend. Under Florus' persecution Christians were driven to the temples of idols; under Macarius the reluctant were driven into church. Under Florus it was said that Christ was to be denied and idols prayed to; under Macarius, by contrast, the uniform and universal worship of the one God in the church was enjoined on all. Therefore when you see that there was no Christians' war - and God recalls the deaths of some without war, when he says: and dead in thee, not dead in war - and that those must be doubtful martyrs who were not provoked to sacrilege or unholy incense or denial of God's name; and, since there is no route to martyrdom but through confession, on what grounds do you call them martyrs, who were not confessors?[84] Or which of them was compelled to deny Christ and confessed him? If therefore there can be no martyrdom without confession of Christ's name, and no-one confessed, and what you say was done was done for the vindication of God's precepts, and you cannot prove that anything was done by us, when what was done was foretold as such by God and his precepts were vindicated: see whether it be not merely vain but superstitious[85] to set those who died without a war in the same place as those who, having made their confession in Christ, were able to die in the name of God.

Or if you wish them to be martyrs, prove that they loved peace, in which are the first foundations of martyrdom, or that they cared for unity, which pleases God, or that they were in charity with their brethren. For I have proved in my first book that all Christians are brethren, and I am going to prove it beyond doubt in the fourth. Those who, according to you, should be called martyrs would not acknowledge

---

[83] *Parricidium* means any flagrant crime, as at Cicero, *Orationes Verrinae* II (5) 66 etc. For the (conventional) charges against the persecutors cf Constantine, *Oratio ad Sanctos* 25 etc.

[84] A confessor is one who attests his faith by refusal to sacrifice or awear by the Emperor. During their imprisonment, which did not always lead to martyrdom, confessors were visited by suppliants seeking absolution, and Cyprian regarded their prestige as a menace to his own authority: see Epistle 22 etc.

[85] Recalling the Roman description of Christianity as a *vana et prava superstitio*, and the provincial governor Pliny's phrase *superstitionem pravam, immodicam* at Epistle X.96.

their brethren and had no charity.[86] Nor may it be said in excuse for them that they refused to communicate with collaborators, when it has been manifestly proved that they themselves were children of collaborators. There is therefore no excuse, as it is patent and manifest that they did not have charity, without which no martyrdom can even be said to occur, without which the most great and sovereign virtue is ineffectual, without which the knowledge of all tongues is of no value, without which there can also be no fellowship with the angels. As the Apostle Paul says: *If I have within me the power of commanding mountains to transplant themselves from one place to another, and speak with the tongues of all peoples, even of angels, and give my body to the flames, and have not charity within me, I am nothing; but I shall be a brass thing tinkling in the desert, so that the work of the voice perishes for want of any hearing.*[87] If it is so great a matter, if the blessed Paul, the vessel of election, pronounces himself to be nothing even in the sovereign virtue and the fellowship of angels, unless he should have charity, see whether they should not be called martyrs but deserve some other name, who as deserters of charity may have suffered anything on account of that desertion.

9. The whole world rejoices over catholic unity, apart from Africa, where a fire has been blown up from a spark. You complain of I know not what crimes committed by the agents of unity. Italy does not make this complaint, nor Gaul, nor Spain, nor Pannonia, nor Galatia, nor Greece, nor Asia with all its provinces, because there was nothing there to be put right, no-one was sent as, so to speak, a tailor.[88] And here in Africa for a long time the garment had been intact as the population remained in unity, but was rent by the envious hand of the enemy. The strips hung, as it were, from one point in the garment, and branches

---

[86] Another leitmotif of Augustine's case against the Donatists. The example of Cyprian shows that even where the Church is offended, charity demands that we maintain the union.

[87] 1Cor 13.1-3, paraphrased freely at the end.

[88] Alluding, no doubt to the image of the Church as the seamless robe of Christ: see John 19.24. The Donatists may have retaliated by quoting Matthew 9.16 par.

coming from a single root were divided from one another.[89] Why did
one party oppose itself to another? Why did one strip raise itself above
the other strip, when it was not able to prove itself superior? What,
then, if the despised strip should say, "Why do you exalt yourself so
high? Did we not grow up as equals, were we not simultaneously in the
hands of those who formed us, were we not cleaned as equals in the
bath? An enemy has conceived a wish to sever us from one another, an
adversary has conceived a wish to deform our beauty". In part of the
garment we are still one, but we hang at odds. For what is rent is
partially divided, not entirely, since it is justly agreed that there is a
single ecclesiastical intercourse between us and you, and if the minds of
men are at loggerheads, the sacraments are not at loggerheads.

Moreover, we could also say, "We believe as you do and are marked
with a single sign, nor are we baptized in any other way than you. We
read the divine testament as you do, we petition one God as you do, the
Lord's Prayer is one among us and among you,[90] but when parts hang
on this side and that through the rending of a part, then as we have said,
a tailor's work was necessary." And none the less a contriver or minister
of this result, when he wants to return the garment to its pristine
appearance, sews together neighbouring threads. You dislike a tailor
who, when he repairs the breach, causes damage; you should dislike that
person more who made it possible for the tailor to go wrong. And those
crimes which you say were committed against you by the agents of
unity belong either to your parents, because of whom these things were
done, or descend by the will of God; we, however, are not involved in
that.

10. What then if, as we have said, these things, however harsh, are seen
to have been done with God's will? For we read in the prophet Ezekiel
of a whitewashed wall, against which God has threatened tempest, rain

---

[89] The word *pannus* signifies a rag in Jeremiah 38.11-12, and the plural denotes the
swaddling-clothes of Jesus at Luke 2.7. Its meaning here is obscure, although Labrousse
(1996) p. 62 n. 2 effects an ingenious conflation of John 19.24 with Cyprian, Epistle
17.3.1. For the branches and the root cf Cyprian, Epistle 48.3, *De Unitate Ecclesiae* 5 etc.
[90] The importance of the Lord's Prayer in the church is attested as early as *Didache* 8
(first or second century in the Syrian region), and in the third century by the *De Oratione
Dominica* of Cyprian, as well as the treatises *De Oratione* by Tertullian and Origen. The
form favoured by the western church is that of Matthew 6.7-15, sometimes augmented by
words found first in *Didache* 8.2, both differing materially from Luke 11. 1-4.

and thunderbolts and accusations: *There will be*, he says, *false seers, who will build a ruinous wall, saying, "Peace, peace"; and where is peace?*[91] Remember how long ago the members of the mother church were rent apart from one another by you. For you were not able to seduce every household all at once. Either the wife departed and the husband stayed, or the parents were seduced and the children refused to follow, or the brother stood while his sister went off. Through your persuasions both pious bodies and pious names were divided, and you were not able to pass over the legal forms. And so you said "Peace be with you"; while God, by contrast, says, *Peace, where is peace?*[92] That is to say, why do you give greeting in the name of what you do not possess? Why do you speak the name of what you have annihilated? You give greeting in the name of peace, you who do not love peace. *These*, he says, *build a ruinous wall.* The house of God is one; those who have chosen to form a party by going outside have made a wall, not a house, because there is no other God to inhabit another house. Thus the false seers are said to have built a wall, and if a door were fitted in it, anyone who enters is outside.

Nor can one wall have a cornerstone; this stone is Christ, gathering two peoples into himself, one from the Gentiles, one from the Jews, and joining both walls in the clasp of peace.[93] For the disadvantages of a wall are as numerous as the advantages of a house: the house guards its contents, rebuffs the tempest, disperses the rain, refuses admission to the robber or the thief or the beast: so too the church catholic embraces in its lap and bosom all the children of peace. When, on the other hand, a ruinous wall is built, it holds up no corner-stone and has a door without a cause, nor does it guard any contents. It is made wet by the rain, it is brought down by tempests, and it cannot prevent the robber or stop the coming of a thief. The wall belongs to the house, but is not a house; and your party is like a church, but is not catholic. He says, and they whitewash it; that is, that you reckon only yourselves holy.

You complain that you suffered certain things without us; therefore it is patent that you alone suffered certain things, because the time of peace is one thing and the time of persecution another. If you deem it

---

[91] Ezekiel 13.10.
[92] Cf John 20.20.
[93] Cf Ephesians 2.20-22; Isaiah 28.16

a persecution, say what all the other provinces in which the catholic church is established suffered along with you. But because it was vengeance, not persecution, only the wall suffered, against which God decreed tempest, rain and thunderbolts and accusations. For thus he spoke: *Why do you build a ruin? Why do you deface it? Why do you whitewash it? This is against my will, says the Lord.* You dislike the times of Leontius (whoever he is),[94] Ursacius, Macarius and others. Correct if you can the will of God, who says, *I shall arise against the wall with my anger and I shall send upon it a mighty tempest and rain, floods and thunderbolts, and I shall strike the ruinous wall, and its bolts will be dissolved.*[95]

But none of you should say, "If unity is a good, why once made was it so often unable to endure?" For this reason, that the matter has been so ordained by God, who has threatened tempest, rain, stones and accusations, and these four events could not occur simultaneously.[96] First came the tempest under Ursacius; the wall was shaken, but did not fall, so that the rain might have something to work on. Rain followed under Gregory:[97] the wall was made wet, but did not dissolve, so that the stones might have something to work on. After the rain followed stones under the agents of unity: the wall disintegrated, but repaired itself again from its foundations. Already three events are concluded: the accusations are still owing to you, but how and when is known to him whose pleasure it is to proclaim these things about you.

11. And in case anyone should doubt this interpretation, God has added the saying, *The things that I say do not concern mud, a side or a wall, but the false propehts, who seduce my people.*[98] See to which party this word "seduce" is applicable. All were with us, you invaded in our absence; but in order to possess those whom you wished to possess, you could not but seduce them. And what words you used to seduce them everyone knows. It was for you to say, "Look behind you", for you to

---

[94] As at Augustine, *Cresc* IV.62, *nescio quis* implies that the name is unimportant, not that it is unknown.
[95] Ezekiel 13.11, after rhetorical expansion of the theme.
[96] Optatus seems to assimilate Ezekiel's prophecy to the four beasts of Daniel; he may also have in mind Matthew 7.24-7 par.
[97] On Gregory see n. 25 above.
[98] Ezekiel 13.9.

say "Redeem your souls", for you to say to faithful people and clerics, "Be Christians". But when you say "Look behind you", you act against the Gospel, where it is said, *No-one holding the handle of the plough and looking behind him will enter the kingdom of the heavens.*[99] And do you want to know the rewards of the one who looks behind and the one who looks before? Remember the fugitives from Sodom, Lot and his wife: the one who looked behind her was changed into a statue of salt, the one who looked before him escaped.[100] What then is this saying of yours, "Look behind you"?

And likewise when you say, "Redeem your souls", whence did you buy them, so that you may sell them? Who, I wonder, is that angel who markets souls? When you say, "Redeem your souls", you renounce the Redeemer, as Christ alone is the redeemer of souls, which the devil possessed before his advent.[101] These Christ our Saviour redeemed with his own blood, as the Apostle says: *For you are bought at a great price.*[102] For it is agreed that all have been bought with the blood of Christ. Christ has not sold those whom he redeemed; the souls bought by Christ could not be sold, so that, as you wish, they could be redeemed again by you. Failing that, how can one soul have two masters?[103] Or can there possibly be another redeemer? What prophets have proclaimed the future coming of another? What Gabriel has spoken for a second time to another Mary?[104] What virgin has given birth for a second time? Who has created new virtues, or other ones? If there is none but one who has redeemed the souls of those who believe, what is this saying of yours, "Redeem your souls"?

Now what is this that you say to Christian people and even clerics, "Be Christians"? And with some miracle you dare to say to each person

---

[99] Luke 9.62, though the phrase "kingdom of the heavens" is Matthaean. Optatus seems to quote from memory.

[100] Genesis 19.26.

[101] For this "ransom" theory cf Origen, *CommRom.* II.13.

[102] 1Cor 6.20 and 7.23, the prooftexts of Origen's theory, which insists (as Paul does not) upon the size of the price.

[103] Cf Matthew 6.24 par.

[104] Cf Luke 1.28-30. Optatus clearly holds that Christ's cross effected a reconciliation between human beings and God that we could not achieve for ourselves.

severally, "Caius Seius, Caia Sera,[105] are you still a pagan man or a
pagan woman?" The one who has professed his own conversion to God
you call a pagan, the one whom either we or you have steeped, not in
our name or your name, but in Christ's, you call a pagan (for there are
some who have both been baptized by you and have subsequently
transferred to our communion); the one who has prayed to God the
Father through his Son before the altar you call a pagan. For anyone
who has believed has believed in the name of the Father and the Son
and the Holy Spirit; and you call him a pagan after his profession of
faith! If any Christian - God forbid! - should fall away, he can be called
a sinner, but he cannot be a second time a pagan.[106] But all these things
you would have to be of no account; and if the one whom you seduce
has agreed with you, this one consent and the stretching forth of your
hand and a few words forthwith make a Christian of the Christian for
you; and the one who seems to you to be a Christian is the one who has
done your will, not the one whom faith has brought over.

12. And if a rather more belated assent is given to your seduction, you
are not wanting also in those arguments make it quite easy for you to
persuade even the unwilling to comply with your wishes. You say that
those who had been a long time in your college were heard to declare
that, when the sacrifice of unity arrived, one who partook of it would
be regarded as having tasted of a pagan ritual.[107] We do not deny that
these things were said by certain people, who are well-known to have
subsequently done that from which a little while before they had
deterred the populace. But there was one reason that called for these
expressions, another that led to the deed. For those who are said to have
spoken thus were induced to say this by a false conjecture which had
filled their ears and that of the whole populace. For it was said at that
time that Paulus and Macarius would come to be present at the sacrifice,
so that, while the altars were being solemnly prepared, they might bring

---

[105] Standard terms for John Doe and his wife in Roman legal usage. At Tertullian,
Apologeticum 3 (c. 197 A.D.) they stand for any of the innumerable pagan converts to
Christianity.

[106] The argument is stronger if *paganus* is understood to denote a civilian in contrast to
a *miles* (cf Pliny, Epistle X.18.2), since a soldier's brand is indelible. For the comparison
cf Augustine, *Sermo ad Catechumenos* 16; Tertullian, *De Corona Militis* 11.

[107] Translating *sacrum*. Cf Hurter (1870), p. 164 n. 1 and Hanson (1985) on the early
aversion to sacrificial imagery.

out an image, which they would first put on the altar and thus the sacrifice would be offered.[108] When this reached people's ears, they were stricken in spirit, and everyone's tongue was excited in response to these words, so that all who had heard them said, "The one who tastes of this tastes of a pagan rite."

And what they said was right, if the true sequel had resembled such a rumour. But when the aforesaid men arrived, nothing was seen of what rumour had fabricated a little while before. Christian eyes saw nothing to be abhorred, seeing proved none of the things that had upset hearing. What was seen was a pure act, and the customary solemnity was conspicuous under the usual rite, as they saw that nothing was changed in the divine sacrifices, nothing added or taken away. The peace proposed by God to those who wanted it was found pleasing; so no-one ought to be challenged for having made the transition from your college to peace. Those who had been disturbed by ominous conjecture were comforted by pure and simple truth. Nor should it be said that they turned the bitter into the sweet or the sweet into the bitter.[109] The bitterness, which was seen to have been falsely prophesied, stayed and remained in the bosom of conjecture; the truth conspicuous to the eyes, having in itself its own sweetness, was separated from the domain of false conjecture. Therefore it is not true either that the bitter was made sweet or the sweet made bitter, because what seemed to have been heard had been far astray, and what was seen was something different and beyond it. So you see that you made your reproaches groundlessly, fabricating what you wished as your opinion, so that you could wound Macarius and Taurinus. You have lost sight of what you would see in your right mind, as spleen has debauched your senses and closed the avenues to your intellect.

---

[108] Images are forbidden in the 36th canon of the council of Eliberis/Elvira (?c. 305), and, as Thummel (1992) confirms, were still deprecated by orthodoxy in the fourth century.
[109] Possibly a reference to Moses' use of wood to sweeten the waters of Marah; cf Justin, *Trypho* 86.1 and Tertullian, *Bapt.* 9. Or else Optatus has in mind Jeremiah 15.18.

OPTATUS:

Fourth Book against the Donatists

1. Brother Parmenianus, we have openly and clearly proved to you that the story about the requisitioning of an armed force is an empty slander. You must also learn that what you said of the oil and sacrifice of a sinner is more applicable to you.[1] For a person does not have to be a sinner because you want him to be; after all, we too can imitate your presumption, and say that you are sinners. Yet, let presumption do its work on both sides, none of us can damn another with a human judgment. It is for God to know the criminal, for him to pronounce the verdict. Let all us human beings be silent, let God point out the sinner, whose sacrifice is a canine victim[2] and whose oil inspires the fear of the one who desires anointing.

2. You must know the patent truth about this matter, brother Parmenianus. If, however, you disdain[3] to hear with goodwill this name of brother which I frequently pronounce, let it be distasteful to you, but to me it is imperative; otherwise I should commit the crime of silence with regard to the demonstration of this name. For if you do not wish to be a brother, I begin to be impious if I am silent as to this name. For you are our brothers, and we yours, as the prophet says: *Did not one God create you and one Father beget you?*[4] For you cannot but be brothers, when it is said to all, *You are gods and children of the Most High.*[5] And we and you have accepted one precept, in which it is said, *Call no-one your father on earth, because you have one Father, in heaven.*[6] Our saviour Christ is the only one born a son of God; but we and you have become children of God by a single means, as it is written in the Gospel: *The Son of God came; to all those that accepted him he*

---

[1] Optatus anticipates the argument of II.6-7 below. The oil had been identified by the Donatists with baptism administered by catholic priests, since this involved *chrismation*; by the sacrifice of the sinner they may have understood the Eucharist.

[2] Anticipating the quotation of Isaiah 66.5 below.

[3] Reading *dedignaris*, rather than the *dignaris* of Ziwsa's text. As his *apparatus* shows, this passage is more than usually confused.

[4] Malachi 2.16.

[5] Psalm 81.6; cf John 10.54.

[6] Matthew 23.9.

gave power, that those who believe in his name might become sons of God.[7] We have both become and are called sons, you have become but are not called sons, because you refuse to be peacemakers or to hear the Son of God himself saying, *Blessed are the peacemakers, because they themselves shall be called sons of God.*[8] When Christ came he called God and man back to peace, And he made them one, *taking away the dividing wall in the midst.*[9] You refuse to have peace with us, that is, with your brethren.

For you cannot but be brothers, when one mother church brought you forth from the same sacramental womb, when God the Father accepted you as his adopted sons by the same means.[10] Therefore Christ, foreseeing this present time when you were destined to fall into discord with us, gave such rules for praying that in prayer at least unity should abide, that those parties who were going to differ should conjoin their prayers. We pray for you because we want to, and you for us even thought you do not want to. Otherwise, each one of you should say, "My Father, who art in heaven", and "Give me today my daily bread", and "Forgive me my sins, as I my debtor".[11] If, then, rules cannot be changed, you see that we are not completely separated from one another, while we pray for you willingly and you for us, albeit unwillingly. You see, brother Parmenianus, that the bonds of sacred kinship between us and you cannot be completely broken.

3. Now we must seek the sinner whose oil can be feared or whose sacrifice rejected. Let human suspicion rest, let the presumption of each party fall silent; who the sinner is, God alone must tell. We read under the second rubric of the forty-ninth psalm that the Holy Spirit said, *God has said to the sinner.*[12] To this place we must apply the whole attention of our intellects, to see who the sinner is. For suppose that, after the lesson, *God has said to the sinner*, words of this kind followed, "You have taken up arms, you have sallied forth from the camp, you have

---

[7] The latter part of this is from John 1.11-12; the first appears to be inferred from John's Christology.

[8] Matthew 5.9.

[9] Ephesians 2.14.

[10] For baptism as a second birth see Titus 3.5; at John 3.4-5 natural birth is contrasted with birth from water and the Spirit.

[11] Parodying Matthew 6.9-12 and Luke 11.2-4.

[12] Psalm 49.12. The quotation continues.

stood against enemies in battle": the soldier would have to fear, because
he himself might seem to be a sinner. Or suppose it said, "You have
procured riches, you have travelled, you have marketed, you have sold
what you bought for gain": the merchant would have to fear, because he
himself might seem to be a sinner. Or suppose it said, "You have built
a ship, you have furnished it with ropes, you have adorned it with sails,
you have caught at favourable winds in order to sail": the sailor would
have to fear, because he himself might seem to be a sinner. Or suppose
that after the lesson, *God has said to the sinner*, there followed these
words, "You have been averse to dissension and schism, you have
entered into concord with your brother, and with the one church which
exists throughout the whole world, you have communicated with the
seven churches and the memorials of the Apostles, you have embraced
unity": if this were the content of the subsequent lesson, we should have
to fear, we might be sinners.But when God says, *Why do you expound
my righteous ways and take my testament into your mouth? Yet you
have despised discipline and have cast my speech behind you; you have
sat opposite your brother to denounce him, and you have put a
stumbling-block in the way of your mother's son. You saw the thief and
ran with him, and you have cast your lot with adulterers*: all these
things are said to you. Acquit yourselves of all these, if you can.

4. For you have despised discipline; why do you recite the testament,[13]
when you do not obey the testament in which is described the discipline
that you refuse to observe? For you cannot say that you serve that on
which you make war. God says, *Seek peace and pursue it;*[14] you have
rejected peace. Is that not to despise discipline? In the Gospel we read,
Peace on earth to people of good will;[15] you will not have either good
will or peace. Is that not to despise discipline? Again in Psalm 122 we
read, *See how good and pleasant it is for brethren to dwell in unity;*[16]
you will not dwell in unity with your brethren. Is that not to despise

---

[13] Meaning the Scriptures, this translation of the Greek *diatheke* being justified by
Hebrews 9.17. The New Testament writers argued that the "covenant" which God made
with his people through Abraham was in fact also a "testament", which could not be
fulfilled without the death of the testator but was then inviolable (cf Gal 4.17). Thus
Christ's death both confirmed the promises and revealed that they pertained to Christians.
[14] Psalm 33.15.
[15] Luke 2.14.
[16] Psalm 132.1.

discipline? Christ says in the Gospel, *He who has once been washed has no need to be washed again*;[17] you by rebaptizing wash again. Is that not to despise discipline? God says, *Do not touch my anointed, or lay your hand on my prophets*;[18] you have stripped divine honours from so many priests! Is that not to despise discipline? Christ says, *By this I know that you are my disciples, if you love one another*;[19] you feel hatred towards us, though we are your brothers, and have refused to imitate the Apostles, who loved even Peter the renegade. Is that not to despise discipline? You expound God's righteous ways and take his testament in your mouth. How do you urge, *Seek peace, when you have no peace*?[20] How do you recite the testament without obeying the testament in which discipline is described?

5. You have been appointed to sit and teach the people, and you disparage us, your brothers. When, as I said above, one mother church brought us forth, one Father has accepted us, you none the less put stumbling-blocks in our way, commanding people severally not to greet us, not to accept an honour from us. Consider the utterances of your pride, consider its treatises, consider its ordinances, ponder your actions also, and you will find that your oil caused fear in him who asked. There is none of you who has failed to mix reproaches of us with his treatises, who does not either initiate one or expound another. You begin to read the Lord's text and you expound treatises in our despite; you produce the Gospel, and you reproach your absent brother; you pour hatreds into the souls of hearers, you persuade them to feel enmity by your teaching, by saying all this you put stumbling-blocks in our way.

Therefore the saying is addressed to every one of you: *Sitting opposite your brother you denounce him, and you put a stumbling-block*

---

[17] John 13.10.

[18] Psalm 104.15; cf II.25. Optatus distinguishes between God and Christ as speakers in the Bible, not because he denies the divinity of Christ, but becasue he accepts the principle that, in order to understand the Scripture, we must know in what "person" (i.e. character) it is spoken. It is possible that the use of the term *personae* to differentiate Father, Son and Spirit in the Triune God derives from this exegetic commonplace.

[19] John 13.34, substituting "I" for "all people". Optatus seems to have written this book at least without a text of the Scriptures.

[20] Psalm 33.15, contrasted with Jeremiah 8.11. cf Augustine, *Petil.* II.157 for a Donatist citation of the latter.

in the way of your mother's son.[21] When God attacks the sinner and upbraids the one who sits, it is patent that this is said specially to you, not to the people, who do not have the right of sitting in the church.[22] Therefore it is without doubt to be imputed to you when God says, Sitting opposite you have put a stumbling-block in the way of your mother's son. I have proved time and again that we have one mother, and you cannot deny it, though you put stumbling-blocks in our way when some of you produce lessons that they do not understand in order to take away what is usually common to all, I mean of course the duty of greeting. For there are some of you who themselves deny the usual kisses in a conventional greeting,[23] and there are many who are taught not to say "Hello" to any of us. And it seems to them that this is commanded by a lesson, which, however, they do not understand, not knowing of whom the Apostle said this: *Do not even take meals with these people, do not say hello to them, for their speech creeps like a cancer.*[24] He said this of the heretics, whose doctrine had begun to be pernicious at this time, as the subtle seduction of their words corrupted the health of the faithful with creeping diseases. Such as Marcion, who having been rendered apostate by the bishop, introduced two Gods and two Christs;[25] such as Praxeas, who urged that the Father suffered, not the Son;[26] such as Valentinus, who tried to suppress the flesh of Christ.[27]

---

[21] Psalm 49.20. The word translated "stumbling-block" is the Greek *scandalon* (cf 1Cor 1.23), the root of our word "scandal".

[22] Cf Justin, *1Apol* 67, Tertullian, *De Corona Militis* 3. The 18th canon of Nicaea (325) implies that presbyters sat, while the 20th enjoins standing prayer. On the enthronement of bishops in the fourth century see Athanasius, *De Fuga* 24, and on that of presbyters Eusebius, *HE* X.5; see further Bright (1882), pp. 59-64 and 72-8.

[23] Christians are told to greet one another with a kiss in the Holy Spirit at 1Thess 5.26; cf Justin, *1Apol* 65. Hippolytus, *Apostolic Tradition* p. 29 Dix and Chadwick, says that this privilege was restricted to the baptized.

[24] Conflating 1Cor 5.11, 2John 16 and 2Tim 2.17.

[25] See Book 1 n. 30. For the two Christs at the crucifixion see Tertullian, *Adversus Marcionem* III.24.5. Marcion is said to have been excommunicated by his own father, who was a bishop by Epiphanius (*Panarion* 42.1, where the implication that Rome was governed by presbyters and unable to reverse a provincial judgment seems to betoken a tradition going back to the second century). Irenaeus, *AH* IV.6 speaks of frequent altercations between Marcion and the Roman bishop Hyginus.

[26] See 1.9, and for this charge, Tertullian, *Adversius Praxean* 1.

[27] See 1.9 with notes on this heretic and others.

Theirs was the speech which contained a cancer to vex the members of the faith. Such too was the speech of the heretic Scorpianus, who denied the necessity of martyrdoms.[28] But let them keep their own venom, and let no account of them even lightly vex the simple intellects of our hearers. To this then belongs the speech which is to be avoided, lest it creep like a cancer.

This is said also of Arius, who tried to teach that the Son of God was made out of no substance, rather than born from God; had not his doctrine been exploded by 318 bishops at the Nicene Council, it would have entered the breasts of many like a cancer.[29] This is said also of Photinus, a heretic of the present times, who dared to say that the Son of God was only a man, not God.[30] This could also be said of you, since your speech has induced an acute cancer in the souls and ears of some. For it is your speech which you maintain towards the sons of peace, when you say "you have perished, look behind you; your soul will perish; how long will you hold back?" By this you have made penitents of the faithful, by this you have put to death the honour of priests. See, it is also your speech which creeps like a cancer today, so that greeting and intercourse may be forbidden. What similar effect could our speech have, when we hold on to the sons of peace with simple doctrine, without seducing those elsewhere or excluding anyone? Therefore it is evident that you daily put stumbling-blocks in our way, and it is a long

---

[28] If the reading offered by Ziwsa is correct, this seems to be a misreading of the title of Tertullian's *Scorpiace*, a work attacking docetic heretics for their evasion of martyrdom.
[29] Condemned in 325 by the Nicene Council. His doctrine was that God the Father possesses his nature uniquely, and produced the Son from nothing. He thus denied the application of the epithet *homoousios* (consubstantial) to the persons of the Trinity. The figure of 318 Bishops, which appears e.g in Hilary of Poitiers, *De Synodis* 86, is fictitious, being based on the number of Abraham's household at Genesis 14.14. For a similar appeal to numbers, this time on behalf of the Donatists, see Augustine, *Cresc.* IV.31 etc.
[30] Bishop Photinus of Smyrna, a pupil of Marcellus of Ancyra, was deposed by the Council of Sirmium in 351 (see Hilary, *De Synodis* 37-8; Epiphanius, *Panarion* 71), having already been deposed by the western Bishops at the Council of Milan in 345. The ninth anathema of Sirmium is directed against those who believe that the Sonship of Christ did not precede the incarnation; in Eusebius, *Contra Marcellum* I.14 this was construed as the doctrine attributed to Paul of Samosata, that Jesus was simply an inspired man, not God incarnate. Photinus died in 376, a fact that has little bearing on the date of composition of Optatus' work: see my introduction.

task to recount all the means whereby you disparage us and all the ways
in which you lay stumbling-blocks.
6. For when he says, moreover, *You saw the thief and ran with him*,
what do you suppose this is spoken of? Surely it is not about the
stealing of a garment or the robbing of a bosom[31] or any thefts of the
kind that cause profit or loss among humans? These too are indeed
forbidden; but in this lesson God upbraids those thefts which are
committed against himself. What thefts are committed against himself,
you ask, what thefts are committed against God? They are found among
you. God's possession is the host of the faithful, from which every day
the marauding devil desires to rob something,[32] wishing to corrupt the
character of a Christian man or woman in some degree, and to snatch
away, if not the whole person, yet whatever part of the person he can.
When you see this thief using violence against us, you have helped him
with your actions; for no-one is unaware that every person who is born,
even if he is born of Christian parents, cannot be without an unclean
spirit,[33] which must necessarily be driven out and separated from the
person before the bath of salvation.[34] This is the work of exorcism, by
which the unclean spirit is expelled and driven into desert places. An
empty house appears in the breast of the believer, a clean house appears.
God enters and dwells there, as the Apostle says: *You are a temple of
God, and in you God dwells.*[35] And when any individual is filled with
God, whom the marauding devil aspires to rob of something. you by
rebaptism exorcise the faithful person and say to the indwelling God,
"Accursed one, go out!"

Thus is fulfilled the saying of God through the prophet Ezekiel, *And
they cursed me amid my people because of a handful and a mite of
barley, that they might slay souls who ought not to have died, when the
proclaim to my people lying vanities.*[36] Therefore God hears of injuries
which are not his due, and deserts a lodging of this kind; and the

---

[31] The *sinus* or bosom of a Roman toga was used for the safekeeping of valuables.
[32] Cf 1Peter 5.8
[33] Cf Tertullian, *De Anima* 39.1, which may refer only to pagan households; but *ibid.* 40.1
affirms the universal corruption of humanity, as does Origen, *HomExod* VIII.4.
[34] For the image, which implies an objective effect in the ceremony, cf Titus 3.5 and 1Cor
6.11.
[35] 1Cor 3.17.
[36] Ezekiel 13.19.

person, who had entered the church filled with God, goes out as an empty vessel. The devil, who like a thief wished to rob something,[37] helped by your actions, sees the person made entirely his own from whom he wished to steal a little. Therefore God said of you, *You saw the thief and ran with him.* Moreover, in the Gospel it is written thus: *Now when God has deserted a person, he is left an empty vessel. However, the unclean spirit, wandering hungry through desert places, says, "My house is empty" - that is to say, the one who had driven me out is driven out - I shall return there and dwell. And he brings with him seven others more savage and he will dwell there and the last times of that person will be worse than the ones before.*[38]

This is (the equivalent of) *You saw the thief and ran with him, and you have made your little portion with adulterers.* By adulterers he means heretics, and by adulteresses those people's churches which Christ spurns and rejects in the Song of Songs. It is as if he said, *"Why do you bind to me those who are not my kin? My beloved is one, my bride is one, my dove is one"*[39] - that is the catholic church, in which you could have been when you chose, by rebaptizing, to have your little portion among adulterers. And since it is most evidently proved by divine testimony that you are sinners, it is also shown that your own auxiliaries have made war on you; for you had taken as an auxiliary the prophet, in whom we read, the sacrifice of the sinner, like one who makes a dog his victim.[40] Now, if there is any shame, recognise that you are sinners.

7. This too you must learn, whose voice it is that says, *Let not the oil of the sinner anoint my head.*[41] For you have not understood whose voice this is; in fact it is Christ's, who had not yet been anointed when he asked that the oil of the sinner should not pollute his head. Not understanding this, you have said, "David the prophet feared the oil of the sinner". He had long before been fully anointed by Samuel; there

---

[37] Cf John 10.10.
[38] Matthew 12.43-5, though it is not God but the daemon who leaves the man. Perhaps Optatus' text should be emended. Origen (n. 33 above) quotes this passage to illustrate the soul's subjection to demons from the time of birth.
[39] Song of Songs 6.8; cf 1.10.
[40] Isaiah 66.3.
[41] Psalm 140.5; cf Augustine, *Cresc.* II.29 etc

was no reason for him to be anointed again.[42] Therefore the voice is that of Christ, saying, *Let not the oil of the sinner anoint my head.* These are prayers, not orders,[43] they are desires, not precepts. For if it were an order, he would say, "The oil of the sinner shall not anoint my head". The voice is therefore that of the Son of God, who at that time feared to encounter the oil of the sinner, that is of any human being, since no-one is without sin save God alone. The reason why his son feared the oil of a human being is that it was indecent that God should be anointed by a human. Thus he begs the Father that he should not be anointed by a human, but by God the Father himself.

The Son therefore asks; let us see if the Father has agreed. This the Holy Spirit indicates plainly in Psalm 44, where he says to the Son himself, *Let God your Lord anoint you with the oil of exultation otherwise than your companions.*[44] His companions were the priests and kings of the Jews, who are well known to have been anointed severally by humans. But because the Son was to be anointed by the Father, God by God, according to the Son's prayer and the promise proclaimed by the Spirit was the Father's consummation in the Jordan. When the Son of God, our Saviour, came there, he was revealed to John with these words: *Behold the Lamb of God, who takes away the sins of the world.*[45] He stepped down into the water, not because there was anything to be cleansed in God, but water had to go before the oil which was to come, in order to institute, direct and fulfil the mysteries of baptism.[46] When he had been washed in John's hands, the order of the mystery succeeded and the Father consummated what the Son had asked and the Holy Spirit had promised.

The sky opened as the God the Father performed the anointing, the spiritual oil forthwith descended in the likeness of a dove, and sat upon

---

[42] See 1Kings 16.11f.

[43] By this reasoning, Optatus would have to say that Genesis 1.3 is spoken by the Son to the Father; cf Origen, *De Oratione* 24.5, where the second-century heresiarch and apologist Tatian is attacked for holding this view. See also Book 5, n. 12

[44] Psalm 44.8. Addressed to the Son, the "King of Kings", because it is a royal Psalm.

[45] John 1.29, though in fact it is the Baptist himself who says this; the words spoken to him are at John 1.33.

[46] On baptism as a mystery cf Gregory of Nyssa, *Oratio Catechetica* 33 etc. The term initially means a secret revealed by God (Ephesians 1.9 etc.), but later by assimilation to pagan usage comes to denote the revelatory sacrament.

his head and suffused him; the oil was dispensed, and so he began to be called Christ when he was anointed by God the Father.[47] And so that he would not seem to lack the imposition of hands, the voice of God was heard saying from the cloud, *This is my Son, of whom I have thought well; hear him.*[48] This, therefore, is (the meaning of) the lesson, *Let not the oil of the sinner anoint my head.* Late though it is, learn the true interpretation, brother Parmenianus, since now you have found a time to learn.[49]

8. As for this which, you say, we read in the prophet Solomon, *The sons of adultery are abortive and bastard vines cannot put down deep roots*[50] - this can be understood also as a literal saying. If you make a figure of it, you have excused the true adulterers. But let it be said figuratively: this is said of heretics, among whom are false sacramental nuptials, and in whose beds iniquity is found, as their seed is corrupted for the annihilation of faith.[51] While Valentinus asserted that the Son of God was in a phantom, not in flesh, he corrupted his own faith and that of his school. The annihilation of the seed is the nativity of those who did not believe that the Son of God was born in the flesh from the virgin Mary and suffered in the flesh.

9. And you also recall reading this in the prophet Jeremiah, that heaven abhorred the evils done by the people of God, *That they forsook the fount of living water and they dug for themselves hollowed lakes, which could not hold water.*[52] You read it indeed, but, as matters are, you refused to understand. All your argumentation being driven by your zeal to cast incriminating reproaches on the catholics, you have tried to wrest a great deal to your own way of thinking. For if you think that everything is said through the prophets in such a way as to apply to our own time, you have excused the Jews, who are well known to be the subject of these words, having put away the living God, the true God, the God who bestowed goods on them, and made for themselves idols,

---

[47] Based on Matthew 3.16-17 par, the oil being added from the baptismal service. The Greek *christos* means "anointed", and Jesus is here confirmed as King by the reference to Psalm 2.7.

[48] Combining Matthew 1.17 par with Matthew 17.5 par.

[49] Accepting the reading proposed in Ziwsa's apparatus: *tempus discendi invenisti.*

[50] Wisdom 3.6.

[51] On the fornication of heretics see Clement of Alexandria, *Stromateis* III.25-39 etc.

[52] Jeremiah 2.13.

that is hollowed lakes which cannot hold water. In God perpetual majesty teems forth, just as in a fountain water teems forth widely through flowing veins; but idols, unless they are made, cannot exist, and lakes if they are not dug cannot have capacious inlets; a lake cannot be excavated without art and machinery, nor can an idol come to be without artifice. In idols there is no natural power, but it is joined and entwined with it by human error; a power is reckoned in idols, which was not born there.[53] A lake is hollowed by art, and if the fabric is shaken,[54] it neither has water from itself nor can hold it when it receives it; in the same way, an idol is nothing of itself and, while it is worshipped, is nothing.

This is what God meant by saying that his people had committed two evils, because they had forsaken the fount of living water and had made for themselves dug out and hollowed lakes. For indeed the Jewish people had deserted the true water, it had ignored the majesty of God and had followed a religion polluted by idols. For God shows the same grief in the prophet Isaiah, when he declares that this has two elements, saying, *Hear, heaven, and earth, mark with your ears: I have begotten sons and raised them up, and of themeselves they have abandoned me.*[55] Why, brother Parmenianus, have you said nothing of this lesson? Is it because water is not named here? For it is palpable that in your zeal to incriminate you have so abused the Law that, wherever you have found water written, you use certain wiles to apply it invidiously, and with a sort of dragnet interwoven with the malice of arguments,[56] you have drawn to yourself whatever good things there are.[57] For what are you

---

[53] For the argument that, though an idol is nothing, it is wrong to worship it, see 1Cor 8.4 and 10.18-20.

[54] Accepting a reading in Ziwsa's *apparatus*, since I can make nothing of the text.

[55] Isaiah 1.2.

[56] Perhaps an ironic reference to Matthew 13.47-50, where the net of the Kingdom catches both good fish and bad, to be separated only at the last day. Such passages are regularly quoted against the Donatist aspiration to perfection: see e.g. Augustine, *Cresc.* IV.33 and *Caths* 35.

[57] Since Optatus believes that the Bible is the prophetic word of God, he can apply many passages in a way that we would regard as figurative. None the less he seems to exclude the possibility of multiple meaning, affirming that every prophecy has one historical reference and one speaker; and he assumes that the primary meaning is the one determined by the literal context, though without reference to the historical circumstances of the writer.

thinking of in this chapter of Jeremiah, when God exclaims that he has been deserted and thus lakes have been hollowed - he is angry for himself, not for his possession; for the water of baptism is God's possession, not God. And if you think yourselves deserted, were those baptised among us ever among you, so that they might properly seem to come to us as deserters from you? It is therefore proved that what you have said about the oil and sacrifice of the sinner has been spoken not against us but against yourselves.

OPTATUS:

Fifth Book against the Donatists

In my first book I have shown by the plainest documentary evidence who collaborated against the Law[1] and who were the authors of the schism, and in the second I have demonstrated that the one true catholic church is among us. And in the third I have proved that we are the least responsible for the harsh acts that are alleged, and have shown by a divine token that it is rather you who are the sinners. At this point we have now to speak of baptism, which is the substance of the whole question now in dispute, since you have profaned baptism by your presumption, when you have chosen to repeat what Christ said was to be done once. And you do not deny this, brother Parmenianus, because at the opening of your treatise, you have said many things against yourselves and in our favour, since serve to our cause.

For you have recalled, in analogy with baptism, that the flood occurred once, and there was one circumcision for the Jewish people.[2] And when you had treated these matters at the beginning of your treatise, you became, however, unmindful of them in the course of your treatise, by introducing two waters;[3] and, since you were going to speak argumentatively about the true water and the false, you adopted an unwise method in constructing the opening of your oration. By attacking the unity of holy baptism, you confirm it; with regard to Jewish circumcision you wanted to boast, as a sort of founding principle, that the baptism of Christians had been foreshadowed in the circumcision of the Hebrews. You have defended the catholic church while you impugn it. For in the course of your treatise you have declared that you are

---

[1] Presumably the Christian Law (cf James 1.25; Augustine, *Brev.* III.8), or the laws of baptism, defined below. Fourth-century commentators on Galatians 2.16ff (Marius Victorinus, Jerome, Theodoret) distinguish between the ceremonial law, which is abolished, and the moral or natural law, which remains both binding on and possible for Christians. The "collaboration" mentioned here is, as usual, *traditio*, handing over of scriptures.

[2] Optatus' memory fails him here: a second circumcision was performed by Joshua (Joshua 5.2), and explained by Origen as a type of baptism (*HomJosh* V.6).

[3] The Donatists alluded to the *aqua mendax* of Jeremiah 15.18. Cf Ambrose, *Myst.* 23; Augustine, *Cath.* 64, *Petil.* II.235 etc.

making one baptism empty so that you may seem to make the other full. When you say that, apart from heretics' baptism, there is one sort and another sort, then even though you have tried to show that they are of different species, you could not deny that there are two. When you try to take away one of these, you have been striving to turn the second visibly into a kind of first.

Now circumcision was sent forth as a type[4] before the arrival of baptism, and your treatise argues that among Christians there are two waters; therefore show that there were two circumcisions among the Jews also, one better, the other worse. If you look for this, you will not be able to find it. The race of Abraham, to which the Jews belong, glories in being marked by this seal. Therefore the truth that follows should be such as the image sent before it. And furthermore God, as he wanted to show that a single thing ought to come later when truth succeeded, did not choose that anything be taken from the ear or from the finger, but that part of the body was chosen where the abstraction of the foreskin on one occasion produced a sign of health, which cannot happen again.[5] For when done once it preserves health; if it happens again it may bring ruin. So too the baptism of Christians, jointly performed by the Trinity, confers grace; if it is repeated it causes life to be cast away.

Why then, brother Parmenianus, have you decided to propose a single thing, and compare to this two baptisms, albeit of different species, one true and one false? For this was what you subsequently argued, asserting that yours was the only true one, while you wished to ascribe the other to us as a lie. After this you also mentioned the Flood; this was indeed an image of baptism, whose purpose was to drown sinners and by means of washing to restore the world, which was completely soiled, to

---

[4] The notion that an episode or character of the Old Testament prefigures Christ or the Church is expressed by the word *tupos* at Romans 5.14 and by *antitupon* at 1Peter 3.21.
[5] Various interpretations of circumcision were proposed by early Christians: thus Justin, *Trypho* 16, treats it as a sign that the Jews would be cut off from their salvation; the *Epistle of Barnabas* 9.4 regards it as a false commandment; Origen, *CommRom* II.13 says that Christ has offered his own blood so that we need not offer the blood of circumcision. Antoninus Pius' law against the circumcision of proselytes at *Digest* 48.8.11 shows that the Roman government saw the rite as a species of castration such as was practised by illicit eastern cults.

its pristine cleanliness.[6] But, as you were going on to say later that apart from the diseased fountains of the heretics there is yet another water, that which tells lies against the true one, why have you chosen to recall the Flood, which occurred once? If the case is so, show first that there were two arks, albeit dissimilar, and two unlike doves carrying different branches in their beaks,[7] if you are going to prove that there is true and false water.

Therefore the only water, and the true one, is that which is founded not upon the place or upon the person, but upon the Trinity. And since you have said that there is also a lying water, learn further where you will be able to find it: it is with Praxeas the Patripassian, who completely denies the Son and maintains that the Father suffered.[8] And, seeing that the Son of God is truth, as he himself witnesses, saying *I am the way, the truth and the life*,[9] therefore if the Son of God is truth, where he himself is not there is a lie. Seeing that the Son is not with the Patripassian, neither is truth, and where there is not truth, there is the lying water. And so, late though it is, stop inventing crimes, and do not transfer to the catholics what is said against the Patripassians.

Now, since it has been plainly demonstrated that what you have said about the Flood and circumcision could be said by us and for us,[10] the next task is to show how you have bestowed on baptism praise of such a kind that there is much in it that tells in our favour and yours, but also something that tells against you. That which is common to us and you tells in favour of both sides - of yours for this reason, that you spring from us. In sum, there is a single ecclesiastical intercourse between both us and you, common readings, the same faith, the same sacraments of faith, the same mysteries. Therefore you did well to praise baptism; for which of the faithful does not know that baptism is the life of the

---

[6] Cf 1Peter 3.20. The paucity of the redeemed appeared, however, to support the Donatists: cf Augustine, *Cath.* 33.
[7] Referring to the account of the end of the flood at Genesis 8.8-10. The one dove is a symbol of the united church (Song of Songs 6.8 at I.10 etc.) and of the uniting Spirit (Matthew 3.16 at IV.7). According to Augustine, *Brev.* III.16, catholics argued that the dove represents the elect who will remain after the last day, while the raven, who did not return, is a symbol of future damnation for the unrighteous.
[8] See Tertullian, *Adversus Praxean* 1 and Optatuts I.9.
[9] John 14.6.
[10] Reading *nobis*, from Ziwsa's *apparatus*, not *vobis* from his text.

virtues, the death of crimes, the birth of immortality, the means of imparting the heavenly kingdom, the port of innocence and, as you have said yourself, the shipwreck of sinners?[11] It is not the agent of the rite who vouchsafes these things to every believer, but the faith of the believer and the Trinity.

2. Then you ask what you have said against yourselves in the praise of baptism. Listen, but first you must confess what all of you will be quite unable to deny. For you say that that the Trinity is of little account where your presence has been wanting. If you slander us, at least show respect for God, who holds first place in the Trinity, who with his own Son and the Holy Spirit performs and fulfils all things, and even in the place where no human being is present. But you, brother Parmenianus, in your praise of water from the readings in Genesis, said that waters first brought forth living souls. What, were they able to generate them of their own accord? What, was the whole Trinity not there too? Certainly the Father was there too, as he deigned to give an order, saying *Let the waters bring forth swimming creatures, flying creatures* etc. But if what happened happened without an agent, God would say "Bring forth, waters".[12] So the Son of God was also there as an agent, there was the Holy Spirit, as we read, *And the Spirit of God was moving above the waters.*[13] I see no fourth there, nothing less than than three; and yet what the Trinity performed came to birth, and you were not there. Otherwise, if nothing should be allowed to the Trinity without you, call the fish back to their origin; now submerge the flying birds in the waves, if in your absence the Trinity ought not to perform anything.

3. When, therefore, you said that both there was one flood and that circumcision could not be repeated, and we have taught you that the heavenly gift is conferred on every believer by the Trinity, not by a human, why have you thought proper to duplicate baptism, not after us but after the Trinity? No little strife has grown up about this sacrament,

---

[11] For these metaphors cf Romans 6.3-4, Titus 3.5, John 3.5; and for the last two possibly 1Peter 3.21 and 1Tim 1.20. Once again, the Donatists will have read the symbolism of the ark as a mandate for the exclusion of evil elements from the Church.

[12] Genesis 1.20. Cf Origen, *De Oratione* 24.5, which, however, insists that the verb is to be taken as an imperative, not as a request. Christian writers usually maintained that Christ was the Word of creation rather than its addressee: see Irenaeus, *AH* V.32.1, Augustine, *De Genesi ad Litteram* I.10 etc.

[13] Genesis 1.2. Cf Augustine, *De Genesi ad Litteram* I.6-7.

and it is doubtful whether it is granted to do this again after the Trinity
in the same Trinity. You say, "it is granted"; we say, "it is not granted".
Between your "it is granted" and our "it is not granted" the souls of the
people tack and veer. Let no-one believe you, no-one believe us; all of
us are people at loggerheads. Judges must be sought; if Christians,
neither side can give them, because truth is hindered by zeal. A judge
must be sought from those without; if a pagan, he cannot know the
secrets of Christians, if a Jew, he is an enemy of Christian baptism;
therefore in the world no judgment on this matter can be found; a judge
must be sought from heaven.

But why do we batter heaven, when we have here a testament in the
Gospel? For in this place earthly things can rightly be compared to
heavenly ones. The case is the same as with any person who has a lot
of children: so long as the father is present the father himself commands
them individually; no testament is necessary yet. And so too Christ, so
long as he was present in the world, while he was not yet wanting, gave
whatever commands were necessary for the time to his disciples. But
when an earthly father feels himself to be on the brink of death, fearing
lest after his death the brothers should break the peace and be at odds,
he brings witnesses and transfers his will from his dying breast to
tablets which will last a long time; and if any dispute arises among the
brothers, they do not go to the burial-place, but seek the testament, and
the one who rests in the burial-place speaks silently from the tablets;
just so, the one whose testament [the Gospel] is alive in heaven, and
therefore let his will be sought in the Gospel, as in a testament.[14]

For Christ in his foreknowledge saw what you are now doing even
when it was yet to come. When he was washing the feet of his disciples,
the Son of God said to Peter, *What I do you do not know; later,
however, you will know.*[15] By saying you will know later, he referred to
the present times; therefore among the other articles of his testament he
set down this article about water also.

When he was washing his disciples' feet, the others were silent, and if
Peter too had been silent, he would simply have enacted a type of
humility, and said nothing about the sacrament of baptism. But when

---

[14] For this notion of the Scripture as the testament of the dead Christ cf Hebrews 9.15-19.
[15] John 13.7ff; cf Ambrose, *Myst.* 31. It is not clear that this means baptism, any more
than the numerous other references to water in the fourth Gospel. Cf Augustine, *Cath.* 65.

Peter refused and did not allow his feet to be washed, Christ denied him the kingdom unless he accepted service. But when mention was made of the heavenly kingdom, where part of his part was demanded for service, he offered his whole body to be washed.

Now come here, all Christian people, singly and together; learn what is granted. When Peter provokes him, Christ teaches. He who doubts learns. For the voice of Christ says, *He who is once washed has no need to be washed again, because he is wholly clean.*[16] And he said this about that washing which he had commanded to be celebrated in honour of the Trinity, not about that of the Jews and heretics, who when they wash are filthy, but about the sacred water, which flows from the fountains of the three names. For the Lord himself gave this precept, saying, *Go, baptize all nations in the name of the Father and the Son and the Holy Spirit.*[17] It was about this washing that he said, He who is once washed has no need to be washed again. By saying *once*, he forbade a repetition, and he said it about the act, not the person. For if there had been a gradation, he would say, "He who has once been well washed"; but as he has not added the word "well", he indicates that whatever has been done in the Trinity is well done.

This is the reason why we have accepted those who come from you without reservation. When he says, *he has no need to be washed again*, this statement is general, not particular; for if he were saying this to Peter, Christ would say, "Because you have once been washed, you have no need to be washed again". Hence, whenever anyone baptized by you has elected to cross over to us, we have received his arrival without reservation, according to this authority and example. For let it be far from us ever to exorcize one who is sound in faith, let it be far from us ever to call back to the font one who is already washed; let it be far from us ever to sin in the Holy Spirit,[18] a crime which is denied forgiveness in the present and future age; let it be far from us to repeat that which is once done, or to duplicate that which is one. For thus it

---

[16] John 13.10; cf Augustine, *Cath.* 63, with the same reservations as in n. 15.
[17] Matthew 28.19.
[18] Matthew 17.31-2 par; though Optatus strangely speaks of sinning in the Spirit, rather than against him.

is written, where the Apostle says, *One God, one Christ, one faith, one immersion.*[19]

As for you, who aspire quite readily to duplicate baptism, if you gave another baptism, give another faith; if you give another faith, give also another Christ; if you give another Christ, give another God. You cannot deny that God is one, lest you fall into Marcion's pit.[20] Therefore God is one, and from one God there is one Christ. The one who is rebaptized was already a Christian; how can he be called a Christian again? In this passage the one faith is separated from that of the heretics, and the unique faith from their diversity of faith. It is written to you as well, who after it is once done do it again, placing everything in the gifts, nothing in the sacraments, when this title of faith belongs to the believer, not the agent. For whoever asks, the one who believes in God believes, and after this one's single "Credo", you exact another "Credo".[21] Then follows the one baptism, so that, because what is one is sacred by virtue of being one, it should not only be separated from the profane and sacrilegious baptisms of heretics, but should not be duplicated, as it is one, or repeated, since it happens once.

4. In the celebration of this sacrament of baptism, there are three aspects, which you will not be able to augment, diminish or omit. The first aspect concerns the Trinity, the second the believer and the third the agent. But we are not to accord the same weight in the scale to each of these. For I see two as necessary and one as all but necessary: the Trinity, without which the rite cannot be carried on, holds the prime place; this is followed by the faith of the believer; next now comes the person of the agent, which cannot be of similar authority. The two first remain always immutable and unmoved; for the Trinity itself exists for ever, the faith in individuals is one, and both always retain their force. But we understand that the person of the agent cannot be equal to the

---

[19] Ephesians 4.5.

[20] See Book I.9. Marcion is the arch-heretic for Africans, being the object of Tertullian's *Adversus Marcionem* and the author of the heresy named most frequently in Cyprian's Epistle 73. Augustine, *Cath.* 79, ironically suggests that the Marcionites could justify their position as well as the Donatists.

[21] The opening word of creeds recited at baptism and after; cf Ambrose, *Myst.* 28. On the Roman versions see Kelly (1972), 100-204. The Latin creeds would begin with the words *Credo in Deum patrem omnipotentem* (cf Book I.1); those who used the Nicene Creed of 325 would add the word *unum*.

two former aspects by the fact that it alone is clearly mutable. You desire that you and we should differ in respect of this same person, and reckoning yourselves more holy, you do not scruple to put your pride before the Trinity, seeing that the person of the agent can change, while the Trinity cannot change.

And when it is baptism that should be desired by those who receive it, you advance yourselves as the objects of desire. Since you are [merely] agents among others, show what place in that mystery you have and whether you can be of the same body. The character of baptism is unique, and it governs a body of its own, which body has certain members, and nothing can be either added to or taken from them. If the agent is found to hold a privileged place among these members, the whole body belongs to the agent.[22] All these members of this body are together once and for all, and cannot change; but the agents change every day with regard to places, times and persons. For neither is there one person who baptizes always and everywhere. In this work many were engaged long ago, others are now, and others will be later; the agents can change, the sacraments cannot change.

When therefore you see that all who baptize are agents, not masters, and the sacraments are holy through themselves, not through human beings, why is it that you claim so much for yourselves? Why is it that you try to exclude God from his own gifts? Let God vouchsafe the things that are his. For that gift which is divine cannot be given by man. If you think so, you are trying to make void the words of the prophets and the promises of God; by these it is proved that God, not man, does the washing. Against you here is David the prophet, who says in Psalm 50: *You will wash me and I shall be made whiter than snow.*[23] Again in the same psalm: *God, wash from me unrighteousness and cleanse me from my wrongdoing.* He said *Wash me*; he did not say, "Find me someone through whom I may be washed". And Isaiah the prophet spoke as follows: *Since God will wash away the filth of the sons and daughters of Zion*[24] - we have proved in the third book that Zion is the

---

[22] Paul argues at Col 2.19 that the head of the Church is Christ.

[23] Psalm 50.9f.

[24] Isaiah 4.4. On Zion as the Church see III. 2. While commending Optatus at *Cath.* 50, Augustine prefers to argue, on the basis of Luke 24.47, that the true Church must retain contact with the earthly Jerusalem.

church - therefore God washes the sons and daughters of the church - he did not say, "Those who deem themselves holy will wash them". You must either deign to be vanquished by the prophets, or you must recognise that it is God, not man, that washes.

When you keep saying "How can he give who has nothing to give?", acknowledge that God is the giver, acknowledge that God cleanses each one; for no-one but God can wash the filth and blemishes of the mind. Or if you do think that the washing belongs to you, say what kind of mind it is that is washed by means of the body, or what form it has, or in what part of the human being it dwells; this human beings are not allowed to know. How is it, therefore, that you think you do the washing, when you do not know what sort of thing it is that you are washing? It is for God, not human beings, to cleanse; for he himself through the prophet Isaiah promised that he would wash, when he says, *And if your sins were like scarlet, I shall make them white as snow.*[25] He said *I shall make them white*, not "I shall have them made white". If God promised this, why do you want to bestow what it is not granted to you to promise or to bestow or to have? See, in Isaiah God promises that he will make white those stained by sin, not through a man. Turn back to the Gospel, see what Christ has promised for the salvation of the human race. When the Samaritan woman refused him water, then the Son of God said something directed to your own presumption. *The one who drinks the water that I give*, he said, *shall never thirst.*[26] *The water that I give*, he said: he did not say, "that will be given by those who deem themselves holy", as you think yourselves, but he said that he would give it. He therefore is the one who gives, and what is given is his. What is it that you are trying to claim for yourselves with the greatest importunity?

5. John the Baptist enhanced this case, having come as a herald of salvation and immersing many in repentance and forgiveness of their sins. When he announced that the Son of God was about to come, these are his words: *See, there comes one to baptize you.*[27] And yet we do not read that after John Christ rebaptized anyone. As to this saying of his,

---

[25] Isaiah 1.18.
[26] John 4.13.
[27] John 1.33. Yet John's disciples were rebaptized in Ephesus by those of Jesus (Acts 19.2) - a fact adduced against Jerome by a schismatic interlocutor in his *Alt.* See below.

to baptize you, therefore, Christ when he came at that time baptized no-one after John. It was promised to our times that he would give what today is given, in accordance with what he says: *The one who drinks the water that I give will never thirst.* For moreover, when the disciples of John said to their master, *See, he whom you baptized is baptizing*,[28] he was baptizing indeed, but through the hands of his Apostles, to whom he had given the laws of baptism. After all, we read in another place, *For he himself baptized no-one, but his disciples did.*[29] In this matter we are all his disciples, so that we may be the agents of his giving what he promised to give.

And yet when John was baptizing countless thousands of people and Christ was already present, the servant acted as agent and the master was idle, before he gave the form of baptism. Over no small period of time, thousands of people were immersed in penitence and forgiveness of their sins. Yet no-one had been immersed in the [name of the] Trinity, no-one had heard that there was a Holy Spirit.[30] And when the time of fulfilment came, at a certain time the Son of God gave laws for baptism and gave a way by which to go to the kingdom of heaven. At that very time he gave the precept, saying, *Go, teach all nations, baptizing them in the name of the Father, the Son and the Holy Spirit.*[31] From that day, what was commanded had to come to pass; before the time he would not correct the previous ministry, lest he give a warrant for rebaptism, notwithstanding that the baptism of John is one thing and that of Christ another. Before [giving] the law, he wished the baptism of John, which was not full, to stand for the full one; and yet because the aforementioned thousands of people had believed in God, even though they did not know the Son of God and the Holy Spirit, he could not deny them the kingdom of heaven. Hence the voice of the Son of God says, *From the days of John until now the kingdom of God suffers*

---

[28] John 3.26, paraphrasing so as to obscure the fact that Jesus' baptism is not described in this Gospel.
[29] John 4.2.
[30] Looking forward to Acts 19.2 below. The "countless thousands" are an exaggeration of the Biblical testimony.
[31] Matthew 28.19 again.

violence, and those who use violence bear it away.[32] He said they use
violence, because hitherto John was baptizing. In sum, because there
was one time before the precepts and another after the precepts, those
who were baptized after the precepts in the name of the Saviour entered
lawfully into the kingdom of God; those who [were baptized] before the
precepts used violence without a law, but were not excluded. Therefore,
while the baptism of John before the precepts was imperfect, it was
judged perfect by him whom no-one judges, and because his ordinance
fixed, as it were, a sort of boundary between the former and the latter
times.

When certain people at Ephesus were being baptized in John's
baptism after the precepts, the most blessed Paul on seeing them
inquired whether they had received the Holy Spirit.[33] They said that *they
did not know whether there was a Holy Spirit,* and he told them that
after the baptism of John they should receive the Holy Spirit. For they
were baptized in the way that many had been baptized by John. But
those who were baptized before the law had a right to indulgence,
because he who could give indulgence was present; those who had not
been overtaken by the laws were not totally culpable. But those who are
said to have been baptized in Ephesus after the law by the baptism of
John, had erred in the sacrament after the laws, because the baptism of
the Lord had now been introduced and that of the servant ousted. And
so, after the divine commandments, it was their duty to go to heaven
lawfully, not by violence; for now Christ had fixed an end to the times,
saying, *From the days of John until today.* Now after today what was
granted yesterday was no longer granted.

So do not flatter yourselves with the saying of the Apostle Paul, who
was not inquiring about the person of the agent, but about the fact; it
was the fact, not the person, that displeased him. In short, he enjoined
the baptism of the Saviour, so that those who had not known it might
learn it, because they had received not it, but another. But as for you,
what do you change? If you were able to change the fact, you would

---

[32] Matthew 11.12. The meaning of the verse is highly obscure: Optatus has *deripiunt* for
the Greek *biazetai*, which Jerome renders more literally by *vim patitur* ("suffers
violence").
[33] Acts 19.2-4. Augustine sees the difference between the baptisms in the form, not the
agent: *Petil.* II.75-6 etc.

have done well - if, that is, you did anything according to the law. Paul said, *By what baptism were you baptized*? And they said, *That of John.* He persuaded them to acept the baptism of Christ. You say not "What did you receive?", but "From whom did you receive it?", and you pursue people's characters, and wish to repeat what is done once. Those who were baptized at Ephesus had believed in repentance and the forgiveness of sins; it was rightly said to them that they should be baptized in the name of the Father, the Son and the Holy Spirit. But as to you, what do you change in people, who have already declared their belief in the name of Father, the Son and the Holy Spirit? Whether you inquire about this or another thing, you will necessarily be convicted of sin, whether you make inquiries about what is not commanded, or wish to do that which is already done.

6. I return now to that saying of yours, "He who has nothing to give, how can he give?" Whence comes this expression, from what lesson can it be recited? The expression is culled from common speech,[34] not read from the book: "He who has nothing to give, how can he give?" These words are not written in the law; for if, as you would have it, a person gives, God is idle, and if God is idle and everything that is to be given is with you, let the conversion be to you. Let those whom you baptize be immersed in your name. Blush when the most blessed Paul exclaims and declares his exultation: *What, were you baptized in my name*?[35] He rejoices, because he has baptized only two people and one household; and you aspire to rebaptize [whole] peoples, and rejoice in the fact that you have sinned and go on sinning, saying "What is given by one who has nothing to give?" The one believed in is himself the one who gives what is believed, not the one through whom belief occurs. To sum up: under John a countless mutlitude of people was baptized. Prove either that John received or had something to give. Rather, it was by his ministry that God gave, as he never fails in giving; and now, when all are agents, the ministry is human, but the gift divine.

7. Now what a ridiculous thing this is, which is always heard from you, as if it were to your own glory: "This gift of baptism belongs to the giver, not the receiver". And I wish that you were saying this of God,

---

[34] Literally "from the neighbourhood" (*vico*). Since *vicus* often denotes a village in contrast to an urban area, this may be another sneer at the rusticity of the Donatists.
[35] 1Cor 1.13. Augustine stresses Paul's disclaimer at *Cresc.* III.6, *Petil.* III.63 etc.

who is the giver of this thing! But the absurdity is that you call yourselves the givers. If it is so, then we and you should possess our proselytes separately. You who call yourselves holy, inquire of the one in your possession whether he renounces the devil and believes in God; and let him say, "I will not". On the other hand, let us sinners, as you would have it, inquire of another proselyte whether he renounces the devil and believes in God etc., and let him say, "I renounce him and believe", etc. When you immerse the unwilling and we the willing, let it be said which of them has a share in God's grace. Without doubt the one who obtains it is surely the one who believes, not the one for whose will you subsitute your own holiness.

Either confess yourselves to be agents, though belatedly, or if the substance of the matter is in the agent and not in itself, let certain people claim this for themselves in their own arts - that we may, on your provocation, compare even human arts to divine matters. When a precious dye is applied, the nature of a white fleece is often changed, as it is made purple artificially. Thus white wool passes into purple, in the same way as a catechumen passes into one of the faithful. Certainly when he begins to be what he was not, he ceases to be what he was. The wool changes both its colour and its name,[36] and the person changes both appellation and cast of mind. The effects must be considered, the efficient causes reviewed. You say that it is is by your gift that a person is made one of the faithful; if this is entirely your doing, let the agent whose art produces purple also say that he has the precious colour in his own hands; that he does not procure from the Ocean precious pigments unknown to many, immersed in which the fleeces are promoted by their colour to an admirable dignity; that he makes the purple solely by his touch without the admixture of fishes' blood.

If therefore this agent cannot give colour solely by his touch, so neither can the agent of baptism give anything from himself without the Trinity. Such is the case in the matter now being debated. For the form of baptism for proselytes is commanded by the Saviour; the agent of

---

[36] The word *conchylia*, derived from a fish which yielded purple dye (Pliny, *Natural History* IX.86) could be applied to the coloured garments (Juvenal, *Satire* III.81). In the light of the citations in Constantine, *Oratio* 20 and Lactantius, *Div. Inst.* VII.24, Optatus may have attached an allegorical significance to Virgil, Eclogue IV.43-44. See further Courcelle (1957).

baptism is not defined by any exception. He did not say to the Apostles, "Do this yourselves, let not others do it"; whoever has baptized in the name of the Father and the Son and the Holy Spirit has fulfilled the work of the Apostles. Indeed we read in the Gospel where John says: Master, we saw one expelling demons in your name, and we forbade him, because he does not follow with us: Christ says, *Do not forbid him, for whoever is not against you is for you.*[37] For what is enjoined upon them is that their work should be sanctification by the Trinity; and that they should not baptize in their own name, but in the name of the Father and the Son and the Holy Spirit; therefore it is the name, not the work, that sanctifies.

Understand, though belatedly, that you are agents, not masters. And if the church is a vineyard, and the vines are human beings and cultivators are appointed, why do you invade the domain of the father of the household?[38] Why do you claim for yourselves that which is God's? Why do you want everything to be yours, where you cannot even have a part? For it is on account of the way that you puff yourselves up against us that the most blessed Paul reproaches the Corinthians; in himself and Apollos he adumbrates the acts of our own times. *Let none, he says, be puffed up against another.*[39] So as to show that this whole sacrament of baptism belongs to God, so that the agent can claim there nothing for himself, he speaks as follows: *I indeed planted* - that is, I made a catechumen of a pagan - *Apollos watered*[40] - that is, he baptized the catechumen. But that what had been planted and watered grew was God's work. For it is also true today that anyone who wants to prepare his vineyard hires an agent at an agreed wage, who, with bent back and sweating sides, is to make a hollow in the earth where he can put down the plants that have been chosen and bring water over the flattened hole. He can dig the hole and put in the plants; he can introduce water; he cannot order [the hole] to retain it; for it belongs to

---

[37] Luke 9.49-50.
[38] See Matthew 20.16 for the parable of the vineyard and John 4.35-6 for the application to Christian mission. Cf Matthew 22.33-41 par. For the interpretation of the Church as the vineyard see Origen, *HomMatth* XV. where Optatus' terms *operarius* and *paterfamilias* appear in Rufinus' translation.
[39] 1Cor 4.6.
[40] 1Cor 3.6.

God alone to bring forth roots from the middle of the stems to grow together in the earth, and to elicit oozing buds and increase of leaves.

Thus the blessed Apostle Paul, in order to prevent your being presumptuous and puffed up, and lest the agent of baptism should either reckon himself to be its lord or claim a tiny part of such a great gift for himself, speaks as follows, indicating that everything is of God: *Neither the one who plants nor the one who waters is anything, but* only God, who leads it on to increase.[41] You are agents among others; when the sun comes, that is at the end of the age, you can strive with us about the wage in the day of retribution. Do not claim for yourselves the royal domain. For if it is so, let the agents who serve at God's table[42] also claim that the guests should show gratitude to them for the generosity that has been extended. The voice of Christ says in the invitation: *Come, my Father's blessed ones, behold the kingdom which is prepared for you from the beginning of the world.*[43] The nations come seeking grace; the one who exhibits it is the one who deigned to invite them; the crowd of those who serve has the ministry; thanks are to be given not to those who serve but to the one who provides the meal. You, when you are agents, impudently claim the whole lordship of the feast for yourselves, when the most blessed Paul humbly confesses himself and others to be servants. Lest anyone should think that his hope should be placed in the Apostles or bishops, he speaks as follows: *For what is Paul, or what is Apollos? Surely the agents of him in whom we believe.*[44] Therefore among all those who serve there is not lordship but ministry.[45] You see, therefore, brother Parmenianus, that of the three aspects mentioned above, that first third is immovable, unconquerable and changeless, but the person of the agent is temporary.

8. It remains now to say something about the merit of the believer who has the faith that the Son of God has put before his own holiness and majesty. For you cannot be more holy than Christ is; but when that

---

[41] 1Cor 3.7.
[42] Introducing the parable of the Great Supper (Matthew 22.1-14), but perhaps with an allusion to 1Cor 9.13.
[43] Matthew 25.34.
[44] 1Cor 3.4 (expanded).
[45] Using the word *operarius*, which I have elsewhere rendered as "agent". For the thought cf Mark 10.42-5 and John 13.13-15.

woman whose daughter was dead came to him and asked him to revive her, he promised nothing from his own power, but inquired about another's faith, so that, if the woman believed, the daughter would revive on account of the mother's faith, and if she did not believe the power of the Son of God would be stilled by the blow.[46] The woman was asked, she replied that it was possible for her to believe what was asked. When ordered to go, the woman returned home, she found the girl alive whom she had left dead. She did not run to kiss her, she did not hurry to embrace her, but returned to give thanks to the Saviour; and so that the Son of God might show that he had been idle, and faith alone had done the work, he said, *Go in peace, woman, your faith has saved you.* Where is that saying of yours, "It belongs to the giver, not the receiver"?

And what do you think of the faith of the centurion? When his boy was poorly, he begged the Saviour to come and turn death away from him. Christ was already coming to the boy when the centurion restrained him, as confessing the unworthiness of his house. The Son of God ought not to enter it with his whole person [he said], but send his power, by which death could be put to flight and the boy could revive. It was not the courage, nor the wisdom of the centurion that was praised, but his faith: *and the boy was cured in that hour.*[47] Evidently "it belongs to the giver, not to the receiver".

There are many testimonies of this kind in the Gospel concerning perfect faith, but anyway three testimonies of faith should be completed. What do you think also of that woman, who had suffered for twelve years for a hidden cause peculiar to the female sex, and had expended all her substance on doctors? When she saw that the Son of God was honoured for such great powers, she entered the crowd, she saw the doctor, and saw also the people, and sorrow impelled her to seek the doctor, while shame hindered her from revealing her case before the

---

[46] The quotation is from Luke 8.48 (the woman with the issue of blood), but Optatus appears to have confused this with the surrounding context (the raising of Jairus' daughter) and with Mark 7.29 (the Syrophoenician woman returns home to find the demon gone from her daughter). Conflation with Luke 7.11-17 (raising of the widow's son, memorable because of the OT parallels) may also have occurred.

[47] Matthew 8.13, rather than Luke 7.2, where the *pais* ("boy" or "slave") becomes a *doulos* ("slave").

male sex.[48] Her silent faith devised a plan. *I shall put forth my hand,* she said, *and shall touch the hem of his garment, and I shall become healthy.* Amid the crowd, seen by no-one, she put forth her hand, touched and was made healthy; and she did not dare to reveal what she had not dared to ask. But lest the fruit of faith should seem to lie low among those who were ignorant of it, the Saviour spoke as follows: *Who touched me? His disciples were amazed, saying, The crowd presses on you, and you say, "Who touched me?"! And Christ said, Who touched me, I say? I have felt power go out of me.*[49] So the woman confessed that she had touched him and was healthy. Long before the woman had begged on her daughter's behalf, the centurion had petitioned on his boy's; in this place, the woman did not beg, nor did Christ promise, but what faith had presumed upon it obtained. Evidently "it belongs to the giver, not the receiver".

9. For as to this description of Naaman the Syrian as a raw mass of the most obstinately pullulating wounds,[50] with which you have elected to enlarge your treatises, brother Parmenianus, what has this to do with the present matter? This would be well said, and you could have been right to make use of a long discourse, if you found some catechumen of the foulest character, maintaining an extremely obstinate cast of mind, who declined to accept the most tender grace of the water of life. These words that you have spoken would serve well to show the regeneration of the person, they would serve well to demonstrate the possibility of changing and softening the inveterate obstinacy of our nature into childlike flesh. But in this dispute which is being carried on at the present time between the parties, for what reason have you recalled a lesson like this? We do not read here that anyone washed this leprous Syrian before Elisha's saying or by his order, so that he might be duly washed a second time. And even if this did happen, nothing even so would accrue to you which you could rightly imitate. For we do not read that he first washed in the rivers of Syria and was washed by

---

[48] Matthew 9.20-22 par, with characteristic speculation on the woman's motives. Like other orthodox writers of the fourth century, Optatus assumes that any profession of ignorance by Christ is for our benefit (cf Basil, Epistles 10 and 236 etc.).

[49] Luke 8.45; Mark 5.31.

[50] See 2Kings 5.1-16. Parmenianus was clearly another of those who enjoyed rhetorical embellishment of the Scriptures.

anyone and got no profit.⁵¹ And if this were the reading, it would not redound to the praise of Elisha, who did not wash him but gave the advice, but to the glory of the Jordan, in that an early grace had come to that man in that river, in which later, through John's offices, the sins of the people would be put to death by confession to repentance.

10. Finally, what is that part of your treatise about the heavenly wedding, where, cutting off hope of future things, you have made everything rest on the present time, saying that "the person who deceived your doormen and agents" has been cast out from your society, so as to be sent abroad with injury?⁵² If that is so, there is nothing that faith may hope for, nothing to be conferred by the resurrection, nothing more to look forward to in heaven, nothing to be recognised by God, that king and head of the household, at his own feast, when he rejoices in the presence of a multitude and is grieved by the absence of some.⁵³ And he says that *many are called, but few chosen*; he will have no cause to be angry with one who has no wedding-garment, when Christ himself, the Son of God, is the bridegroom and the garment and the robe, swimming in the water which clothes many and awaits a countless number and does not fail in clothing.

But in case anyone should call it rash in me to say that the Son of God is the garment, let him read the Apostle's saying, *All you who have been baptized in Christ have put on Christ.*⁵⁴ O robe which is always one and changeless, which properly clothes all ages and types, and is neither wrinkled in infants nor stretched in youths nor changed in women! In due course that day will come for the celebration of the heavenly wedding to begin; there those who have preserved the one baptism will recline securely. For when anyone has consented to be rebaptized by you, there is no denying the resurrection of this person, since he has believed in the resurrection of the body; he will arise

---

⁵¹ Though at 2Kings 5.12 he considers the experiment. Naaman is a type of the baptized at Ambrose, *Myst.* 16.
⁵² Cf Matthew 22.12 for the ill-dressed wedding-guest. Doorkeeper was the name of a clerical order: cf John 10.3, Synesius, Epistle 3 and canon 24 of the Council of Laodicea (4th century).
⁵³ Matthew 22.1-14 is the version followed. At 22.7 the Lord of the Feast is enraged by the refusals of invited guests. The saying that many are called and few chosen appears at 22.14.
⁵⁴ Galatians 3.21, though 1Cor 15.53 is required to justify the mention of the Resurrection.

indeed, but naked. But because he has allowed his wedding garment to be stripped off by you, he will hear the voice of the head of the household say this: "Friend" - that is, I recognise you - "you had renounced the devil at one time, and had turned to me, and I had given you a wedding garment; why have you come here without the thing that I gave you in your possession?" That is to say, "Why do you not have that which I gave you?" For no-one can be angry with someone for not having a thing that has not been given. "You received the wedding garment among the rest, and you are the only one who does not have it? Why have you come naked and mournful? Who has taken these spoils from you? What dens of fraud have you approached? What robbers have you encountered?" All those who come in this guise will have no place in that feast.

11. And so that I may be concise, even though belatedly, I believe that even this will suffice, without my adducing any of these numerous proofs at all: in your absence a thousand have been baptized, so far as words go; of these a hundred have died according to their own lot.[55] Hold back your hands a little while from this abomination. It is your holiness, as you say, that will first revive those who are buried; let it, if it can, correct the dead and then turn back to the living. If you cannot revive the dead, why do you try to lay your hands on the living, unless to fulfil what God has said of you through the prophet Ezekiel, saying, *that they may kill souls who ought not to have died.*[56]

---

[55] The argument seems to be that if the Donatists cannot confer immortality on the body, they cannot give eternal life to the soul. Cf n. 30 on the "countless thousands" baptized by John, whose rite would now be inefficacious.

[56] Ezekiel 13.19.

OPTATUS:

Sixth Book against the Donatists

1. In my view, your profane acts with regard to the divine sacraments have been clearly demonstrated. Now we must expose the cruel and stupid conduct which you will be quite unable to deny. For what is so sacrilegious as to break, level or remove the altars of God where you too at one time made your offerings, where both the prayers of the people and the limbs of Christ are borne up,[1] where Almighty God is invoked, where the Holy Spirit descended at the prayer,[2] where many accepted the pledge of eternal salvation and the protection of faith and the hope of the resurrection?[3] The altars, I say, on which the Saviour forbade us to lay the gifts of brotherhood, except those that were founded on peace. *Lay your gift down, he says, before the altar, and first return, agree with your brother, so that the priest may offer on your behalf.*[4] For what is the altar but the seat of the body and blood of Christ? All these your madness has either levelled or broken or removed. This inexpiable profanity, therefore, if it issued from any cause, should have happened in one way [only]. But so far as I can see, in one place the abundance of wood demanded to be broken, whereas shortage of wood bade others to level the altars; it was partly awe, however, that persuaded others to remove them; everywhere,

---

[1] Cf Ambrose, *Sacr.* VI.1-4 for the (then common) view that the eucharist was the true flesh and blood of Christ. The Biblical warrant is found at Matthew 26.26-8 par and John 6.48-56. Some Latin writers (e.g. Tertullian, *Adversus Marcionem* IV.40) appear to regard the sacrament more figuratively. The notion that the eucharist, when a bishop presides, cements the unity of the Church can be traced back to Ignatius, *Ephesians* 20 etc., but the suggestion that it repeats Christ's sacrifice is rejected, e.g. in Origen's *De Pascha*, and was not, according to Hanson (1985), common doctrine during the first three Christian centuries.

[2] Cf Ambrose, *Sacr.* V.19ff on the Lord's Prayer. The descent of the Spirit occurs at the action called the invocation or *epiclesis*. Optatus is an early witness to the western innvoation, whereby it is the Spirit, not the Word that is asked to descend. See Dix (1945), pp. 188-9.

[3] Cf Ambrose, *Sacr.* V.5-17 on the benefits of baptism. The hope of the resurrection is confirmed at John 6.54.

[4] Matthew 5.24.

nevertheless it is a profanity when you have laid your sacrilegious and impious hands on something so great.

Why should I recall your hiring of a host of abandoned people, and the wine that you gave as wages?[5] So that this could be drunk in sacrilegious draughts by unclean mouths, a stove was made from the fragments of the altars. If in your rancorous judgment we seemed filthy, what had God, who used to be invoked there, done to you? How had you been offended by Christ, whose body and blood dwelt there on certain occasions? How had you offended yourselves, so as to break the altars where over long stretches of time before us, you made offerings which in your own view were holy? When you impiously persecute our hands in the place where Christ's body dwelt, you have also dealt a blow to your own. In this way you have imitated the Jews; they laid hands on Christ on the cross, you have beaten him on the altar. If you wanted to go after catholics there, you should have spared your own ancient offerings in that place. Now you are found to be proud in the place where long ago you made humble offerings;[6] you sin readily in the place where you used to pray for the sins of many.

By doing this you have entered readily into the number of sacrilegious priests, you have associated with the wickedness of profane folk, about whom the prophet Elijah made his complaint before the Lord. For he spoke in these words, by which you among others deserve to be accused: *Lord, he said, they have broken down your altars.*[7] When he says "your", he indicates that when any offering is made to God by anyone, the thing is God's. It should have been enough for your insanity to have mutilated the members of the church, to have divided the people of God by your seductions when they had long been in a state of unity. In all this you should at least have spared the altars. Why have you broken down people's prayers and desires with the very altars? For the prayer of the people used to ascend from those places to the ears of God. Why have you cut off the road for their petitions? And was it to

---

[5] Further atrocities of the circumcellions, for whom, as Augustine also argues (*Cresc.* III.49 etc.) the Donatists must hold themselves responsible by their own logic.
[6] On the pride of the Donatists cf Augustine, *De Unico Baptismo* 7 etc. On pride as the root of sin see Augustine, *De Natura et Gratia* I.33 etc.
[7] 1Kings 19.10. Augustine, *Cath.* 33 implies that the Donatists cited the story of Elijah's exile to justify their small numbers and isolation from the main Church

prevent the supplication from rising to God in the usual manner that you stole away the ladder, as it were,[8] with your impious hands? And yet, when you are all involved in one conspiracy, your wrongdoing in this affair has been diverse, though your error is much the same. If it was enough to remove, it was wrong to break; if it was obligatory to break, it was a sin to level; for if it was wrong, as you held, the one who broke seems to have been right to break. Now that person is a criminal who, by his levelling, preserved the greater part.

What is this new and stupid wisdom that seeks novelty in the bowels of antiquity and having, as it were, removed the skin from the body, seeks a sort of new skin in the recesses of the body? That gift, which belongs to itself and rests wholly in itself, because it is one, can be diminished, but cannot be changed, when anything has been taken away from it. You have indeed levelled what you saw, but there still remains there what you hate. Well, what if you have conspired to make the elements appear unclean which we have touched in God's name in our very ministry? Which of the faithful does not know that in the performance of the mysteries the wood itself is concealed by a linen covering?[9] In the course of [administering] the sacrament itself it was possible to touch the veil, not the wood; otherise, if the veils can be penetrated by touch, the wood is therefore penetrated too; if the wood can be penetrated, the earth too is penetrated; if you level the wood, let the earth be dug up also, make a deep hole, as you are seeking purity according to your own judgment. But take care that you do not descend to the nether regions and find there the schismatics Korah, Dathan and Abiram, who are obviously your masters.[10] Therefore it is agreed that you have both broken and levelled altars. How is it that in this matter your madness seems, as it were, to have subsequently languished? For we see that you later changed your policy, and now you no longer break or level altars, but merely remove them. If this was enough, you too indicate that those things that you formerly did should not have been done at all.

---

[8] Probably alluding to the equation of the Son of Man with Jacob's Ladder at John 1.51.
[9] For the *velamen*, called *kalumma* in Greek, cf the *Liturgy of John Chrysostom* p. 360 Brightman.
[10] The story from Numbers 16 again. See below, nn. 16-17.

2. Yet you have doubled this dreadful outrage, when you broke even the chalices which bore the blood of Christ, whose form you reduced to a mass, obtaining funds in profane markets - for which funds you did not even choose the buyers - acting sacrilegiously, in that you sold them without recklessly, avariciously in selling them [at all]. You have even allowed your own hands, which you used before us to handle the same chalices, to be burned along with them.[11] All this, however, you ordered to be sold everywhere; perhaps lewd women bought it for their own use, pagans bought it to make vessels, in which they might burn incense to their own idols. What profane wickedness, what an unheard-of outrage, to take from God in order to furnish idols, to steal from God what will serve for sacrilege!

3. But at see at this point that, forging an invidous falsehood against us, you would take refuge in the prophet Haggai, where it is written, *Those things that the polluted one has touched are polluted.*[12] When rancour comes into play, it is easy to cast reproach in anger; but in every case where a crime is alleged, manifest proof is necessary. For which of us entered the temples? Who saw sacrilegious ceremonies? People can be polluted by smoke, odours, sacrilege, sacrifices, blood; but in this case who entered the temple? Who gave incense to idols? Who was spotted by unclean odours? Who saw the blood of an unclean beast or a person being poured out? Whom can you prove to have bent his mind to any outrage? Convict just one bishop of association with any wickedness, if you can. You raise suspicions about some primate or other, who was said to have walked at that time.[13] Suspicion is not an adequate charge.

---

[11] Optatus would appear to be alluding to the traces of the Donatists' hands, unless this is an unfeeling reference to their willing martyrdoms. The breaking of a chalice was a serious breach of ecclesiastical law; cf the charges against Athanasius (298-373), bishop of Alexandria and defender of the Nicene creed, recorded in his *Apologia Contra Arianos* 63.

[12] Haggai 2.14. In this Book, as in the rest, Optatus assumes that the Jewish priesthood is continued in the Christian ministry. This is a dubious reading of the New Testament, which reserves the good sense of *hiereus* for Christ himself.

[13] "Walked" appears to mean simply "held office". Since, as Labrousse (1996) p. 169 observes, this use of *primas* for "primate" in Optatus is unique, it is not clear whether Caecilian or Mensurius is meant. Optatus' *nescio quis* implies that the facts are of no importance in comparison with the obligations of charity, a point much laboured by Augustine (cf. *Cresc.* IV.62).

When did he either blush or suffer exposure? Keep your suspicions to yourselves.

Therefore, as I said above, whatever harsh acts may have been committed in this case, we have demonstrated, when the matter has been retraced to its origins, that they belong to your leaders. On what grounds do you refer to catholics as polluted? Is it because we have followed the will and bidding of God by our love of peace, communicating with the whole world, associated with the Orientals,[14] where Christ was born according to his humanity, where he impressed his sacred footprints, where his venerable feet walked, where all those great miracles were done by the very Son of God, where so many Apostles followed him, where the sevenfold church is, from which you have cut yourselves off, not only without sorrow, but with a certain self-congratulation? Because we have been in accord with the Corinthians, Galatians and Thessalonians and maintained communion with them,[15] you call us polluted; because we do not read lessons with you in secret, you call us polluted - or deny, if you can, that you read the lessons of others. Why do you dare to read letters written to the Corinthians, when you refuse to communicate with the Corinthians? Why do you recite writings addressed to the Galatians, to the Thessalonians, when you are not in their communion? Since all this is patently so, understand that it is you who are cut off from the holy church, not we who are polluted. Where, then, is the succour that you think the prophet Haggai can give you?

The aforementioned altars and vessels, therefore, had long been both in your hands and in ours; if you denigrate our hands, why do you therewith condemn yours also? Yet you say that we read, *What the polluted one has touched is polluted*. Suppose that anyone is polluted, so that things touched by him will seeem polluted. Let it be so, if there is only touch, and no invocation of the name of God occurs, those things that the polluted one has touched may be defiled, if nothing is said of God. For if there is an invocation of the name of God, the very invocation sanctifies even what seemed to be polluted. After all, 250 thuribles were borne in the hands of sacrilegious and sinful people, but

---

[14] Cf Augustine, *Cresc.* III.38 and III.77.

[15] On the seven churches of Revelation 2-3 and the seven Pauline churches see II.6 and II.14..

when the earth was swallowing those same sinners, the thuribles remained, struck from their hands.[16] And when Aaron the holy priest was wondering what he should do about these, he heard the voice of God saying, *Aaron, take these vessels and make plates from them, and put them in the corner of the ark of God's testament, because, even if those who bore them sinned, they are none the less sacred vessels, because my name has been invoked there, says God.*[17] And certainly bearing them is more than touching. Therefore it is now clearly apparent that something can be sancitifed by the invocation of the name of God; for touch cannot have the same force as the invocation of the divine name.You also, who presume upon your holiness, say whether touch or invocation sanctifies. Certainly invocation, not touch; or if you presume upon the touch alone, touch a table, a stone, a garment; let us see if they can be holy, when nothing is said of God.

4. How stupid and vain it was in you to decide that your will, and as it were, your dignity, demand that virgins of God should do penance,[18] that those who had long since taken the tokens of a vow on their heads should subsequently change them at your bidding, that they should throw off one head-covering and adopt another. Tell us first whence you received any commands about head-coverings. For virginity is a voluntary matter, not a compulsory one. Moreover, that innkeeper the Apostle Paul,[19] to whom the people of God, lacerated with the wounds of sin, was confided, had requested and received two denarii, obviously the two testaments; these he laid down and as it were spent by teaching, and he taught how Christian spouses ought to live. When it was inquired of him what precepts he gave about virgins, he replied that about virgins nothing had been commanded.[20] He declared that he had requested two

---

[16] Numbers 16.17.

[17] Numbers 16.36, but to Eleazar the son of Aaron.

[18] Virgins were a consecrated order, who were expected to practice rigorous self-denial while they wept for the sins of others and themselves. Cf Ambrose, *De Institutione Virginitatis* 75-82. The Donatists were asking them to do penance for a virginity which had itself been a strict and vicarious penance.

[19] Paul is being compared here to the innkeeper in the Parable of the Samaritan at Luke 10.34-35. Ziwsa notes a parallel in Fulgentius, *Ad Monimum* II.13. In this reading, the Samaritan is Christ, as John 8.48 might seem to imply, and Augustine (*Quaestiones Evangeliorum* II.19) affirms.

[20] 1Cor 7.25.

denarii, that is the two testaments; his expenditures were exhausted, so to speak, but because the one who had confided the wounded person to him had promised to return, whatever he requested further as payment for the cure after the two denarii were exhausted, Paul requested not as precepts but as advice to the virgin state. It was neither an obstacle to those who wanted it, nor did it coerce or compel those who did not: he who has given his virgin does well, and he who has not does better.

These are his words of advice, and no precept is added, either as to what wool the head-covering should be made of or as to what purple it should be dyed in.[21] For virginity cannot be assisted by this little headband,[22] it is not this that allays the heat of the mind, which is inflamed from time to time in the course of age, it is not this that relieves the mind which is frequently oppressed by the burdens of desire. For if that were the case, not one but a great many would be placed on the virgin's head, so that, whenever the desires of the flesh pierced her mind, the number of head-coverings would fight against the piercing of the mind. The thing was devised as a token for the head, not as a medicine of chastity.[23] After all, such a little headband can grow old and be eaten away and perish; and yet virginity, if it remain inviolate, can be safe without a head-covering. This kind of marriage is spiritual. They had already come to the bridegroom's wedding by their will and declaration; and so that they may demonstrate their renunciation of wordly marriage and their union with the spiritual bridegroom, they had unbound their hair; they had already celebrated the heavenly wedding.[24] Why is it that you have compelled them to

---

[21] Cf Ambrose, *De Institutione Virginitatis* 109.

[22] On the *mitra* and the *castimoniales* see II.19 and notes.

[23] Alluding perhaps to Ignatius' description of the eucharist as "medicine of immortaility" at Ephesians 20.2. Tertullian, *De Virginibus Velandis* 14-16 rests his argument for veiling on the perils of incontinence; but the exhortations in Ambrose, *De Inst. Virg.* 112 imply that the veil does not suffice to make the virgin.

[24] For the bridal imagery cf Matthew's parable of the virgins as 25.1-13; Methodius, *Symposium* VI.5. For (spiritual) virginity as the condition of marriage with Christ cf Revelation 14.4 and 21.2. Optatus seems to be the sole authority for the custom of unbinding the woman's hair at a Christian wedding; but the 17th canon of Gangra (4th century, post 325) cites 1Cor 11.10 to show that a woman's hair should be worn long as a token of subjection. Labrousse (1996) p. 175 n. 1 cites a letter of Pope Siricus at *Patrologia Latina* XIII p. 1182 on the replacement of the virginal with a matrimonial veil in the ceremony.

unbind their hair again? Why, I say, have you exacted from them a second declaration? What other spiritual bridegroom is there with whom they could marry again? When did the one whom they had married die, so that they could marry again? You have renewed the nakedness of heads already covered, you have taken from these the visible tokens of their declaration, which had been devised against abduction or solicitation. In the head-covering is a token of the will, not a help to chastity; [the purpose is] to prevent a betrothed suitor from continuing to woo an object devoted to God[25] or a rapist from daring to violate her. It is therefore a token, not a sacrament.

You have thus found virgins of a kind who had already married spiritually, whom you forced into a second marriage and ordered to unbind their hair once again. Even women who marry in the flesh do not suffer this. If it should happen to any of these to change her °husband after matrimonial bereavement, this temporal ceremony is not repeated, she is not raised aloft, a popular gathering is not arranged.[26] You have therefore taken off not head decorations, but, as I said above, tokens of the better choice. You have showered unclean ashes on hair already consecrated to God, you have even ordered that salt water be poured over them.[27] And I wish that you would at least swiftly replace what you have taken; you have increased the delays, so that some waited a long time after being reduced to their previous state of dress, deprived of the tokens by which they had long defended themselves against solicitation and abduction. When these saw that the ban which had long been in place against them had now been lifted, they turned betrothal into abduction. Nor was any of them a sinner in his own eyes,

---

[25] Thecla, who in the *Acts of Paul and Thecla* renounces her betrothal to Thamyris, was widely commended in the Church.

[26] Though 1 Tim 4.11-15 expresses the wish that younger widows should marry, this is only a concession to avoid scandal, and Tertullian, *De Monogamia* argued that all Christian men and women should waive this privilege. The seventh canon of Neocaesarea (c.315) forbade presbyters (and therefore bishops) to attend the feasts of those who contracted a second marriage, and Augustine, *De Bono Viduitatis* 6, says that second marriages, though lawful, are held in less honour.

[27] A purificatory ritual, which may be based on the use of salt in Jewish sacrifice and covenant (Leviticus 2.13; Numbers 18.19) or on Matthew 5.13 par. The use of salt in the eucharist is attested at *Clementine Homilies* 14.1.

since he abducted her in the same state that she was in when he asked to receive her as his wife.

5. How much damage of this kind you have done to God, how much revenue you have made for the devil! You have impiously melted down chalices, you have cruelly broken and mindlessly levelled altars; not without insults, you have forced wretched girls to accept a second head-covering, when no reading can be recited about a first. Nor can I omit this fact, which was displeasing to God, and cannot be excused by your fellow-worshippers or defended by any person. In many cases you have thought it right to use secular tribunals and public laws to snatch away the instruments of the divine law through the executive power of officials, wishing to have by yourselves what peaceful times had posssessed in common.[28] I do not fear as a Christian to say what the pagan executive, at your petition, was unable to ignore: you have snatched away the Lord's coverings and instruments, which had long been a common possession; you have snatched away the curtains with the codices;[29] in your own proud judgment you deemed both to be polluted. If I am not mistaken, you rushed to purify all these; undoubtedly you washed the curtains; tell us what you did about the codices. In everything your oversight ought to exercise equal judgment; either wash both or leave both alone. You wash the curtain, you do not wash the codex; if you do well in one, you do ill in the other. You cannot deny that you offend in one if you act worthily in the other, and if you rejoice in appearing to be religious in one, you should weep because you are caught being sacrilegious in the other.

6. Now what about the fact that in many places you have chosen to wash walls and have required the spaces between to be sprinkled with salt water? O what a sweet creation of God's is water, above which the Holy Spirit was borne before the very nativity of the world![30] O water, which to make the world pure, didst wash the earth! O water, which Moses sweetened with wood so that you lost your natural flavour and satisfied the cravings of so many people with delicious draughts![31] After such exaltation no light degradation awaited you. Through Moses'

---

[28] Cf 1Cor 6.1ff and the remarks of Constantine at Appendix 5, p. 209 20ff Ziwsa.
[29] The veils referred to in n.9, and the copies of the Scriptures.
[30] Genesis 1.2; cf Ambrose, Myst.s 9 etc.
[31] See Exodus 15.23ff and Ambrose, Myst. 14.

presence your bitterness died, and today your sweetness is troubled by schismatics,[32] along with the host of catholics. We suffer war equally, and equally we look for the judgment of God. Tell us, brother Parmenianus, what have the place and the very walls done to you that they should suffer this? Is it that God was prayed to there? Or that the Holy Spirit was invoked there? Or that the prophets and sacred Gospels were recited there in your absence? Or that there the minds of brothers who had long been at odds came into accord? Or that the unity pleasing to God had found a home in which to dwell? Tell us what there was there that you could wash.

If we catholics have trodden our footprints into the neighbourhood and the street, why do you not clean everything? For it is equally true of our people and yours that they washed themselves with the same intention of looking after the body, and many of ours washed frequently before you. If you think that everything should be purified in our wake, wash the water also, if you can. Or if our footprints, as I said above, seem to you to be polluted, let the earth be enough; why have you chosen also to wash walls, on which human footprints cannot be placed? We cannot tread on walls, but only look at them. If you judge that what strikes the eyes must be washed, why have you left the rest unwashed? We look at the roof, we look at the sky; these cannot be washed by you. By washing the former you have pleased God, by failing to wash the others you appear to have committed an inexpiable sin. When, therefore you want to seem diligent in one place, you are found negligent in another - if, that is, your stupidity and, to give it its true name, vanity, can be called diligence. Or perhaps by doing this you have intimidated ignorant people into believing that, because the column is washed, they should wash their bodies also. If this is the secret policy in your actions, you have imposed a subtle deception on wretched folk; if you acted in such a way without a policy, you are manifestly lacking in insight. Even those whom you have seduced recognise that you acted stupidly in this, and you yourselves cannot deny it.

7. Need I also recall that other impiety which arises from your scheming, that you have formed the desire of invading churches, so that you may claim the cemeteries for yourselves alone, not allowing

---

[32] For accounts of such schisms see Augustine, *Parm.* and *Cresc.* passim. On the actions of the circumcellions see III.4.

catholic bodies to be buried?[33] To intimidate the living, you abuse the dead also, refusing them a place for funerals. If the struggle was between the living, your hatred should at least be assuaged by the other's death. He with whom you were previously at odds is now silent: why do you insult his funeral? Why do you hinder his burial? Why be at odds with the dead? You have lost the fruit of your malice, and if you do not wish the bodies to rest in unity, none the less you will not be able to separate the souls that are at one in God's keeping.

8. It is indeed impossible to recount all your proceedings from the outset, but let them none the less be held to your account, as you hold the role of masters in this error. And as it is, who could be silent about your party, those I mean whom you have been able to seduce by factious or devious talk, so as to make them yours, not only men but women too: once sheep, they have suddenly become wolves, once faithful, now perjurers, once patient, now madmen; once peaceable, now litigants; once guileless, now seducers; once reverent, now shameless; now fierce, although once meek; once innocent, now contrivers of malice. Once these men and women have fallen into your company, they grieve that others should be in the state in which they were born; they invite those who stand well to join their fall; if they knew that they were going to acquire glory, they would enjoy their good fortune silently. But now, desiring to palliate their defection to a state of loss, they invite others to fall likewise, and those who abide in the bosom of their mother the church they accuse of being slow and tardy. For they do not blush to say to these people, "Jack or Jill,[34] how long will you hold back?" That is to say: "now you should imitate my error, now you should forsake the truth. Imitate my fall, imitate my vile defection. How long will you be called faithful? Now forsake your faith, now learn penitence."

You are birdcatchers, and these men and women are the birds.[35] But there is not only one kind of birdcatcher: some, practising a guileless art, look for trees with deep-set roots, spread out in the form of a wood,

---

[33] Similar atrocities are recounted by Augustine, *Cresc.* III.47, IV.31 etc.
[34] Caius Serus and Caia Sera, as at III.11.
[35] This prodigious simile, reminiscent of those employed in the contemporary *Panarion* of Epiphanius (376), may be inspired by the image of the Church as Christ's one dove (Song of Songs 6.8 etc.).

where birds in their guileless flight sit on natural branches. There are no ruses or artificial plots to be related in this case; their one art is merely their expertise in catching. You, I say, resemble that birdcatcher who after the night departs and before the daybreak does not approach natural trees in the way of the others, but carrying a tree himself, whittles down the future wood to a dry stalk, using complex art to make a tree unsupported by any roots. Into this he inserts adulterous branches, and, having by now lost its own branches through the pruning, it receives extraneous leaves. He carries some birds enclosed in the hollow, others stuffed to make images of living ones. He places these birds, already dead, on the deceptive branches as though they were alive. Some are hidden in the hollow, others are seen as if living on the branches. This double ruse is combined with skill, and so that the guileless living birds may be deceived, the birds which are in fact dead seem to extend their necks and make noises, and those who are hidden in their prison sing, as though through another throat. One trick takes effect through the image of the one and the voice of the other: the captives catch the free and the dead kill the living. Such are they whom you have wounded either by rebaptism or by penance: so that these men and women will not seem to have perished alone, they strive with great zeal and labour that other men or women should perish with them.

OPTATUS:

Seventh Book against the Donatists

1. After having revealed the collaborators and shown which is the holy church, after having refuted the calumnies which you were heaping on us, and after [the exposure of] your sins, which deserved the reproach of God, in due order your repetition of the sacraments and your arrogant and intimidatory acts have been revealed.[1] Our answers and assertions should now have come to an end; but since I see that, after the axes of truth have cut down the wood of malignity,[2] the provocations offered by you or your party continue to burgeon - your argument, as I hear, being that we ought not to have sought unity of communion when you were agreed to be children of collaborators - I shall briefly reply to this. It is quite true that the catholic church was self-sufficient, containing countless peoples in all the provinces, and was self-sufficient in Africa too, albeit with few members;[3] but God was not pleased by your separation, since the members of the one body had been rent apart, and against God's will you brothers strayed from your brothers.

Although an internal judgment had taken effect among your parents, so that those who should have been rejected because of their crimes as collaborators withdrew of their own accord, no judgment was pronounced, but the sentence took effect. Expulsion was due to them after the offence of collaboration, which they had confessed among themselves in the Numidian council;[4] but to avoid ill-feeling the severity of judgment was remitted, when your ancestors dealt with their guilt of

---

[1] On the status of the seventh book see now the introductions to the relevant portion of Labrousse (1996) and to this volume. There is no reason to deny that it is by Optatus, though it may not have formed part of the first edition.

[2] Cf Luke 3.9 for the axe, and Tertullian, *Adversus Valentinianos* 39 for the use of a wood as a metaphor for heresy.

[3] If the meaning is that the catholics are a small community in comparison with the Donatists, that does not accord with Augustine's claim, *Brev.* I, that the catholic bishops mustered for a council in 411 outnumbered the full resources of their opponents. The small numbers of the Donatists are a constant theme of the latter: see *Cresc.* IV.63 etc. His *Breviculus* indicates the existence of about 300 catholic bishoprics in Africa - which is, of course, no proof of anything.

[4] Described by Augustine, *Cresc.* III.30; see Book I, n.45.

their own accord by forming a plan to secede as if in pride, concealing their crime when they ought to have been sorry and ashamed. For if at that happy time of peace they ought to have acted for unity, so too they themselves ought not to have been rejected from the church, since their choice had been excused by constraint. For none of them had spontaneously collaborated, nor will it be possible to equate this sin with other misdeeds.[5] For whatever God did not wish to happen, he forbade with his own mouth, as he said, You shall not kill, you shall not commit adultery etc.[6] He could also have forbidden the offence that your parents committed; but since the offence of the mind is one thing and the effect of the outcome another, whatever can proceed from a person's will deserved to be forbidden; whatever is committed by constraint cannot be indicted with great force. Voluntary acts receive punishment, necessary ones pardon.[7] A homicide, when no-one forces the atrocity, is able to do the deed and able not to; the fornicator, when no-one else compels him, can commit adultery or not commit it; and so with other things of this kind where we have freedom of decision. Thus when forbidden things are done, they are destined for judgment; when things not banned take place through some necessity, perhaps the one who declined to forbid them would readily deign to forgive them.

Moreover, while this misdeed could have been alleged against your parents as an almost capital offence, if they had been exposed at that time or summoned to judgment, they could have called more than one example to their aid from the earliest times, when the tables of the Law are said to have been shattered or books handed over, and either cut or

---

[5] Optatus' lenient judgment of *traditores* is upheld by the canons of Ancyra (314), which allow full restoration to the church after five years of prostration and "communication in prayer" even for those who sacrificed under compulsion, whereas adultery requires seven years of penance (canon 20), fornication or abortion ten (canon 21), voluntary homicides cannot be readmitted to full communion until death (canon 22) and even involuntary homicides must wait five (canon 23).

[6] Exodus 20.11-13.

[7] True in the case of the canons of Ancyra on homicide (n.5), but the pardon for the lighter sin does not exempt from penance. In some codes (e.g. Basil's *Canonical Letter to Amphilochius*, III.56-7) both voluntary and involuntary homicide can be forgiven after different terms of penance. The case under discussion here is the handing over of Scriptures, which can hardly be "involuntary" in our sense; but Optatus clearly means "performed under constraint".

burnt,[8] and no-one was condemned. If, as I said above, your parents had been exposed at that time, or summoned to judgment, they would undoubtedly have said that they did no more than the legislator Moses. Although will and constraint do not resemble each other but are mutually repugnant, your parents' cause and that of Moses would have been identical in that both have the same reference to the Law. Your parents would be able to say that they had done by constraint what Moses had formerly done wilfully. When he was indignant with the people, he did not reflect that God had written with his own finger[9] - and what has been written in heaven is more than what has been written on earth, and the writing of God's finger is not the same as that of a pen that human hands have fashioned. Moses was carrying what he had received through the cloud,[10] and your parents handed over what they had composed for a given fee. Your parents would rightly defend themselves, urging that it was not a capital crime if each of them, in the terror of great fear, did what Moses had done in anger. And we do not read that God was indignant with Moses or that he avenged the shattered tablets,[11] which he had indited with his own hand, nor was he either called a sinner or punished. The Law came forth from God in the same way as water flows from a fountain, or like fruits which are plucked from the tree while the root is preserved.[12] That which is destroyed does not perish, if its origin is preserved.

Moreover Moses, after the tablets of the Law had been scattered and broken, was not deemed worthy of condemnation, and subsequently, when recalled, ascended Mount Sinai, and was deemed worthy to speak with God again, and received a second new-fashioned Law, as is revealed by the title of the book which in the Greek vocabulary is

---

[8] Described below: Exodus 32, Jeremiah 36, 1Maccabees 1.59ff.
[9] The phrase is found at Exodus 8.15 and Deuteronomy 9.10.
[10] Exodus 19.18-25.
[11] Exodus 32.16-19.
[12] Recalling Cyprian's metaphors for the unity of the Church (*De Unitate Ecclesiae* 5), as well as those of Tertullian for the procession of the Spirit (*Adversus Praxean* 8 etc.). Biblical authority can perhaps be found at Matthew 13.23 (the Word bears fruit when sown) and John 4.13.

written as Deuteronomos.[13] See, the content of the Law did not perish,
as its origin had been preserved. But in case anyone should think that
Moses had an entitlement, like a certain bond with God on account of
their intercourse and that therefore God was not angry; since, then, if
this were so, friendship should always have claimed its entitlement and
reward, why was vengeance subsequently taken on him for an offence?
Was it not to show that what he had committed in anger was trivial?
The Law remained sound in God, even after it had been shattered by a
human being with tablets of stone; when the worship which a human
being owed was not displayed, Moses deserved that punishment of dying
in mid-journey and not entering the land of promise;[14] hence it is
apparent that we cannot reckon that sin a great one which in the present
instance could be committed with impunity.

If your parents had said this, who would have been able to deny them
communion? What if they had advanced that subsequent instance, in
which we read that when the new-fashioned law was kept in the ark,
and the people of Israel was being vanquished in war, the law was
carried against the enemy by the vote of the people, and the very elders
and the other children of Israel were unable to defend it; it was handed
over to the enemy, while lesser things were carried back.[15] When the
law was handed over, those who had said it should be carried forth fled
in fear, and we do not read that they later suffered anything in revenge.
If this argument had been offered by your parents, who would have
been able to reject them from his communion?

What if your leaders had also not kept silent about the instance in
which we read that Baruch handed over to Judin the scribe the book
which he had taken down from the mouth of the prophet Jeremiah, that
the chief men of the king ordered that both Baruch, who had taken it

---

[13] Exodus 34.28; cf Jerome, *Liber de Situ et Nominibus* 183. In fact the Greek word
Deuteronomos is a mistranslation of the Hebrew, meaning "copy"; but the notion of two
covenants at Sinai is used for a different purpose in the second-century *Epistle of
Barnabas* 14, where the Christians are said to have received the first (broken) covenant
which the Jews never possessed. See V.1 on the distinction between the moral and the
ceremonial law.

[14] Numbers 20.12, however, says that Moses had angered God by failing to honour him
before the people, and 20.24 alludes to his lack of steadfastness when the people
demanded water.

[15] 1Kings 4.3-11.

down, and Jeremiah, through whom God had spoken, should flee and hide.[16] Jeremiah had been dictating, Baruch handed it over, both had fled; the book was carried to King Jehoiachin, and since this king had before him a blazing hearth because of the coldness of the weather, and had not listened gladly to the book recited by the scribe Judin, he cut it into small pieces from the end and put it on the fire. And God was not angry either with Jeremiah, who had fled, nor with Baruch, who, fleeing with him, had handed it over; if God had been angry with them, he would have spoken to some other prophet; he spoke not to another, but to Jeremiah himself. For thus we read: *And the word of God came to Jeremiah, after the king had burnt the title and the speeches of the book which Baruch wrote from the mouth of Jeremiah. God said to Jeremiah: "Take yourself another scroll, and write all your speeches, which were written at that time in the book that Jehoiachin the king of Judah burnt"*.[17] See then, God was not angry, neither did that which burnt perish, nor was Baruch punished, nor was Jeremiah despised by God; whence it appears that in this matter the guilt was never grave when no vengeance could follow it.If your parents had alleged this, who would have been able to exclude them from communion?

Indeed, when God saw that Moses had shattered the tablets and that the ark had been left to the enemy, and that the book of the Law, after being handed over by Baruch, had been cut up and burnt, he displayed his providence and promised that he would now write the law not on tablets nor in books, but in the very inner man, that is in the mind and heart of every single believer,[18] as he had written it in the heart of Noah, Abraham, Isaac and Jacob and the other patriarchs, who are well-known to have lived lawfully without the Law.[19] This the blessed

---

[16] Jeremiah 36.11-26.
[17] Jeremiah 37.28.
[18] For the inner man see 2Cor 4.16 etc. In Augustine's anti-Pelagian treatises the law of the inner man is that of love or *caritas* (*De Spiritu et Littera, passim*), which in the anti-Donatist writings is the cement of the church. The Donatists have failed to cultivate the inner man, which would enable them to make light of manifest vices in their neighbours.
[19] Noah is said to be righteous at Genesis 6.9; but, as Optatus notes below, even he cannot be said to have merited his salvation, and, even if Abraham was justified by his own faith (Gen 15.6), nothing but God's unlimited mercy could have justified Jacob. Optatus must be taken to mean that the patriarchs believed in Christ (John 8.56 etc.) or that they followed the law of charity.

apostle Paul proves, saying: *written not by ink, but by the spirit of the living God, not on tablets of stone but on tablets of fleshly hearts.*[20]

After the Law, before Christian times, had been shattered by Moses and left to the enemy by the children of Israel, and cut up and burnt when Baruch offered it to King Jehoiachin, God through his prophet showed where he was later going to write the law better, saying: *Since this is my testament, which I shall dispense to the house of Israel and the house of Judah, and after those days, says the Lord, giving my laws I shall write them in their heart and in their minds.*[21] He made this promise long since and recently fulfilled it in Christian times. Therefore the scroll is in the second place, the writing-material is in second place. If the Law has been written by God in a place from which it cannot be handed over, so that your parents, who already believed in the Trinity, though handing over books, did not hand over their hearts and minds, in which God wrote his Law, just as he had promised to write it, where, brother Parmenianus, is that statement of yours that the Law was completely burnt up by collaborators? See, it has not been completely burnt up or entirely removed, when it remains in the hearts of believers and thousands of books are recited everywhere; whence it is apparent that, albeit in ignorance, you have chosen to make a vain accusation against your parents.

If, therefore, your parents could have met the time of unity with so many instances reasonably offered, and could not themselves have been rejected from communion, how much [more true this is of] you, who are well-known to be not collaborators, but children of collaborators, when fathers and sons are distinguished both by person and by name, and if there is no common guilt between the persons, there cannot be a single sentence? Though even if they had entered into union and had come of their own accord to the catholic church - not like you, who, as is well-known, have been led not without God's will to return from your wanderings and are none the less still wandering - if, as I said, they had come of their own accord to the catholic church, our ancestors would perhaps have hesitated to receive such people because they had been collaborators; but we should be glad that few if any of such people have lasted up to our own time. Today, then, it is a new situation, as we

---

[20] 2Cor3.3., citing Jeremiah 31.33.
[21] Jeremiah 31.33; cf Hebrews 10.16.

have to do with you, not with them. Although it may seem that the hereditary blot had been passed on from them to you, you cannot even so be criminals under this charge along with your ancestors according to God's judgment. He spoke through the prophet Ezekiel, saying, *The father's soul is mine and the son's soul is mine; the soul that sins shall be punished alone.*[22]

This was already proved in an ancient period, at the very birth of the world, when the father's offence did not accrue to Seth, the son of Adam.[23] But in case anyone should should say that in another place it is written, in God's words, *I shall requite the parents' evils up to the fourth generation,*[24] both these voices undoubtedly are his, but they do not both address the same people. The first is given through Moses to a particular race of humans, the second through Ezekiel to another race of humans. As God knew that the Jews under Pontius Pilate would make a declaration, saying, *His blood be upon our heads and the heads of our children,*[25] God in his foreknowledge saw that what they would say fell short of the magnitude of their guilt, and so that the offence might be expiated with condign penalties, threatened the Jews themselves with the statement that he would requite the parents' evils up to the fourth generation. Therefore this voice is addressed to the Jews in particular, but the other to Christians; by this he deigned to promise that if the parents sinned in anything he would not avenge it upon the sons, nor on the parents, if there chanced to be some wrongdoing by the sons.

When in Moses' time the Law was repeated without any penalty and the ark of the testament was returned by the enemy of their own accord and another scroll was written, at God's behest, by Jeremiah: why is it thought that among your ancestors alone that sin was capital, for which no-one, in so many instances, was condemned? For if the purpose of giving the Law was that humans might be taught, not that the Law itself

---

[22] Ezekiel 18.4, correcting the' earlier misuse of Ezekiel 18.2.
[23] This may contradict the Augustinian notion of original sin, which maintains that both the *vitium* and the *reatus* of Adam descend to all his offspring. The claim that we all inherit guilt from Adam was regarded by Augustine as an ecclesiastical commonplace, at least in Africa, but he receives no report from his countryman here. See Book II n. 74
[24] Exodus 20.5.
[25] Matthew 27.25.

should be worshipped as if in God's place, the host of believers has suffered no loss after what your ancestors did; every one of them in fear gave up his own codices. For the Law, which was necessary, is flourishing among teachers of the people and worshippers of God. The libraries are full of books; there is nothing lacking to the church; the divine call sounds everywhere through each locality; the mouths of readers are not silent; the hands of all are full of codices; nothing is lacking to those people who desire to be taught, albeit the Law would seem to have been written no more for the sake of teaching than on account of the future judgment, so that the sinner might know what he could suffer if he has lived unjustly.

It is indeed written and read that *The Law was not given to the just, because every single just person is a law to himself.*[26] And in another place the same blessed apostle Paul says that the law does not make people just, but itself loves justice.[27] In all efficient causes the effects are always sought; the Law, which works the effect, becomes idle if what it effects is brought about through a short way. It was not, after all, said to Abraham, "Believe"; rather, he believed on his own initiative, whereby the effect of the Law was fulfilled without the Law. We do not read, "Abraham heard the Law and believed"; but we read, *Abraham believed God and it was reckoned to him as righteousness.*[28] And in the earliest times Noah the patriarch did nothing to make himself righteous, and was elected as the righteous one who would build an ark and voyage successfully in the flood. It is a long task to go through the individuals who without the Law were found righteous. If your parents had said this in their own time, who would have rejected them from his own communion?

What if they had said that one should not pass over in silence the Apostle's words about those outside the Law: *the nations, who do not know the Law, do those things which are in the Law, for they have a*

---

[26] 1Tim 1.9, combined with Romans 2.14.

[27] The place will never be found in the letters of Paul ; but Ziwsa suggests Romans 3.20 and Galatians 2.16. If the point is that the Law condemns us by asking what we cannot do, it is sound theology. Cf Romans 7.14 etc.

[28] Genesis 15.6; cf Romans 4.3.

Law written in their own hearts.[29] For many are proved to have sinned in the Law and many to have lived well without the Law. The Law and humanity are two things, but cannot be equal; for humans are not made for the sake of the Law, but the Law for the sake of humans.[30] Nowhere do I see damage done to God, when the origin of the Law remains with him, and after the scripture was allegedly handed over by your parents, nothing is lacking, all the members of the Law are sound, they are preserved, they are recited; there is no less of the Law for those who desire to teach and be taught. Or was this more necessary, that a human being should be killed in order that no scripture should be handed over? Why, when human beings have escaped death without the loss of any scripture?

The Law and God are not one. If it was a duty to die for God, who is able both to raise the dead and to award the prize,[31] a book not handed over cannot do either one of these two things. Constraint therefore deprives itself of power. We see negligence no less frequently producing the result that constraint produces. For if books or writing materials in which the lawful scripture is contained, should be preserved entirely intact, why are some not condemned for negligence?[32] Handing them over is not far from storing or handling them ill. One person stores the book in his home, and this home is incinerated by fire; let the one who stored it negligently be condemned, if we are to condemn the one who when a book was demanded gave gave it up in terror. Let us also condemn those who stored writing materials or books in such a way that the little animals of the house, that is mice, gnawed them so much as to make it impossible to read them. Let us also condemn the one who stored it in his house in such a way that through excess of rain the roofs let fall enough drops to obliterate everything with damp and make it impossible to read it. Let us also condemn those who when carrying books of the Law rashly trusted themselves to the greedy waves of

---

[29] Romans 2.14. One lesson which a catholic might draw from this passage is that the church of the inner man is diffused throughout the nations, and that Donatists, like Jews, deny themselves the mercy of God. Cf Origen, *CommRom* II.9ff.

[30] Combining Galatians 3.23 (pedagogic office of the Law) with Mark 2.27 (the Sabbath made for man).

[31] Cf 1Cor 9.24; Romans 8.11 etc.

[32] Adopting Casaubon's conjecture *quare* from Ziwsa's *apparatus*, in preference to the *quasi* of his text.

rivers, and in their desire to free themselves let the scriptures fall from their hands amid the waves.

Therefore if scripture is one, and the one who failed to preserve this is a criminal: one has handed it over to the waves, another has left it to gnawing animals, another has negligently left it to be corrupted by water-drops, another in his human fear of death has handed it over to a human being: if it is one offence that all have committed, why do we choose to condemn the one, when the guilt of collaboration is smaller than that of negligence? The one who stored it in front of mice or left it under dropping water was wilfully negligent, and the one who lost it in the river sinned by rashness; the one who handed anything over through fear of death gave it up as a human to a human; it was whole in the giver's possession, whole in that of the recipient. If the one who received it handed it over to the flames, the sin is in the one who burned it rather than in the one who handed it over. If your ancestors had said this, when would we have been able to reject them from our communion?

If they had also chosen to recall the times of King Antiochus, in which all the Jews were forced to consign their books to the fire,[33] and thus the whole scripture was so consigned, so that not a single jot in any book remained? None of the Jews was condemned at that time, and neither God nor any angel pronounced any sentence against any Jew,[34] because the sin was in the one who used commands and threats, not in the people who handed them over with trembling and sorrow. In order that this Antiochus would not seem to have done any harm to the ancient people, God at once provided that through the human Ezra, who held the post of reader at that time, the whole Law, as it had been before, should be dictated to the last jot.[35] Thus the tyrant Antiochus was unable to reap the fruit of his malignity, when apart from seven brothers and one old man who all refused to eat pig's flesh,[36] he killed

---

[33] IMacc 1.59. On the Maccabees as examples to the Christian martyrs see Frend (1965).
[34] The possibility of an angel is introduced because such beings are the agents of God's communication in the Old Testament (Exodus 3.2 etc.), and Galatians 3.19 states that the Law was given by angels through the hand of a mediator.
[35] Labrousse (1996) p. 214 n.2 suggests a conflation of Ezra 7, Nehemiah 8 and 2Maccabees 8.23. Optatus may be thinking of the tradition recorded in IV Ezra 14.37-48 that the scribe recovered 24 books from heaven. See Charles (1913),pp. 623-4.
[36] 2Maccabees 7.

no Jew and it was impossible that the Law should perish. So also in their own time your parents themselves were not killed, and the books of the Law of the Lord are recited everywhere in their entirety.[37] If your parents, as I said above, had said this, who would not have received them withour misgiving into his communion, where, as has been said, the sin was one of constraint, not of will? In the times of unity your leaders, who are proved to have acted thus, had already gone out from among the living, leaving to you a sort of hereditary blot, which God in his providence washed away from you in the first instance when, as I said above, he distinguished between parents and children. Since therefore it is a sin to hand over, let your parents consider what they are to say at God's tribunal; the sin, however, cannot be yours, as you are of another time.

2. Hence it is that we have wished to receive you into our communion, because at that time it was not you but your leaders who sinned. For a sinner of the same kind as your ancestors, if he should come to the church and show the nature of his constraining circumstances, should first be received, then cherished in the pious bosom of the mother church. Nor should one judge another, as though entirely holy, beacause it is written in the Gospel, in Christ's words, *Do not judge, lest judgment be passed on you*[38] - especially when no-one entirely holy can be found. For if there are some who could be without sin, they lie in the Lord's Prayer, if without cause they beg indulgence, saying to God the Father, *Remit our sins, as we also remit those of our debtors*,[39] while the Apostle John uncovers all consciences and surrenders his own with these words: *If we say, he says, that we have not sin, we deceive ourselves*

---

[37] Different lists of the "entire" Old Testament were compiled by Christian authors of the fourth century. Josephus had said (*Contra Apionem* 1.8) that books written since the Persian period were of less authority, and limits the canon to twenty-two. Cyril of Jerusalem, *Catechetical Homily* IV.36 reconciles this with our present list, except that he includes Baruch and the Letter of Jeremiah; Athanasius, *Festal Letter* 39.4 appears to omit Esther. But Optatus, who cites Tobit, Wisdom and 2 Maccabees, seems to accept the whole Septuagintal corpus, which, even after Jerome's translation from the Hebrew, was endorsed by African councils of 393, 397 and 419. See Munier (1972/3).

[38] Matthew 7.1; Luke 6.37.

[39] Matthew 6.12; Luke 11.4. Cf Augustine, *Cresc.* II.35 etc.

and truth is not in us.[40] We have explained the reason for this statement
more plainly in the fourth book.

But suppose that some are also totally perfect in holiness: it is not
granted that they should be without brothers, against whose rejection the
precepts of the Gospel speak loudly when describing a field, which is
the whole world where the church is, and Christ the sower, who gives
precepts of salvation.[41] On the other side is the evil person, that is the
devil, who sows unseasonable sins, not in light but under darkness; and
in one field diverse seeds spring up, just as in the church the host of
souls is not homogeneous. The field accepts good and bad seeds, there
is a diversity of seeds; but the creator of all souls is one, the lord of the
field is one; where the weeds are born, there are two authors of the
seed, but the field has one lord, the Lord God himself. His is the earth,
his are the good seeds, his too is the rain.[42] And so we have agreed to
lead you back and receive you in unity, because it is not granted to us
either to separate or to reject those, though they be sinners, who were
born with us in the same field, that is were fed by the same baptism -
just as it was not granted to the Apostles to separate the wheat from the
weeds,[43] as separation cannot take place without annihilation, the danger
being that while one uproots what is not needed, one tramples on what
is needed.

Likewise Christ commanded that throughout the whole world, in
which there is one church, both his seeds and the foreign ones should
grow. After this common growth will come the day of judgment, which
is the harvest of souls; sitting as judge will be the Son of God, who
knows what is his and what is foreign. It will be for him to choose what

---

[40] 1John 1.8. Cf Augustine, *Petil.*. II.241 etc.

[41] Matthew 13.24-29 (perhaps using 13.19 to prove that the seed is the word). This is
Augustine's favourite parable, and he defends its application to the Church, against the
objections of the Donatists, at *Brev.*. III.10. The Donatists cited Jeremiah 23.28,
maintained that the field was the world rather than the Church, and distinguished between
conscious and unconscious toleration of the sinner. See further n. 76 below.

[42] Cf Matthew 5.45 (God rains on just and unjust alike).

[43] Optatus boldly uses the story of Peter's denial, whereas Augustine is content to note that
the Apostles bore with Judas (*Cresc.* II.24 etc.) and that Jesus forbade the disciples to
prevent a stranger from using his name in exorcism (*De Unico Baptismo* 12). Cf *Brev.*
III.11. The strength of Optatus' example is that the disciples knowingly associated with
Peter after his denial.

he stores in the barn and what he hands over to the fire, which ones he destines to endless torments and on which ones he bestows the promised rewards. Let us all ackowledge that we are human; let no-one arrogate to himself the power of the divine judge. For if any bishop claims everything for himself, what is Christ to do in the judgment? Let it be enough for a human if he is not guilty of a sin of his own, rather than that he should desire to be the judge of another. We declare, in short, not only that we do not reject you, but would also not have excluded your parents from the boon of peace, had it been present at that time and unity had existed. For it is wrong that we should do as bishops what the Apostles did not do,[44] not being permitted either to separate the seeds or to uproot the weeds from the wheat.

3. But if the catholic church should have hesitated to receive you, should you not have followed the practice of unity? But you declined to advance the examples which we read in the gospel, such as the lesson about the most blessed Peter himself, from which we recite the description of the practice for maintaining or creating unity. Certainly it is bad to do anything against a prohibition; but it is worse not to have unity when you can, since we see that Christ preferred this unity to his own vindication, wishing rather that his disciples should be at one than that they should avenge the offence to him.As he did not want to be denied, he promised that he would deny before the Father the one who denied him in human company[45] - and yet he did not promise to punish the one who had handed over any scripture. It is therefore more serious to deny the one who spoke than to have handed over the words that he spoke. And, whereas this is written thus, none the less for the good of unity, the blessed Peter, for whom it was enough, after his denial, that he might obtain forgiveness, had the reward of being preferred to all the apostles, and was the only one to receive the keys of heaven and vouchsafing them to others.[46]

---

[44] The only indication in the text that the author was a Bishop.

[45] Matthew 10.33; Luke 12.9.

[46] Matthew 16.19, with an additional clause implying the apostolic succession of bishops. Augustine's anti-Donatist writings do not quote this verse, and when citing Matthew 16.18 he assumes that the united faith of the Church is the rock upon which it is founded (*Cath.* 60-61).

We are given to understand that sins should be buried for the good
of unity by the fact that the most blessed apostle Paul says that charity
can cover a multitude of sins: *bear one another's burdens*, he says; and
in another place, *Charity is long-suffering, charity is benign, charity
invites no envy, charity is not puffed up, it does not seek its own.*[47]
And he spoke well. For he had seen all these things in the other
apostles, who for the good of unity charitably refused to withdraw from
communion with Peter, the one, that is, who had denied Christ. But if
the love of innocence had been greater than the utility of peace and
unity, they would have said that they ought not to communicate with
Peter, who had denied his master, our Lord the son of God. As I said
above they could have avoided communion with the most blessed Peter;
they could have recited against him the words of Christ, who had
promised that he would deny before his Father one who had denied him
in human company. To this practice we should pay close attention; and
if I recall a few details of it, may the same holy and blessed Peter show
me pardon if I seem to recall what is well-known to have happened and
is read.

I hesitate to say that such great holiness sinned, yet he himself proves
that it happened by grieving bitterly and weeping abundantly; he would
have neither grieved nor wept if there had been no offence in the
meantime. Certainly the chief of the apostles could have controlled
himself in such a way as to prevent any occurrence that he would grieve
for; but in this single case of his many faults are visible, so that it may
be shown that for the good of unity everything should be reserved for
God. And I do not know whether in another person this kind of sin
could have been so grave as it manifeslt was in the blessed Peter. For
anyone who happens to have denied the Son of God in some persecution
will be seen, in comparison with the blessed Peter to have done a lesser
wrong, if he has denied the one whom he has not seen, denied the one
whom he has not known, denied the one to whom he has promised
nothing, denied him only once.

For in the blessed Peter this kind of sin is aggravated: first, because
when Christ was asking all of them who people said he was, one said
Elijah, another said a prophet; then we read that Christ said, *Who do*

[47] Galatians 6.2; 1Cor 13.4-5, with small omission.

you say that I am?, and Peter said to him, *You are the Christ the Son of the living God.*[48] For this acknowledgment he deserved praise from him, because he had said this at the instance of God the Father. See, when the others did not recognise the Son of God, Peter alone recognised him. Then on the day of the Passion, when Christ said, *See, I am taken and you will all flee,*[49] while the others were silent he alone promised that he would not go away. In his foreknowledge the Son of God said, *Peter, before the cock crows, you will deny me three times.*[50] Something was added to the gravity of the sin, namely the promise which he was not going to fulfil. After Christ was led to the house of Caiaphas, to fill up the measure of his wrongdoing, no-one else out of so many was interrogated except the blessed Peter. He denied him on the first interrogation, he denied him again on interrogation, and on the third he said that he did not know Christ at all. And the cock crowed, not so that it might mark the time by its crowing, but so that the blessed Peter might recognise his sin. Then indeed he grieved bitterly and wept abundantly.[51]

See then, as was said above, he alone recognised him when the others did not recognise him, he alone promised when the others did not promise, he alone denied him three times when the others did not deny him once; and yet for the good of unity he was not rewarded by separation from the apostles. From this we understand that all things are ordered by the foreknowledge of the Saviour, so that this same man might receive the keys. The path of malice was stopped, so that the Apostles would not form the notion of judging his laxity and condemn him severely for his denial of Christ. So many innocent ones stood by and the sinner received the keys, so that a practice of unity might be established. It was provided that the sinner should open to the innocent, so that the innocent would not turn the keys against the sinners and the unity which is needed could not come into being. If you had recalled this with a desire for unity, when would the church have hesitated to

---

[48] Matthew 16.15-16, the praise following at 16.17.
[49] Cf. Matthew 26.31 ("all shall be ashamed") and 45 ("the Son of Man is betrayed"). Two misquoted phrases misleadingly combined.
[50] Matthew 26.33-4.
[51] Matthew 26.69-75 par.

receive you in its pious bosom, when it is patent that you are not collaborators, but children of collaborators?

4. For some of you, wishing to prove us contemptible in the eyes of their own people, also mingle with their treatise the statement of the prophet Solomon: *Dying flies destroy the odour of the oil;*[52] and they call us dying flies and designate the oil as that ointment which is seasoned in the name of Christ, since after it is seasoned it is designated chrism.[53] Before it is seasoned it is still oil of a simple nature; it becomes sweet when it is seasoned in the name of Christ. Therefore there are three things which are designated by the prophet Solomon: the oil, the sweetness and the dying flies which destroy the sweetness. These three things have their place in due order: in the first place is the oil, in the second sweetness from refinement, in the third the dying flies which destroy the sweetness. Let any such writer of treatises among you show by what method he calls us the dying flies. If you think that the refinement which gives sweetness to the oil belongs to you, the oil and sweetness belongs to you. How can we destroy your oil, so that you would rightly call us dying flies? What is yours belongs to you. And if anyone passes from you to us, he is preserved by us in the state in which you let him go. On what grounds do you say that we are the dying flies who destroy the sweetness of the oil, when in your wake we do nothing of the kind?

If, on the other hand, you say that the sweetness of the oil can be corrupted by us, then either we have some power and we give sweetness to the oil, or if, as you would have it, we have no power, the oil remains such as it was in origin. On what grounds do you say that we are the dying flies who corrupt the sweetness of the oil? Therefore the oil before we refine it is such as it was in origin; once refined, it can receive sweetness from the name of Christ. How can we by one act refine and corrupt it? The remaining possibility is that, if the oil is sweet in itself, human action is idle, if it undergoes human refinement in the name of Christ. The same agent cannot perform two mutually

---

[52] Ecclesiastes 10.1. The Donatist application of the verse to themselves may have been assisted by 2Cor 2.15.

[53] Christ means the "anointed", i.e. for God's favour and sevice. Psalm 104.15, already quoted at II.25 refers to "christs", though Optatus translates *unctos*. For the wordplay, cf 2Cor 1.21 and Theophilus, *Ad Autolycum* I.12.

repugnant and contrary things at once. If we refine in your absence, we do not corrupt. If we corrupt, who refined before us what we could corrupt? Therefore, lest the prophet's utterance should be idle, if so it is [to be interpreted], understand that you are the dying flies. For you have destroyed, not what is original but what has been refined; for we read that it is sweetness, not the nature, that can be corrupted. For oil is simple and its own name is the single one that belongs to it; when refined it is now called chrism, and contains the sweetness which soothes the skin of conscience by expelling the pain of sins, and and produces a new ease of mind which prepares a seat for the Holy Spirit,[54] so that, bitterness having been ousted, he may gladly deign to dwell there by invitation. If we destroyed the oil that you refined, you would be able rightly to call us dying flies. But since we preserve what you have anointed in the state in which we accepted it, we cannot be the dying flies.

But since, driven by the storms of ill-feeling, you fall as if into oil, you destroy by rebaptism the sweetness of that oil which has been refined in the name of Christ for the seasoning of character and the kindling of the mind's light into true and saving knowledge. You have destroyed the thing which contained the oil and sweetness. How could we corrupt the sweetness, which no-one refined before us? You have seduced people, you have rebaptized them, you have anointed them again. Alas! You have destroyed that which had been refined in the name of Christ, not without dying yourselves, in the manner of flies which perish as they destroy. Because sin which is unforgiven is death. It is written that *He who has sinned against the Holy Spirit will not be forgiven either in this age or in the next.*[55] Therefore, when you both falsely call us flies and hasten to undo all that we have done, and say

---

[54] Since Paul speaks of the anointed Christian as receiving a seal and the pledge of the Spirit (2Cor 1.22),. chrismation, or anointing with oil, became an indispensable rite before and after baptism, first for exorcism, then for thanksgiving and confirmation. See Hippolytus, *Apostolic Tradition* pp. 34-39 Dix and Chadwick.

[55] Matthew 12.32. Cf the use of this phrase by the Donatists in Augustine, *Cresc.* IV.10. Caecilian was obviously considered by them an apostate, a sin which was pronounced unforgivable by the first canon of Eliberis (?305) even after Cyprian's defence of the readmission of the lapsed in his *De Lapsis*. Optatus, however, remains true to his argument that schism is the worst sin for a Christian; as Augustine was frequently to argue, a schismatic sins against the love of God.

that we are contemptible and despicable, claiming holiness for yourselves alone, you advance your innocence as a pledge that you can forgive the sins of others.[56] You see therefore that it was not, as you urge, about us, but about you, that the most blessed apostle Paul said, *There will be people who love themselves, glorying in themselves, proud, blasphemers, disobedient to parents, ungrateful, vicious, not preserving peace, without affection, slanderers, cruel, without kindness, etc.*[57]

5. For by what sort of arbitrary decision have you chosen to apply to yourselves the character of Moses, who, as the apostle Paul recalls, was withstood by Jannes and Mambres?[58] If this is so, what truth can be found among you, which the catholic church is seen to withstand, or what lie can you prove to be among us? Can you possibly prove it a lie to say that we are in one communion with the whole world? Can you possibly prove it a lie to say that we retain and defend the true and unique creed? Can you possibly prove it a lie to say that the see of Peter and the keys of the kingdom of heaven were bestowed by Christ where our society is? In the very lesson that you have recalled, consider the order of things, and note which of the characters came first. Certainly Jannes and Mambres are in the second place, wilfully taking arms against Moses and the truth with their false arts, and they tried in vain to undermine the virtues of Moses, who had come before them. As Moses was first, so the catholic church is first; as Jannes and Mambres opposed and withstood him, so you are rebels who take up arms against the true catholic church.

Why is it, therefore, that you wish to interchange our names and yours, unless it is to make yourselves the equal of your associates? For there are some of you who, forgetful or ignorant of times past, say against us what appertains to those who long ago fell away from the catholic church and ordained Majorinus, that is to say those authors of schism and collaboration.[59] While they still maintained peace, before they

---

[56] The Donatists evidently took less note of Matthew 16.19 John 20.23, where the power of binding and loosing is promised to all the Apostles, and maybe to all who possess the Holy Spirit.

[57] 2Tim 3.2-3.

[58] 2Tim 3.8, giving a name to the Egyptian sorcerers who reproduced some of the miracles of Moses at Exodus 7.11 etc. Mambres in Optatus is a variant of the more usual Jambres.

[59] See the account of the origins of the controversy in I.16ff.

set about destroying the unity which is pleasing to god, they were deservedly called the light of the world and the salt of the earth.[60] While they taught peace, they were still called peacemakers; before they were puffed up, they were blessed through poverty of spirit, they were part of the seasoning; they were blessed while they were meek, they were part of the seasoning; they were blessed while they were righteous, they were part of the seasoning; the blessed, while they were peacemakers, were the whole of the seasoned.[61] Then they stowed the riches of error in their spirit and their breasts, creating a schism, they were found to be cruel and lacking in mercy, as they impiously divided the members of the church and, following injustice, held the kingdom of God in disdain, and by dividing the church refused to be peacemakers. After this they made themselves the salt of folly, by which nothing could be seasoned which would have pleased God by its sweetness.

And when this evil appertains to your ancestors, certain of your associates argue otherwise, so as to say that those people were fools who, though belatedly, acknowledged the truth and, returning from schism, sought peace by acknowledging the mother church. Some of your party think that these people erred, they reckon that in their folly they turned away from wisdom. From this is it apparent that all of you err in the same way by interchanging names, as you also have compared Jannes and Mambres to the peaceable catholics and yourselves, the schismatics, to Moses, which has nothing to do with truth. And some of your associates have wished to judge the wise in their unwisdom, so that they say that the fools became peacemakers and refused to perceive the folly of their own parents in raising discord.

6. Your ill-will reaches such a point that you say that Macarius, after those deeds, should not have been taken into communion, but the catholic bishops should rather have abstained.[62] First, though the name of communion is one, the modes are different: it is one thing for a bishop to communicate with a bishop, and another for one of the laity to communicate with a bishop. Next, it would have been a serious

---

[60] Matthew 5.13-14.

[61] Cf Matthew 5.9-10.

[62] A voluntary homicide, should be excommunicated for a term, if not for life; see nn. 5 and 7 above. Augustine, *Cresc.* III.55 contends that over-zealous catholics should be tolerated, like Donatists, for the peace of the Church.

matter if Macarius had done what he is said to have done of his own will;[63] because the deed is avenged on the doers by public tribunals and Roman laws. For the homicide is the person who, under the force of no constraint, at no behest, under no power, but driven by his madness has done of his own will what the laws forbid. Macarius, however, did what he is said to have done at your provocation, nor was he a bishop, nor did he hold the office of a bishop, nor did he lay his hand on anyone or offer sacrifice. Since, then, it is patent that he had nothing to do with the bishops' acts, no bishop is seen to have been polluted by him, as he did not make an offering with the bishops. It remains for you to say that he communciated with the people - and it is well-known that he said something among the people, but for the sake of introducing some matter, not of treating it [formally] which belongs to the bishops.[64] For he could only speak, if at all, in isolation.

By contrast, the episcopal treatise is agreed by all to have been clothed with sancitity, doubled indeed by its words of greeting.[65] For the bishop does not begin to say anything to the people, unless he has first greeted the people in the name of God. The closing words resemble the initial ones. Every treatise in the church begins from the name of God and is terminated by the same name of God.[66] Which of you dares to say that Macarius used to greet the people in the manner of bishops? Therefore, since he neither greeted them before saying anything nor dared to greet them after he had spoken, nor laid on hands no sacrificed to God in the episcopal manner, why do you say that the episcopal college could have been polluted, when you see that Macarius had nothing to do with any episcopal office?

---

[63] For the claim that defenders of the catholics did only what the Donatists forced them to do, cf Augustine, *Cresc.* IV.61.

[64] Not true for Irenaeus, who frequently cites presbyters; see Molland (1950). But the custom of declaring doctrine by synods and, in Egypt at least, of enforcing it by Festal letters, inevitably gave rise to the view that speech on maters of doctrine was an episcopal prerogative. Cf the declaration by the bishops at Antioch in 341 that they cannot be followers of Arius, beacuse it would be absurd for Bishops to follow a presbyter. Macarius received support in the preamble to the Carthaginian council under Gratus in 348 (Jonkers, p. 74).

[65] We have no other record of this treatise.

[66] It is hard to believe that this means what it says. The statement is not true even of Festal Letters (see e.g. Athanasius no. 4), let alone of most surviving treatises on doctrine.

Trampled in this place by the foot of truth, your ill-will seems once again to raise its head. For you say that he should not have communicated even among the people. It is indeed patent that he, as the apostle Paul proves, was the minister of God's will; and what wonder, if even pagan judges deserved to be reckoned ministers of God's will, as the apostle says: *Not without cause does the judge bear the sword?*[67] For he is the minister of God's will. The point is that Macarius also is seen to have been a judge in his [role]. But if he was not a judge in what he did, according to the Roman laws he should have suffered vengeance from judges. Or if you say that even so he should not have communicated, we do not see any duty of abstaining in the case of one who did the sort of thing that Moses did; God did not treat him with contempt and abstinence after the deaths of twenty-three thousand people, but invited him again to speak with him.[68] We do not see cause for abstinence in the case of one who did what Phineas did.[69] I recalled a little earlier that he was rewarded for his homicide by the praise of God himself. Still less do we see cause for abstinence in the case of one who did what the prophet Elijah did in killing so many false prophets.[70] For I have already proved above that they were false seers.

7. But let us, to leave these instances in silence, say as you do that Macarius was a criminal; even if he was, we had not the right to abstain when the accuser was silent.[71] For it is written that no-one is to be condemned before the case has been examined. Say who accused him and was not heard. Do you say that Macarius confessed his guilt and our sentence was silent? For we are all judges of some kind in the church, as you also do not deny, because you contend that we should have been severe judges. For we cannot do what God did not do: in judgment he separated the roles, and did not wish the same person to be

---

[67] Romans 13.4. Cf Augustine, *Petil.*. II.45, in answer to the citation of Psalm 104.15.
[68] Exodus 32.28. Cf Book III, n.66.
[69] Numbers 25.9-11. Cf Book III.7.
[70] 1Kings 18.40. Cf Book III.7.
[71] Cf the reasoning of the Council of Carthage in 411, as reported by Augustine, *Brev.*. III.35. Augustine argues that the other provinces could not condemn Caecilian since even if the charges against him were true, they could not know this after the transmarine tribunal.See *Cresc.* IV.32 etc.

accuser and judge.[72] For no-one at the same point in the same case can maintain both roles, so as to be able to be both accuser and judge in the same judgment. Even God did not do this through his omnipotence: so that he might show us the practice of judging, he taught us that the accused should not be condemned without an accuser, nor should the accuser be the one who was to be the judge in that case.

Indeed at the very beginning of the ages, when the birth of humanity had begun anew and Cain had killed his brother Abel, we read: *And God called Cain and inquired of him where his brother was.*[73] He, doubling his sin, as though he could render God ignorant, said that he did not know. And at what time could the Lord not know anything, when all things that are done are under his eyes and countenance?[74] And yet God did not judge without an accuser and inquired anyway about what he knew. And you want us to abstain when we have not seen the person doing anything evil and he has no accuser. I see at this point what your ill-feeling whispers. For you say that what was done is not hidden from us.[75] We confess that we have heard, but it would be a sin to condemn one whom no-one has dared to accuse. But if you say that the deed is not hidden from us, ask God why he inquired when he had seen the parricide.[76] Nor should we have done what God declined to do, when he declined to pronounce sentence except on the acccused. Produce an accuser; otherwise, a sentence could not be just unless the same one who was going to judge made the accusation. Thus he says: *See, the blood of your brother cries to me from the earth.*[77] Therefore,

---

[72] See Deuteronomy 16.18 etc. The having of judges was regarded by the Rabbis as one of the Noachite commandments, binding even on the Gentiles.

[73] Genesis 4.9, translating direct into reported speech.

[74] Questions asked by God were always interpreted by the fathers in such a way as to preserve his omniscience. Cf Philo, *Legum Allegoriae* III.17 and Ambrose, *De Paradiso* on the hiding of Adam.

[75] Donatists held that sin in the church could be tolerated only so long as it was unknown (*Cresc.* II.24 etc.). Augustine replied that this view led to absurdities (*Cresc.* II.22, etc.), that everyone is a sinner (ibid. II.35), that Cyprian himself had refused to judge or excommunicate those who opposed him on the matter of rebaptism (ibid. III.2), and that Donatists themselves had been prepared to tolerate their own schismatics "for the sake of peace" (*ibid.* III.28).

[76] For *parricidium* as the murder of a brother cf Livy, XL.24. Originally signifying the murder of a father, it came to stand for any atrocious crime.

[77] Genesis 4.10.

since you are completely unable to prove that anyone has accused Macarius before us, you cannot condemn our judgment.

APPENDIX ONE:

Proceedings Before the Consular Zenoplilus

1. Here begin the Proceedings, which make it patent that Silvanus, who ordained along with others Donatus' predecessor Majorinus, was a collaborator.[1]

When Constantine Maximus High Augustus and the younger Constantine the most noble Caesar were consuls, on December 13[2] ... with Sextus of Thamugadi,[3] Victor the grammarian having been brought before the court, with the deacon Nundinarius also in attendance,[4] His Excellency[5] the consular Zenophilus[6] said: "What are you called?" He replied, "Victor". His Excellency the consular Zenophilus said, "What

---

[1] Rubrics of this kind may originally have been aded to every item in the appendix, whether by Optatus or by a previous collector. Maier (1987) p. 15 n. 21 cites a similar introduction from *Gesta Collationis Carthaginiensis* III.215 (CCL 149A). The document is included here to incriminate Silvanus, one of the principal accusers of Caecilian. He is shown to have handed over treasures, to have acted for personal gain, and to have been supported by the wealthy Lucilla. His chief accuser, Victor the grammarian, appears to be a member of a Donatist congregation, and is himself incriminated (a) by his failure to withdraw from communion with Silvanus while withdrawing from communion with Caecilian; and (b) by his attempt to deny his own collaboration, which was revealed in the proceedings under Munatius Felix. The account of the election of Silvanus implies that the strength of Donatism was concentrated outside the proconsular province of Africa.

[2] The date is therefore 320 A.D. On the consulships of Constantine's son Constantine I, who received the imperial dignity in 317 and died in 340, see Barnes (1982) p. 95.

[3] See Maier (1987) p. 214 n. 27 for discussion of the emendation *sexto idus decembres Thamugadi in civitate*, which fills the lacuna and removes the name of Sextus, which does not occur elsewhere in this document. According to Maier, however, the state of the lacuna does not support the conjecture, and the name of Sextus already appears in Augustine's citation of these records at *Cresc.* III.33.

[4] Cf Optatus I.14. Nundinarius, named in almost all the letters quoted here, is no doubt the one who divulged them.

[5] That is, *vir clarissimus*, abbreviated to v.c. in this document, and denoting a person of senatorial rank.

[6] A *consularis* is a man sent as the Emperor's legate to govern a province, in this case Numidia. On what may be known or conjectured of Zenophilus' career, see Barnes (1982) pp. 106-7. He seems to have held office in both Sicily, Achaea and Asia as well as Africa, becoming consul in 333.

is your occupation?". Victor said, "I am a teacher of Roman literature, a Latin grammarian".[7]

His Excellency the consular Zenophilus said, "Of what class are you?" Victor said, "My father was a decurion of Constantina,[8] and my grandfather was a soldier. He fought in the imperial army,[9] for we trace our origin from Moorish blood".[10]

His Excellency the consular Zenophilus said, "Mindful of your good faith and your good character, state simply what caused the dispute between the Christians".[11] Victor said, "I do not know how the dispute originated; I am one of the Christian people. However, when I was at Carthage and a time came when Bishop Secundus came to Carthage,[12] they are said to have found that Caecilianus the Bishop had been improperly consecrated by someone or other,[13] and they set up another against him. Hence the dispute arose at that point in Carthage; and hence I cannot be fully acquainted with the origin of the dispute, since

[7] Maier (1987) p. 215 n. 33 says that Victor would teach children between the ages of twelve and fifteen.

[8] A decurion is a local magistrate, made eligible by a property qualification. As Jones, Vol II (1964) pp. 737-8 observes, the office was a burden on poorer incumbents and was not necessarily a sign of culture. Constantina was the title given to Cirta by Constantine after the usuurpation of Domitius Alexander had greatly enhanced its status (Aurelius Victor, *Epitome* 40.28); it had been founded initially as Iulia Cirta by Octavian in 26 B.C. See Teutsch (1962) p. 176ff.

[9] On the imperial *comitatus* see Maier (1987) p. 215 n. 36. It is the military following of the Emperor wherever he is based.

[10] In Appendix II Ingentius confesses to having fabricated evidence on behalf of a Bishop called Maurus, whose name may suggest that he wished to be regarded as indigenous. Diocletian had introduced a Romanizing policy, on which see now Corcoran (1996) pp. 135 and 173. Frend (1952a), pp. 49-58 argues that the strength of Donatism outside the proconsular province may bespeak an adherence to native customs, which would inevitably provoke suspicions of disloyalty to the central government.

[11] Zenophilus implies that he himself was not a Christian.

[12] On Bishop Secundus of Tigisis see Optatus I.19 and especially Augustine, *Cresc.* III.30 and Epistle 43.6ff, where Secundus conspires with other bishops to conceal his misdeeds.

[13] On the Carthaginian council which alleged this see Maier (1987) pp. 128-135; for Augustine's denial of the invalidity see *Brev.* III. 29-30. Cf also Optatus I.19 and notes.

our city has always had one church,[14] and, if it ever had a dispute, we are totally unaware of it."

2. His Excellency the consular Zenophilus said, "do you hold communion with Silvanus? Victor responded, "Yes, with him". His Excellency the consular Zenophilus, said, "Why then do you shun him whose innocence is now free of stain"?[15] And he added, "Moreover, it is asserted that you know another thing for certain, that Silvanus is a collaborator. Confess the matter." Victor replied, "This I do not know".

His Excellency the consular Zenophilus said to Nundinarius the deacon, "Victor claims not to know that Silvanus is a collaborator". The deacon Nundinarius said, "He does know, for he handed over the codices." Victor replied, "I had fled that storm, may I perish if I lie![16] When we suffered a sudden assault of persecution, we fled to Bellona's Hill. I and Victor the presbyter settled with Mars the deacon. When all the codices were demanded from Mars the deacon, he denied that he had them, and Victor then gave the names of all the readers. They came to my house when I was absent. The magistrates went up and my codices were stolen. When I came I found that the codices had been stolen." Nundinarius the deacon said, "You have declared in the proceedings[17] that you handed over the codices. Why are these things denied, when they can be exposed?" His Excellency the consular Zenophilus said to Victor, "Make a simple confession, or you will be more severely interrogated."

---

[14] It seems that no rival had been able to estaboish himself in opposition to Silvanus. When he became a Donatist the catholics wereunable to recover control of the *basilica*, to judge by Appendix 10. See further Augustine, Epistle 53.

[15] Referring to the various acquittals of Caecilian. See Appendices 5, 6, 7, 9, 10.

[16] The proceedings under Munatius Felix reveal that Victor is in fact lying, as one might have gathered from his incoherent repetitions; but flight from persecution would have been consonant with Christ's commands (see Matt 24.16ff etc.), with the teaching of Cyprian's *De Lapsis* and with common practice under Diocletian's persecution. See Nicholson (1989).

[17] That is, the proceedings of the inquisition under Munatius Felix, soon to be read out. For other evidence of these see Maier (1987) pp. 40-41.

The deacon Nundinarius said, "Let the proceedings be read".[18] His Excellency the consular Zenophilus said "Let them be read". Nundinarius gave them to the secretaries,[19] who recited them:

When Diocletian was consul for the eighth and Maximian for the seventh time,[20] on May 19,[21] from the Acts of Munatius Felix the permanent priest,[22] curator of the colony of Cirta.[23] **When they arrived at the house in which the Christians gathered,[24] Felix the permanent priest and curator, said to Paul the Bishop:[25] "Bring forth the writings of the Law, and anything else that you have here, as is commanded, so that you may comply with the edict".[26] Paul the Bishop said, "The readers have the codices;[27] but we give what we have here." Felix the permanent priest, curator of the common weal, said, "Show me the readers or send to them". Paul the Bishop**

---

[18] Parts of what follows appear as Augustine, *Cresc.* III.33 and Epistle 53.4.

[19] The functions of the *exceptores* who kept the court proceedings are alluded to by Ulpian, *Digest* XIX.2.19.9, as well as in inscriptions and papyri. See further Appendix 2, n. 7 on *exceptores*, notaries and scribes.

[20] That is in 303 A.D. On the consulships of Maximian and Diocletian see Barnes (1982) p. 93.

[21] The date is verified by Augustine, *Cresc.* III.33, though his Epistle 53.4 states May 22. Maier (1987) p. 218 n. 49 suggests that the latter date is an erroneous citation from memory.

[22] Schmidt (1892) pp. 125-9 argues that this title, which appears to be peculiar to Africa, is merely honorific.

[23] On the post of *curator rei publicae* see Liebenam (1897). On the distinction implied by colonial status see Appendix II n. 7.

[24] Optatus I.14 and Augustine, *Cresc.* III.30 imply that, up to March/May 7 at least, the Christians of Cirta gathered in a private house.

[25] Predecessor to Silvanus, otherwise unknown.

[26] That is, the first edict of Diocletian, promulgated in Niceomedia on Feb 24 303 A.D., requiring that churches be razed, copies of the Scriptures handed over for burning and Christian deprived of the right to legal representation (Lactantius, *Mort.* 13.1; Eusebius, *Hist. Eccl.* VIII.2.4 and VIII.5.1). For a summary of the four edicts against the Christians, and of modern scholarship on them, see Corcoran (1996) pp. 179-182. As he notes on p. 180 n. 38 and p. 181 n. 47, Optatus is the earliest witness to the promulgation of the first edict in Africa and preserves the only detailed narrative of a confiscation of books. The first edict cannot therefore be proved to have been enforced in Africa before May 19 303.

[27] On the appointment of readers and subdeacons see Hippolytus, *Apostolic Tradition* pp. 21-2 Chadwick and Dix. Readers were to recite those lessons in churches which did not fall to deacons and priests (*Apostolic Constitutions* II.57.7), and the tenth canon of Sardica (343) prescribes reader, deacon and priest as the *cursus honorum* for a bishop.

said, "You know them all". Felix the permanent priest, curator of the common weal, said, "We do not know them". Paul the Bishop said, "The public office knows them,[28] that is the court-notaries Edusius and Junius". Felix the permanent priest, curator of the common weal, said, "Waiting on the list of readers, which the public office will show us, give us what you have".

With Paul the Bishop in session, with the presbyters Montanus and Victor of Densatele and Memorius,[29] the deacons Mars and Helius assisting, Marcuclius, Catullinus, Silvanus and Carosus as subdeacons, Ianuarius, Meracles, Fructuosus, Miggis, Saturninus Victor and other sextons,[30] and Victor son of Aufidus as scribe, the inventory in brief was as follows: two gold chalices, six silver chalices, six silver urns, a silver cooking-pot, seven silver lamps, two wafer-holders, seven short bronze candle-sticks with their own lights, eleven bronze lamps with their own chains, 82 women's tunics, 38 capes, 16 men's tunics, 13 pairs of men's shoes, 47 pairs of women's shoes, 19 peasant clasps.[31] Felix the permanent priest, curator of the common weal, said to the sextons Marcuclius, Silvanus and Carosus,[32] "Bring forth what you have". Silvanus and Carosus said, "What was here we have emptied out in toto." Felix the permanent priest, curator of the public weal, said, "Your response is entered in the proceedings".

4. After empty chests were discovered in the bookroom,[33] Silvanus brought forth a silver and a silver lamp, saying that he had found them behind a coffer. Victor son of Aufidus said to Silvanus, "You would have been dead if you had not found those". Felix the permanent priest, curator of the common weal, said to Silvanus, "Look more carefully, in case anything remains here". Silvanus said, "Nothing remains, we have brought it all out". And when the

---

[28] This would include the scribes and torturers who appear in Appendix 1 and 2 as state servants. See Maier (1987) p. 31.

[29] It is not clear whether three or four are enumerated here: see Maier (1987) p. 219 n. 57.

[30] Maier (1987) p. 219 n. 58 suggests that these would also perform the role of sacristan. The subdeacon Silvanus is the future bishop.

[31] On this rare word, which has also been rendered as "capes", see Maier (1987) p. 219 n. 59.

[32] A mistake for "subdeacons".

[33] That is to say, the place where the readers would keep their copies of the Scriptures.

dining-room was opened,[34] four jars were found there and six pots. Felix the permanent priest, curator of the public weal, said, "Bring forth the scriptures that you have, so that you may comply with the bidding of the Emperors and their edict. Catullinus brought forth one extremely large codex. Felix the permanent priest, curator of the public weal, said to Marcuclius and Silvanus, "Why have you given only one codex?" Catullinus and Marcuclius said, "We have no more, as we are subdeacons; but the readers have the codices". Felix the permanent priest, curator of the common weal, said, "Show me the readers!" Marcuclius and Catullinus said, "We don't know where they live".[35] Felix the permanent priest, curator of the common weal, said to Catullinus and Marcuclius, "If you do not know where they live, tell their names". Catullinus and Marcuclius said, "We are not traitors. Here we are, have us killed". Felix the permanent priest, curator of the common weal, said, "Let them be taken into custody".

5. And when they came to the house of Eugenius, Felix the permanent priest, curator of the public weal, said, "Bring forth the writings that you have, so that you may comply with the edict". And he brought forth four codices. Felix the permanent priest, curator of the common weal, said to Silvanus and Carosus, "Show me the other readers". Silvanus and Carosus said, "The Bishop has already told you that the secretaries Edusius and Junius know them all; they will show them to you at their houses." The secretaries Edusius and Junius said, "We are showing them to you, Sir".

And when they came to the house of Felix the tailor,[36] he brought forth five codices. And when they came to the house of Victorinus, he brought forth eight codices. And when they came to the house of Proiectus, he brought forth five large and two small codices. And when they came to the house of the grammarian, Felix the permanent priest and curator said to Victor the grammarian, "Bring forth the writings that you have, so that you may comply

---

[34] Probably the site of the communal meal or *agape*.

[35] Cf *Martyrdom of Justin* 2 for another case of improbable nescience, indicating the goodwill of the magisrate.

[36] *Sarsor* would appear to be a late variant of *sartor*, though Maier (1987) renders the word as "tailleur de pierre".

with the edict." Victor the grammarian brought forth two codices
and four quiniones.[37] Felix the permanent priest, curator of the
common weal, said to Victor, "Bring out the writings; you have
more." Victor the grammarian said, "If I had had more, I would
have given them".

And when they came to the house of Euticius of Caesarea,[38] Felix
the permanent priest, curator of the common weal, said to Euticius,
"Bring out the writings that you have, so that you may comply with
the edict". Euticius said, "I have none." Felix the permanent priest,
curator of the common weal, said "Your claim has been entered in
the proceedings". And when they came to the house of Coddeo, his
wife brought forth six codices. Felix the permanent priest, curator
of the common weal, said, "Look in case you have more, and bring
them forth." The woman replied, "I have none". Felix the
permanent priest, curator of the common weal, said to Bovis the
public servant, "Enter and look in case she has more." The public
servant said, "I have looked and I have not found any." Felix the
permanent priest, curator of the common weal, said to Victorinus,
Silvanus and Carosus, "If anything is lacking in this work, the
jeopardy is yours."

6. When this had been read, His Excellency the consular Zenophilus
said to Victor: "Make a simple confession!" Victor replied, "I was not
there." Nundinarius the deacon said, "We have read the letters of
bishops made by Fortis".[39] And Nundinarius the deacon read: "Christ
and his angels bear witness that those with whom you have
communicated were collaborators, to wit Silvanus from Cirta is a
collaborator and a thief of goods from the poor; for all of you seniors[40],

---

[37] This word, translated "cahier" by Maier, means a manuscript consisting of five double
leaves. The thing itself is rarer in antiquity than in the mediaeval period, and the term may
not be attested in this sense before the date of this Appendix.
[38] Maier (1987) notes that this is either Caesarea in Mauretania or Caesarea in Numidia.
[39] The meaning of the text as it stands is unclear, since Fortis is merely one of the letter-
writers. Perhaps the original text stated that Fortis had given copies of these letters to the
prosecutors; it seems unlikely that he acted as scribe for the others.
[40] Presumably a reference to the seniores laici, rather than senior bishops, though it is
surprising to find them named before the hierarchy. See n. 46 below.

presbyters and deacons know of the four hundred *folles*[41] of Lucilla, for which you conspired with one another to make Majorinus Bishop, and hence arose the schism. For Victor the fuller also, in the presence of you and the people gave twenty *folles*,[42] so that he might be made a presbyter, as Christ and his angels know".

7. And a copy of the letter was recited: **Greetings in the Lord from Bishop Purpurius**[43] **to Silvanus, his fellow-bishop. Our son the deacon Nundinarius came to me and requested that I should direct this petitionary letter from myself to you, your excellent Holiness, so that, if it should be possible, there should be peace between you and himself. What I indeed desire, so that no-one may know what is going on between us, is that, if you express this wish in your own letter, I myself should in the present case come there alone and put an end to that same dissension between you. For he has given me with his own hand a record of that affair which caused him to be stoned at your behest. It is not true that a father may chastise his son against the truth,**[44] **and I know that what is written down in the document handed to me is true.**[45] **Look for a remedy by which this cancer of yours may be extinguished, before a flame leaps up which after such a long time will not be extinguishable except by spiritual blood. Bring together your fellow-clerics and the seniors of the**

---

[41] On this unit of currency, introduced by Diocletian, see Maier (1987) p. 140 n.8. Coleman-Norton (1966) p. 42, says that the name was applied both to the double denarius and to a bag containing 3,125 of these; after the inflation of Diocletian's time, only the second meaning would denote a very large sum. The following testimonies imply that Lucilla bribed the bishops to vent her own hatred upon Caecilian, who, according to Augustine (Epistle 43.18), foresaw the corrupt decision of the council that ensued, and was condemned in his absence.

[42] Simony, the sale of ecclesiastical offices, is here made the origin of the schism. The offence (described in Acts 8.20) is first condemned formally by the second canon of the Council of Chalcedon (451 A.D.), but it was common to ascribe venal motives to heretics and schismatics. Cf Tertullian, *Adversus Valentinianos* 4; Athanasius, *Historia Arianorum* 73; Eusebius, *Historia Ecclesiastica* VI.43 (on Novatian).

[43] Bishop of Limata, credited at Optatus I.14 and Augustine, *Cresc.* III.29 with an impenitent confession of family murder.

[44] Cf Hebrews 12.5; Proverbs 3.11. The word *verum*, in the barbarous Latin of Purpurius, appears to have taken on the meaning "equitable".

[45] The word *libellus* can signify a written deposition; cf Augustine, Epistle 43.15 on the *libellus* against Caecilian.

people,[46] and let them diligently inquire as to the nature of these disputes, so that what happens may happen according to the ordinances of faith. You will not lean to the right or to the left,[47] but will gladly refuse to lend your ear to evil counsellors, who do not want peace. You are killing all of us .... and by another hand.[48] Farewell.

8. A further copy of a letter: Eternal greetings in the Lord from Bishop Purpurius to the clerics and elders of the people of Cirta! Moses speaks out to the whole assembly of the sons of Israel,[49] and has told them what the Lord commands. Nothing was done without a council of the elders. And so you also, dearly beloved, whom I know to possess all heavenly and spiritual wisdom, must use all your ability to ascertain the nature of this dispute and bring it to a peaceful outcome. For the deacon Nudinarius says that nothing in the cause of this dispute between our beloved Silvanus and himself is unknown to you. For he has handed to me a record in which everything is written down, and has stated that nothing is unknown to you. I know that it is no rumour. Look for a good remedy by which this affair may be extinguished without peril to your souls, lest suddenly, while you show respect of persons, you come into judgment.[50] Judge justly between the parties in accordance with your dignity and justice. Take care for yourselves, that you lean neither to right nor to left; this is God's business, who inspects the thoughts of each.[51] Take pains that no-one may know the nature of this conference. The things contained in the record pertain to you.

---

[46] The word *seniores*, though etymologically the equivalent of the Greek *presbyteroi*, now signifies merely the chief administrators of the Church. See Frend (1961) and Maier (1987) p. 224 n. 81, together with Appendix II n. 27.

[47] Cf. Deuteronomy 28.14 - this allusion to Moses is an index of the august dignity now assumed by bishops.

[48] A lacuna conceals some statement about the dispatch of this or another letter.

[49] Cf Exodus 12.3 for the phrase; Exodus 24.1 for the elders. Whether true or false, the claim that seventy bishops convened at the Carthaginian council against Caecilian (Augustine, Epistle 43.3) may express the desire of the Donatists to imitate the Mosaic constitution.

[50] Cf James 2.1-13.

[51] Cf Romans 2.16.

It is not good, for the Lord says, *You shall be condemned from your own mouth and from your own mouth you shall be justified.*[52]

9. Further, another was recited. Eternal greetings in the Lord from Fortis to his beloved brother Silvanus![53] Our son the deacon Nundinarius has come to me and reported those things which took place between him and you, as being through the agency of a person of ill-will, who wishes to divert the souls of the just from the way of truth. On hearing this, I was disheartened because such a dispute had arisen among us. For a priest of God ought not to arrive at ... let not that which is unprofitable to us occur.[54] Now therefore beg him (it is in his power) that the peace of our Saviour Christ the Lord may be with him. For it is written, *Take care lest, as you bite and accuse one another, you yourselves should be consumed.*[55] Therefore I pray the Lord to take from our midst this stumbling-block, so that God's rite may be celebrated with thanksgiving.[56] As the Lord says, *I give you my peace, I leave my peace to you.*[57] What peace can there be while there is disputing and contention? For when I was ... by a soldier[58] ... separated and had come into that with such an injury, I commended my soul to God, and forgave you, since God sees the minds of men and theirs,[59] and whether I had been led to them by you. But God set me free, and I serve with you. Therefore, just as there is forgiveness between us, you too must be reconciled, so that in Christ's name we can celebrate peace with gladness.[60] Let none know.

---

[52] Matthew 12.37.

[53] The see of Fortis is unknown; the name of Silvanus is lost in the MS, but there can be no doubt of the addressee.

[54] Or something of the sort; the lacuna makes it impossible to offer a confident translation.

[55] Galatians 5.15.

[56] A reference to the eucharist, as becomes plain from other letters. The importance attached to it here suggests that the Easter ceremony is in question. Constantine shared the desire that Easter should be a symbol of peace; see Socrates, *Historia Ecclesiastica* I.8. On the particular importance of removing scandal before the eucharist, cf 1Cor 5.

[57] John 14.27, the first quotation from scripture in Optatus, occurring at I.1 and again at II.5.

[58] The autobiographical passage is impossible to reconstruct.

[59] Cf. Romans 2.1, as above.

[60] Or perhaps *pascham* ("eucharist") should be read for *pacem* ("peace"), though one implies the other and both are anticipated in this document.

10. [Another:] **Eternal greetings in the Lord from Fortis to the
clergy and seniors!**[61] **My son the deacon Nundinarius has come to
me and reported on those things which have been done against you;
it was certainly your duty to compose affairs, so that that which you
and I know should not have come about, as you have reported to
us, seeing that you have suffered the same insanity from those who
stoned them on account of truth.**[62] **And it is written, Is there not a
wise man among you, who could judge between brothers? Yet
brother does indeed go to judgment with brother, but among
infidels;**[63] **as you also do when you contend in judgment.**[64] **Has it
come to this, that we give the heathen such an example as that those
who believed in God through us are the very ones who curse us
when we come into public notice? So that, therefore, it may not
come to this, you who are spiritual**[65] **must ensure that no-one
knows, so that we may celebrate the pasch with thanksgiving and
you may exhort them to be reconciled, and there may be no
dispute; lest, when it has come into public notice, you also should
enter into danger if this has happened, and subsequently blame one
another. You, Possesor and presbyter Dontius,**[66] **will give as much
as possible;**[67] **and you, Valerius and Victor, who know all the
proceedings, will severally take care that peace be with you.**

11. Further, another was read aloud. **Eternal greetings in the Lord!**[68]
Your son Nundinarius has come to us, not only to me but to our

---

[61] Maier (1987) gives this passage in a longer form which conforms with the introductions
to other letters.

[62] I have tried to make sense of an inexplicable passage by some repunctuation. Following
the punctuation of Ziwsa or Maier, the translation would run: "so that it should not reach
the point at which having suffered such insanity from those by whom they were stoned
for the truth. This you and we know".

[63] Cf Matt 7,1; 1Cor 6.5-6; and Constantine's response in Appendix 5 to the Donatists'
appeal.

[64] Reading *contenditis*, with Ziwsa's *apparatus*, for the *non intenditis* of his text.

[65] Cf Gal 6.1, though the duties prescribed are very different.

[66] Or "possessor of Donatus", meaning presumably "champion" of the same. The name
Possessor does not occur again; see Maier (1987) p. 227 n. 91. Dontius, Valerius and
Victor all recur as priests of Cirta.

[67] Or "take all pains", if we take *dabitis* with *operam* in the next sentence.

[68] Maier (1987) p. 228 n. 92-3 accepts the claim of one witness that this letter was
written by Sabinus to Silvanus, as the next is written by Sabinus to Fortis.

brother Fortis, and bringing a serious complaint. I am amazed that one of your authority has dealt thus with your son, whom you cherished and ordained. For if a building is made of earth, is not something celestial added to it, because a priest's hand is responsible for the building? Yet one should not be amazed at you, when Scipture says, *I shall destroy the wisdom of the wise and shall reproach the prudence of the prudent.*[69] And again it says, *Men loved darkness rather than light,*[70] as you also do. Let it be enough for you to know everything. As to that which our brother Fortis also has written to you, now I would beg you, most benign brother, of your charity, to fulfil the saying of the prophet Isaiah, *Drive ill-will from your souls, and come let us dispute, says the Lord.*[71] And again, *Drive the evil one from your midst.*[72] Do so yourself also: subdue and avert the conspiracy of those who do not want peace between you and your son. But let your son Nundinarius celebrate the pasch with you in peace, lest the matter should come to public notice as well as being known to all of us. I would ask you, most benign brother, to accept the prayer of my mediocrity: let no-one know.

12. Further, another was read aloud. Eternal greetings in the Lord from Sabinus to his brother Fortis! I am specially assured what love [you bear] towards all your colleagues; however,[73] I am assured that it is according to the will of God, who said, *I love some above my own soul,*[74] that you have shown respect to Silvanus. Therefore I have not hesitated to give these writings to you, because I have caused what you have written to him to be given over in the case of Nundinarius; and if someone acts quickly, the matter always proceeds at God's instance. Do not attempt an excuse; for in these

---

[69] Isaiah 29.14. I cannot agree with Maier (1987) p. 228 n. 94 that Sabinus betrays his different status by making more frequent use of scripture than other correspondents.
[70] John 3.14.
[71] Cf. Isaiah 1.16-18.
[72] 1Cor 5.13.
[73] Cf Theodoret, Commentary on 1 Corinthians, on 1Cor 1.4: "intending to denounce, he first soothes the ear".
[74] Maier (1987) can offer only *Didache* 2.7 as a parallel. Though the canon of the Gospels had been established since the second century, the quotation of *agrapha* (orally-transmitted sayings attributed to Jesus) was authorised by Paul's statement at Acts 20.35 and was still not uncommon in the fourth century.

days business presses hard on us, and unremittingly urges us with
regard to these matters　right up to the most solemn day of the
pasch, that the most ample peace should come about through you,
so that we may be found worthy *fellow-heirs with Christ,*[75] who said,
I give you my peace, I leave my peace with you.[76] And again I pray
you to do it". And in another hand, "I hope in the Lord's name
that you are well and mindful of me. Farewell, but I ask you, let
no-one know.

13. When these had been read, His Excellency the consular
Zenophilus said, "From the proceedings and letters which have been
read, it is patent that Silvanus was a collaborator." And to Victor he
said, "Confess plainly, whether you know that he handed over
anything". Victor said, "He did, but not in my presence". His Excellency
the consular Zenophilus said, "What was Silvanus' clerical office at
that time?".[77] Victor replied, "The persecution began under Bishop Paul,
and Silvanus was a subdeacon." The deacon Nundinarius said in reply,
"When it came to his being made a Bishop, the people replied, 'Let it
be another; God hear us.'" His Excellency the consular　Zenophilus
said to Victor, "Did the people say, Silvanus is a collaborator'?" Victor
said, "I myself strove {that he be not made} Bishop".[78] His Excellency
the consular Zenophilus said to Victor, "Then you knew him to be a
collaborator? Confess". Victor replied, "He was a collaborator". The
deacon Nundinarius said, "You seniors were shouting, 'God hear us, we
want our fellow-citizen, he is a collaborator'". His Excellency the
consular　Zenophilus　said to Victor, "Did you then shout with the
people that Silvanus was a collaborator and ought not to be made a
Bishop?" Victor said, "I shouted along with the people, for we were

---

[75] Romans 8.17.

[76] John 14.27; see n. 59 above.

[77] The reply agrees with the proceedings of the inquest by Munatius Felix, recited earlier.
For Silvanus to rise so quickly from the status of subdeacon may have been an
irregularity. The functions of the subdeacon (*Apostolic Constitutions* VIII.11.11) were to
guard the doors and assist the higher clerics in the celebration of the eucharist.

[78] The text as it stands implies that Victor himself was a bishop, so something must be
inserted.

asking for our fellow-citizen, an upright man".[79] His Excellency the consular Zenophilus said, "On what grounds did you think that he did not merit it?" Victor said, "We were asking for one who was upright and our fellow-citizen; for I knew that we were going to come to this before the imperial tribunal,[80] when such people were put in charge."

14. Further, after the sextons Victor son of Samsuricus and Saturninus were brought before the court, His Excellency the consular Zenophilus said, "What is your name?". The reply was "Saturninus". His Excellency the consular Zenophilus said, "What is your occupation?". Saturninus replied, "sexton". His Excellency the consular Zenophilus said, "Do you know Silvanus to be a collaborator?" Saturninus said, "I know that he handed over a silver lamp". His Excellency The consular Zenophilus said, "What else?" Saturninus replied, "I know nothing else, except that he took it out from behind a coffer".

15. And, when Saturninus had been taken away, His Excellency the consular Zenophilus said to the one still present, "What is your name?" The reply was "Victor son of Samsuricus". His Excellency the consular Zenophilus said, "What is your occupation?". Victor said, "I am a craftsman".[81] His Excellency the consular Zenophilus said, "Who handed over the silver table?" Victor replied, "I did not see. What I say is what I saw." His Excellency the consular Zenophilus said to Victor, "Albeit it has been made patent from the responses of those who were previously interrogated, confess for yourself none the less whether Silvanus is a collaborator." Victor said, "When Silvanus was asked how he prevented our being taken to Carthage,[82] I heard from the mouth of the Bishop himself, 'A silver lamp and a silver casket were given to me,

---

[79] This person was yet another Donatus. Victor's term *civem nostram* makes it clear that the *populus* mentioned here are those who take a pride in the colonial status of Cirta; they are the superior class who were later shut up in the Casa Maior.

[80] The less urbane supporters of Silvanus were thus expected to excite troubles that would interest even a secular authority. See Schindler (1983) on tensions between the leading Donatists and their supposed partisans in the lower classes. On the use of terms denoting the people in Optatus see Diesner (1961).

[81] Whereas the occupation named by Saturninus implies an ecclesiastical function, Victor assigns himself to a secular trade.

[82] The sentence is obscure. It begins *Secundo petato*, which Maier takes to mean "when he was asked for a second time"; but I would take *Secundo* as a slip of the pen for *Silvano*.

and I handed these over.'" His Excellency the consular Zenophilus said to Victor son of Samsuricus, "From whom did you hear it?" Victor said, "From Bishop Silvanus". His Excellency the consular Zenophilus said to Victor, You heard from the man himself that he had handed them over?" Victor said, "I heard from the man himself that he had handed them over with his own hands."His Excellency the consular Zenophilus said "Where did you hear?" Victor said, "In the basilica".[83] His Excellency the consular Zenophilus said, "In Constantina?" Victor said, "There he began to address the people, saying, 'For what do they call me a collaborator, for a lamp and a casket?'"

16. His Excellency the consular Zenophilus said to Nundinarius, "What other inquiries do you think should be made of these men?" Nundinarius said, "About the fiscal vats,[84] who took them away". His Excellency the consular Zenophilus said to Nundinarius, "What vats?" Nundinarius said, "They were in the temple of Sarapis,[85] and Bishop Purpurius took them; as for the sour wine that they contained, that was taken by Bishop Silvanus, the presbyter Dontius and Lucianus". His Excellency the consular Zenophilus said, "Do those who are present know of this deed?" Nundinarius replied, "They know". The deacon Saturninus said, "Our forefathers used to say that they were stolen". His Excellency the consular Zenophilus said, "By whom were they stolen?" Saturninus said, "By Bishop Purpurius, and the sour wine by Silvanus and the presbyters Dontius and Superius and the deacon Lucianus."

---

[83] A basilica was originally an ornate public building, often used for judicial purposes. The name was applied to major churches when they began to be built in the style of the pagan edifices; the occurrence of the term in this sense here (the first in Latin) suggests that such constructions were possible even before the recognition of Christianity by the Emperors.

[84] The wine appears to have a tax in kind levied by the provincial administration, perhaps an impost on Egyptian merchants (see next note). It is scarcely possible that the bishops had any right or duty to collect it. Maier (1987) speculates that Silvanus stole the wine (*acetum*) for use at the eucharist; this fails to explain what Purpurius did with the vats, or what Silvanus carried the wine away in.

[85] Serapis or Sarapis was a factitious god of Ptolemaic Egypt. That he should have a temple in Cirta is surprising, since Toutain (1896), p. 212 finds little evidence of his cult outside Carthage, and Rives (1995), pp. 212-4 suggests that it was restricted to Alexandrian merchants. Vidman (1969), pp. 331-4 offers a handful of inscriptions from Numidia referring to Isis and Serapis, but only the former in Cirta. The temple was no doubt used as a convenient repository; the bishops are unlikely to have had any religious reason to be there.

Nundinarius said, "Did Victor give twenty *folles* to become a presbyter?" Saturninus said yes. And when he said yes, His Excellency the consular Zenophilus said to Saturninus, "To whom did he give them?" Saturninus said, "To Bishop Silvanus". His Excellency the consular Zenophilus said to Saturninus, "Then, in order to be made a presbyter, he gave twenty *folles* to Silvanus as the price?" Saturninus said, "He did". His Excellency the consular Zenophilus said, "Was it placed before Silvanus?" Saturninus said, "Before the episcopal chair". His Excellency the consular Zenophilus said to Nundinarius, "Who stole the money?" Nundinarius said, "The Bishops themselves divided it between them".

16. His Excellency the consular Zenophilus said to Nundinarius, "Do you desire that Donatus be present?" Nundinarius said, "Certainly he should come, being the one about whom the people shouted two days after the peace,[86] 'God hear us, we want our fellow-citizen'".[87] His Excellency the consular Zenophilus said to Nundinarius, "Did the people really shout this?" He replied, "They did".

His Excellency the consular Zenophilus said to Saturninus, "Did they shout that Silvanus was a collaborator?" Saturninus said, "Certainly". Nundinarius said, "When he was made Bishop, we did not comunicate with him, because he was said to be a collaborator." Saturninus said, "What he says is true". Nundinarius said, "I saw that Mutus the gladiator[88] carried him on his shoulders". His Excellency the consular Zenophilus said to Saturninus, "Did it happen so?" Saturninus said, "Just so." His Excellency the consular Zenophilus said, "Is the

---

[86] Or "after the pasch" (Von Soden). Maier (1987) p. 233 n. 12 suggests that the peace referred to is that accorded to the Church in Africa by Maxentius (see Optatus I.18), between 306 and 312. But Optatus is the sole witness to this event, and in the light of the other letters, I am inclined to think that, whether "peace" or "pasch" is read the allusion is to a Christian ceremony. In any case the dating "two days after the peace of Maxentius" would mean little to an inhabitant of Cirta, who would not hear of it until some time after its promulgation.

[87] See n. 69 above. For the reliance of Donatists on the tumultuous clamour of the plebs cf. Augustine, Epistle 43.14. In general *populus* is less pejorative, in Optatus as elsewhere.

[88] Gladiators were usually condemned criminals or persons of servile status. Christians after the persecutions regarded the arena with peculiar abhorrence (Hippolytus, *Apostolic Constitutions* p. 26 Chadwick and Dix), and in 325 Constantine forbade the gladiatorial shows altogether: see *Codex Theodosianus* XV.12 and Barnes (1981) pp. 51-3.

whole statement of Nundinarius true, that Silvanus was made Bishop by gladiators?" Saturninus said, "It is true". Nundinarius said, "There were prostitutes there".[89] His Excellency the consular Zenophilus said to Saturninus, "Did the gladiators lift him up?" Saturninus said, "They themselves and the populace bore him; for the citizens were shut up in the place of the martyrs".[90] Nundinarius the deacon said, "Surely the people of God was not there?" Saturninus said, "They were shut up in the Great Lodge". His Excellency the consular Zenophilus said, "Is the whole statement of Nundinarius really true?" Saturninus said, "It is true". His Excellency the consular Zenophilus said, "What do you say?" Victor said, "It is all true, My Lord".

17. Nundinarius said, "Bishop Purpurius took a hundred *folles*." His Excellency the consular Zenophilus said to Nundinarius, "Who, in your view, should be interrogated about the four hundred *folles*?" Nundinarius said, "Lucianus the deacon should be presented, since he knows the whole". His Excellency the consular Zenophilus said to Nundinarius, "Do these men know?" Nundinarius said, "They do not". His Excellency the consular Zenophilus said, "Let Lucianus be presented". Nundinarius said, "These men know that four hundred *folles* were received, but they do not know that the bishops divided them." His Excellency the consular Zenophilus said to Nundinarius and Victor, "Do you know that *folles* were received from Lucilla?" Saturninus and Victor said, "We do." His Excellency the consular Zenophilus said, "Did the poor not receive them?" They said, "No-one received anything." His Excellency the consular Zenophilus said to Saturninus and Victor, "Was nothing stolen from the temple of Sarapis?" Saturninus and Victor said, "Purpurius took vats and Bishop Silvanus and the presbyters Dontius and Superius and the deacon Lucianus took the sour wine. His Excellency the consular Zenophilus said, "From the reply of Victor the grammarian and Victor son of Samsuricus and

---

[89] The use of prostitution as an image of idolatry in the Old Testament made it an archetypal sin for Jews and Christians, condemned e.g. in 1Cor 6 and in the twelfth canon of Elvira (?305 A.D.). It is, however, much less frequently denounced in the canons than e.g. adultery, and the gravity of Nundinarius' accusation here may lie less in the heinousness of the sin than in the low social status of the prostitutes.

[90] On the Casa Maior, a "funerary chapel" in the cemetery, see Maier (1987) p. 234 n. 115.

Saturninus it has become clear that everything alleged by Nundinarius is true. Let them be taken away and depart."

18. His Excellency the consular Zenophilus said, "What others do you think should be interrogated?" Nundinarius said, "The deacon Castus, so that he may tell us if he was not a collaborator. He was the one who ordained him". And when the deacon Castus had been brought before the court, His Excellency the consular Zenophilus said, "What are you called?". He replied, "Castus." His Excellency the consular Zenophilus said to Castus, "What is your occupation?" Castus said, "I have no status". His Excellency the consular Zenophilus said, "Granted that the charges of Nundinarius have been confessed through Victor the scribe, as also through Victor son of Samsuricus and Saturninus, you too tell us none the less, whether Silvanus is a collaborator." Castus said, "He said that he found a lamp behind a coffer". His Excellency the consular Zenophilus said to Castus, "Confess also about the vats stolen from the temple of Sarapis and about the sour wine." Castus replied, "Bishop Purpurius took the vats". His Excellency the consular Zenophilus said, "Who took the sour wine?" Castus replied that Bishop Silvanus, and the presbyters Dontius and Superius, took the sour wine from there.

His Excellency the consular Zenophilus said to Castus, "Confess how many *folles* Victor gave, so that he could be made a presbyter." Castus said, "My Lord, he gave a purse, and what it contained I do not know". His Excellency the consular Zenophilus said to Castus, "To whom was the purse given?" Castus said, "He brought it to him at the Great House".[91] His Excellency the consular Zenophilus said, "Was the money not given to the people?" Castus replied, "It was not given, nor did I see it". His Excellency the consular Zenophilus said, "As to the *folles* which Lucilla gave, did the lesser people receive nothing?" Castus said, "I did not see anyone receiving". His Excellency the consular Zenophilus said, "Where did they go then?" Castus said, "I do not know". Nundinarius said, "At least you heard and saw if the people were told, 'Lucilla gives to you also from her own property.'?" Castus said, "I did not see anyone receiving". His Excellency the consular

---

[91] Taking *illo* as a barbarism for *illi*. If Castus too was in the Casa Maior, his testimony is no doubt that of an eye-witness. It is not clear whether Victor's money was part of Lucilla's bounty.

Zenophilus said, "Castus has plainly confessed that he does not know of a division among the people of the *folles* that Lucilla gave; and so let him be taken away."

19. Further, when the subdeacon Crescentianus had been brought before the court, His Excellency the consular Zenophilus said, "What are you called?" He replied, "Crescentianus".[92] His Excellency the consular Zenophilus said, "Confess straightforwardly like the others, whether you know Silvanus to be a collaborator". Crescentianus said, "Those before me, who were clerics, have themselves tesified in detail." His Excellency the consular Zenophilus said, "What have they testified?" Crescentianus said, "They reported that he was a collaborator". His Excellency the consular Zenophilus said, "They said that he was a collaborator?" And he added, "What did they say?" Crescentianus said, "Those who associated with him among the common people said that he had collaborated at some time." His Excellency Zenophilus said to Crescentianus, "They said this about Silvanus?" Crescentianus said, "Certainly". His Excellency the consular Zenophilus said to Crescentianus, "When he was made a Bishop, were you present?" Crescentianus said, "I was present with the people locked up in the Great Lodge". The deacon Nundinarius said, "It was peasants and gladiators who made him a bishop". His Excellency the consular Zenophilus said, "Was it indeed Mutus the gladiator who elevated him?" He said, "Openly."

20. His Excellency the consular Zenophilus the consular said to Crescentianus, "Do you know of vats being stolen from the temple of Sarapis?" Crescentianus said, "Many said that Bishop Purpurius himself took the vats and the sour wine, which [news] had reached our reverend Silvanus,[93] and was stated by the sons of Aelio." His Excellency the consular Zenophilus said, "What did you hear?" Crescentius said, "That the sour wine had been stolen by the reverend Silvanus and the presbyters Dontius and Superius and the deacon Lucianus." His Excellency the consular Zenophilus said to Crescentianus, "Of the four hundred *folles* which Lucilla gave, did the people receive anything?" Crescentianus said, "I don't know of anyone receiving anything from it, nor who distributed them". Nundinarius said, "Did the old women never

---

[92] The inquiry as to his occupation has no doubt been omitted inadvertently.

[93] Taking *senex* to be a title of esteem here, as does Maier (1987) p. 238 n. 137.

receive anything from it?"[94] Crescentianus said, "Nothing." His Excellency the consular Zenophilus said, "Surely whenever anything like this is given, the whole of the people publicly receive from it?" Crescentianus said, "I did not hear or see that any persons gave it out". His Excellency the consular Zenophilus said to Cresecntianus, "Then nothing of the four hundred *folles* was given to the people?" Crescentianus said, "Nothing; or at least some little morsel would have reached us." His Excellency the consular Zenophilus said, "Then where did they go when stolen?" Crescentianus said, "I do not know; no-one received anything."

Nundinarius said, "How many *folles* did Victor give, so that he could be made a presbyter?" Crescentianus said, "I saw baskets being brought with money". His Excellency the consular Zenophilus said to Crescentianus, "To whom were the baskets given?" Crescentianus said, "To Bishop Silvanus". His Excellency the consular Zenophilus said, "They were given to Silvanus?" Crescentianus said, "To Silvanus." His Excellency the consular Zenophilus said, "Was nothing given to the people?" He replied, "Nothing. We would necessarily have received something if they had been distributed in the usual manner."His Excellency the consular Zenophilus said to Nundinarius, "What else do you think should be asked of Crescentianus?" Nundinarius said, "That's it". His Excellency the consular Zenophilus said, "Since the subdeacon Crescentianus has confessed straightforwardly about everything, let him be taken out".

Further, when the subdeacon Januarius had been brought in and sworn, His Excellency the consular Zenophilus said, "What are you called?" He replied .....[95]

---

[94] On the duty of clerics to feed the widows, already implied in Acts 6, see (e.g.) the seventh canon of the (Westerners') council of Sardica (343), which says that such ministrations are impeded by the importunity of the "Africans".

[95] Readers will neither regret the loss of the remainder nor find it difficult to supply from their own conjecture.

APPENDIX TWO:

The acquittal proceedings of Felix Bishop of Abthugni[1]

1. ... in the municipality of the Abthugnians[2] the *duovir* Gallienus[3] said, "Since you are present, Caecilianus,[4] listen to the letter of my illustrious Lord Aelius Paulinus[5] when he was exercising the prefecture as *vicarius*;[6] [hear] what he was pleased to command in the letter given to me, which compelled you to declare the scribe whom you then had at the time of your administration, and the notary.[7] But since the notary of

---

[1] These appear as pp. 175-87 in Maier (1987). The proceedings were also know to Augustine, who argues at *Epistle* 43.13 that if Felix was acquitted Caecilain's innocence must be still more secure. The text is however defective, and many of the characters are otherwise unknown to us. I have annotated only what I can elucidate. On the complicity between imperial officials and Christians revealed here, see Lepelley (1983).

[2] A *municipium*, according to Aulus Gellius (*Noctes Attici* XVI.3) was a civic community which retained self-government and was subject only to whatever laws it chose to accept. In most cases the original magistrates were replaced by *quattuorviri*, or sometimes (as here) the *duumviri* usual in coloniae (see nn.3 and 7). It seems to have been the usual, and perhaps the universal, rule that the Romans incorporated existing communities as *municipia* rather than creating them. See Sherwin-White (1973), pp. 174-6, with the qualifications of Millar (1977), pp. 398-401. On the status and topography of Abthugni (the modern Hr es Souar), which became a *municipium* at some time in the second century, see Toutain (1896), p. 381; Teutsch (1962), p. 31 n.170.

[3] The form *duovir* is preferred in this document to the more usual *duumvir*. On the administrative functions of this senior civic official see Maier (1987), pp. 29-30.

[4] This Caecilianus, *duovir* in 303, bears the full name Alfius Caecilianus, and is not to be confused with the Bishop.

[5] Maier (1987), p.175 n. 33, rightly observes that the epithet *spectabilis* is probably not a later interpolation, but the earliest known occurrence of a title which was more frequently applied to persons of the second senatorial rank in the late fourth century. The name Aelius Paulinus is superseded by that of Aelianus in this document; since Aelianus took over Verus' functions when the latter fell ill, Maier suggests that the latter's full name was Aelius Paulinus Verus.

[6] That is, governing the diocese of African provinces rather than the proconsular province. For the date see n. 13.

[7] The notary is a stenographer, according to Lepelley (1982) p. 226. He thus creates the records which are said to be preserved by the secretraries (*exceptores*) in Appendix 1. The notary appears to have served the court, while scribes such as Miccius and Ingentius served the magistrate and the exceptores served the city itself. See further n. 13 and

that time has passed away, you will have to carry with you all the acts of your administration in faithful accord with the letter of my Lord as aforesaid, and it will also be necessary to travel to the colony of the Carthaginians[8] with your scribe. The curator[9] is present, and in his presence we compel you. What is your reply to this?"

Caecilianus said, "As soon as you brought to me the letter of the illustrious Aelius Paulinus when exercising the prefecture as *vicarius*, I sent forthwith to the scribe Miccius, bidding him come to bring me the proceedings written at that time, and he has been making inquiries up to the present. And since it is no small time since I held the office of *duovir*[10] - it is eleven years - I shall comply with this high injunction when he has found them." The *duovir* Gallienus said, "It is your duty to comply with the command; for you know that the command is sacred".[11] Caecilianus said, "I am bound to your high injunction."

2. Further, when shortly after the scribe Miccius had arrived, the *duovir* Fuscius said, "You also have heard, Miccius, that you as well as Caecilianus are under the necessity of going to the office of the vicarius, so that you may take with you the decision of that time. What do you say to this?" Miccius replied, "At the end of the year, the magistrate took all his proceedings to his own home"....[12]

3. "I am inquiring whether the wax records of them can be found". And when he inquired, the *duovir* Quintus Sisenna said, "What the office knew it has stated in reply".[13] Apronianus said, "If the magistrate

---

Appendix 1.5.

[8] *Coloniae* were originally settlements of Romans, but by the third century the status was largely titular. It was held to be more desirable than that of a *municipium*, especially when conjoined (as in Carthage, Leptis Magna and Utica) with the *jus Italicum*, which exempted it from land-tax and perhaps the poll-tax also. See Sherwin-White (1973) pp. 216-8.

[9] That is, either Calibius Junior or Callidius Gratianus. See Book 1.27 and notes thereon.

[10] That is, he held it in 303/4 A.D, and the date of the present Acts is therefore 314 or 315.

[11] Maier (1987), p. 176 n. 34 claims that the sanctity of the command lies in its coming ultimately from the Emperor himself; but Corcoran (1996) p. 170 observes that the Greek equivalent *theion* is used in Egypt for edicts of the prefect.

[12] A lacuna is indicated in Ziwsa's text, and we therefore have no explanation for this (evidently unusual) proceeding.

[13] The *officium* which is under the authority of Sisenna may consist merely of the *exceptores* (Appendix 1.5).

had taken away all his own proceedings, where, after so long a time, {shall we find} the proceedings which were published or written then?" And when he spoke, the proconsul Aelianus[14] said, "Both my interrogation and the replies of individuals are contained in the proceedings." Agesilaus said, "There are also other letters germane to this case; it is appropriate that they be read". The proconsul Aelianus said, "Let them be read in the hearing of Caecilianus, so that he may acknowledge whether he himself dictated them."

4. Agesilaus read aloud: **In the consulship of |Volusianus| and Annianus, 14 days before the Kalends of September,[15] in judicial proceedings before Aurelius Didymus Speretius the priest of Jupiter Optimus Maximus,[16]** *duovir* **of the distinguished colony of the Carthaginians, Maximus said, 'I speak in the name of the senior figures of the Christian people under the catholic religion. Before the Most High Emperors a case will be brought against Felix and Caecilian, who are trying with all their might to usurp the primacy of the same religion.[17] Against them records of his crime are being sought out. For when an edict of persecution had been issued against the Christians, namely that they should sacrifice or hand over to the flames whatever scriptures they possessed, Felix, who**

---

14 See note 5 above. On the likelihood that the proconsulate of Aelianus ran from 313 to 315 see Barnes (1982) p. 170

[15] That is, August 19 314 A.D if the insertion of Volusianus' name is accepted. On the acts of this consulate, one of the last not to include either Emperor, see Corcoran (1996) pp. 303-5. Appendices 3, 4 and 5 will also fall under this year. Augustine, *Post Gesta* 56 gives a date of 15th February under these consuls for the acquittal of Felix, but Maier (1987), pp. 171-2 argues that he was referring to their postconsular year. In that case the trial was a long one, running from August 314 to Feb 315.

[16] Jupiter Optimus Maximus is the highest cult-title, and in Carthage, as in Rome, the holding of his priesthood is combined with distinguished political office. Speretus appears as *duovir* in the current proceedings; Maximus (who appears by mistake for Apronianus in Augustine, Epistle 88.4), was also present at the later proceedings, so that those under Aelianus, now being read, must have happened only a little earlier.

[17] The intended appeal must be to Constantine and Licinius (though the presence of the latter will be notional) but was not heard in the aftermath of the Council of Arles (see Appendices 5 and 6). It appears that the accusers wished to go directly to the Emperor (either in Rome or Africa), but were required to submit to a preliminary hearing. See Corcoran (1996), pp. 216-8 on Constantine's attempts to restrict direct appeals.

was then Bishop of Abthugni,[18] had vouchsafed consent that scriptures should be handed over by the hand of Galatius so that they might be burnt by fire. And at that time the magistrate was Alfius Caecilianus, whose presence may it please you to notice. And since he bore at that time the duty of ensuring that all should sacrifice according to the proconsular edict,[19] and if any had scriptures they should present them according to the sacred religion, I request, as he is present and you see him to be an old man and he cannot come to the sacred court,[20] that he may testify in the proceedings, whether he did indeed, as his own proceedings show, give a letter by agreement, and whether what is contained in the letter is true, so that the certified proceedings may be disclosed at the sacred tribunal.

The *duovir* Speretius said to Caecilianus, who was present, "Do you hear what is testified in the proceedings?" Alfius Caecilianus said, "I had gone to Zama with Saturninus to procure linen, and when we came there the Christians themselves sent people to me in the praetorium[21] to say, "Has the sacred command reached you?". I said, "No, but I have already seen tokens of it, both the destruction of basilicae[22] at Zama and Furnae and the burning of scriptures. Therefore set out, if you have any scriptures, to comply with the sacred command." Then they sent people to the house of Bishop Felix, to take scriptures from it so that they could be burned according to the sacred command. So Galatius proceeded with me to the place where prayers had been customarily offered. We took the throne from there and the letters of greeting, and

---

[18] Maier (1987), p. 177 n.44 raises the question of whether this reference to Felix in the past tense indicates that he was dead. He was absent in 314/5 (Augustine, *Breviculus* III.42), but *tunc* here merely indicates the cause of his prominence in 303.

[19] The imperial decree of Feb 24 303, requiring destruction of churches and Scriptures, had to be promulgated in the province by the proconsul, and then enforced by minor officials. See further Corcoran (1996) p. 180 and n. 43.

[20] The *comitatus* is here the imperial court, to which the Donatists wished to appeal. On its sanctity see n. 11 above.

[21] The word *praetorium*, once a general's camp, had come to signify the residence of a provincial governor, though it was also used of the Emperor's bodyguard.

[22] Maier (1987), p. 178 n. 51, remarks that this is the earliest occurrence of the term in a document.

all the doors were burnt in accordance with the sacred command.[23] And when we sent to the house of the same Bishop Felix, the public officials announed that he was absent. For at a later time, on the arrival of Ingentius, scribe of Augentius with whom I administered the aedileship,[24] I dictated a letter to this same colleague, which I had sent to the same Bishop Felix." Maximus said, "He is present; let the same letter be presented to him. so that he may acknowledge it as the same". He replied, "It is the same". Maximus said, "Since he has acknowledged his own letter, I say and request that the full text be inserted in the proceedings". And he recited:

5. **Greetings from Caecilianus to his father Felix![25] When Ingentius came to his friend my colleague Augentius and inquired whether in the year of my *duovir*ate any scriptures of your religion were burnt in accordance with the sacred law[26] ..... after my servant Galatius, of your religion, had publicly taken the letters of greeting out of the church. With good wishes, farewell.' This is the seal, which the Christians, and the same person whose praetorium it is, sent to me in intercession[27] and you said, 'Take the key, and take any books that you find on the throne and any codices on the stone. Take good care that the officials do not take oil and grain.' And I said to you, 'Do you not know that, where the scriptures are found, the house itself is destroyed?' And you said, 'What are we to do then?' And I said to you, 'Let one of your people take them to the area where you make your prayers,[28] and let them be deposited**

---

[23] Maier (1987), p. 179 follows Von Soden in amending to "before all the doors"; but he also quotes Lepelley (1979), p. 338 on the burning of church doors in Egypt. I have therefore thought it best to translate Ziwsa's text as it stands.

[24] Ingentius was decurion of Ziqua in 313/4. The office of aedile is now equivalent to that of *duovir*.

[25] As an honorific, the title is strange, as Alfius Caecilianus does not profess to be a Christian. The problem would not be solved, however, if, following a tentative suggestion of Maier (1987), p. 179 n.56, we take Felix to have been his natural father, since (a) the references to "your religion" then become absurdly cold; and (b) the evidence of Caecilianus here would be compromised if he were actuated by filial piety.

[26] A lacuna is indicated here by Ziwsa.

[27] Ziwsa indicates no lacuna here, but a subsequent passage shows that there is one, which is not eliminated even there (n. 39 below). We have the right to entertain a suspicion of subsequent tampering by parties friendly to Felix.

[28] Maier (1987) p. 180 n. 57 argues that the word *area* denotes a cemetery.

there. And I shall come with the officials and take them.' And we came there and took everything in accordance with the sacred command.

Maximus said, "Since the reading of this letter, which he himself admits to having sent, has been recorded in the proceedings, I request that what he has said should stay in the proceedings." The *duovir* Speretius said, "What you have said has been written down."

6. Agesilaus said, "He has acknowledged the present letter. The remaining part, which he is now reading, he declares to be false." Caecilianus said, "My Lord, I dictated up to this point where it has, 'With good wishes, dearest father, farewell."

Apronianus said, "Such falsification, through terror, through duplicity, through irreligious attitudes, is always the way of those who refuse to agree with the catholic church. For when Paulinus was holding the office of vice-prefect here,[29] a certain private man was suborned, with the pittance of a courier, to go to those [faithful] in the catholic faith and cajole and intimidate them. Therefore the conspiracy was exposed. For there was a lying plot against Felix the most pious bishop to make him appear to have handed over and burnt sacred scriptures. Since, indeed, all of these doings were prejudicial to the sanctity and piety of Caecilian, Ingentius was suborned to go with a letter supposedly from Bishop Felix to Caecilianus the *duovir* and pretend to him that he had been commissioned by Felix.[30] Let him say the very words of this fabrication". The proconsul Aelianus said, "Speak".

7. Apronianus said, **'Tell my friend Caecilianus', he says, that I have received eleven precious holy codices, and because it now behoves me to restore them, say that in the year of your magistracy you burnt them, so that I need not return them'. Therefore you must inquire of Ingentius about this matter, how far this intrigue and fabrication went, and how far he wanted to implicate a magistrate in a lie, so that he might stain Felix with infamy. Let him say who sent him, but also if this intrigue against the conscience of Felix .... by which he might detract from the honour**

---

[29] That is, Aelius Paulinus held the office of *vicarius*.
[30] The first is the Bishop, the second the magistrate.

of Caecilian.[31] **For there is a certain man who was sent as a legate through Mauritania and Numidia from the opposite party.**

8. And, Ingentius being present, the proconsul Aelianus said, "At whose bidding did you undertake to do these acts of which you are accused?" Ingentius said, "Where?" The Proconsul Aelianus said, "Since you pretend not to understand what is asked of you, I shall speak more plainly: who sent you to Caecilianus the magistrate?" Ingentius said, "No-one sent me." The proconsul Aelianus said, "Then how was it that you went to the magistrate Caecilianus?" Ingentius said, "When we had come and the case of Maurus the Bishop of Utica,[32] who had bought back his bishopric, was in progress, Felix the Bishop of Abthugni came up to the city to take part, and said, 'Let no-one communicate, because he has admitted a falsehood'. And I said in opposition to him, 'Neither with him nor with you, since you are a collaborator.' For I grieved for the cause of Maurus my host, since in evading persecution I had communicated with him in great jeopardy. Thereafter I went to the territory of that same Felix, and took with me three seniors,[33] so that they could see whether he had truly collaborated or not."

Apronianus said, "It is not so, he went to Caecilianus. Ask Caecilianus." The proconsul Aelianus said to Caecilianus, "How was it that Ingentius came to you?" Caecilianus replied, "He came to me at home; I was dining with my staff. He came there, he stood in the doorway. He said, 'Where is Caecilianus?" I replied 'Here'. I say to him, 'What is it? Is all well?'. 'All, " he says. I replied to him, "If it does not displease you to dine, come and dine.' He says to me, 'I shall return here.' He came there alone. He began to say to me, 'See that you take note of me',[34] and to inquire whether the scripture had been burnt

[31]I.e. the Bishop. Allegations of fabrication were frequent in the fourth century (see Rufinus, *De Adulteratione Librorum Origenis*).

[32] The name of Maurus is otherwise unknown, the charges against him illustrate the rigour of Christian policy at this time.

[33] For the *seniores* cf Optatus I.17. Maier (1987), p. 224 n. 81 defines these as "notables of the comunity". The antiquity of the office is shown by Tertullian, *Apologeticum* 39.4, while Augustine, Epistle 78 asserts that they precede the *plebs* but rank below the clerics. Cf Acts 7.3 for the civic use of the term, and for the views of scholars see Rankin (1995), pp. 139-41..

[34] Translating *ecce sic mihi curare*, on the assumption that, here as elsewhere, the spoken Latin is ungrammatical. However, Ziwsa indicates a lacuna in the middle of *curare*.

in the year of my magistracy.[35] I say to him, 'You are obnoxious to me, you are a corrupted man, relieve me of your presence here.' And I spurned him from me. And he came, repeating this, with my colleague, with whom I had been aedile. My colleague says to me, ""Our bishop Felix had sent a man here so that you may produce a letter for him, since he has received codices and does want them taken back. Could you write to him that they were burnt in the year of your *duovir*ate.' And I said, 'Is this the truthfulness of Christians?'[36]

Ingentius said, "My Lord, let Augentius come. And I am honourable, and stake my honour that I have his letter."[37] The proconsul Aelianus said, "You are refuted on another point." The proconsul Aelianus said to his officer, "Make him ready". And when he was ready, the proconsul Aelianus said, "Suspend him." And when he had been suspended, the proconsul Aelianus said to Caecilianus, "How was it that Ingentius came to you?" He replied, "He said, 'Our Felix has sent me here so that you may write to him, since (he says) there is some worthless good-for-nothing who owns extremely precious codices in my possession and I do not wish to restore them. And so produce a letter for me saying that they have been burnt, so that he will not ask for them back.' And I said, 'Is this the truthfulness of Christians?' And I began to chastise him, and my colleague says, "Write to that Felix of ours". And so I dictated the letter which is in evidence, as far as I dictated it."

9. The proconsul Aelianus said, "Do not be afraid to hear the reading of your letter; acknowledge up to what point you dictated it." Agesilaus read aloud ....[38] **With wishes for a long life, farewell, most beloved father**. The proconsul Aelianus said to Caecilianus, "Did you dictate up to this point?" He replied, "Up to this point; the rest is false". Agesilaus

---

[35] Maier (1987) p. 183 n, 64 believes that this phrase is still in the mouth of Ingentius, and therefore that it should refer to "your magistracy". He believes that Caecilianus himself is guilty of a strange lapse of the tongue. But Caecilianus would not need to make any such inquiry.

[36] Or "faith (*fides*) of Christians " - a pagan testimony (ironic or otherwise) to the known virtues of the sect.

[37] Reading *litteras*, with Masson in Ziwsa's *apparatus*. But Maier retains the MS *latera*, translating "entourage".

[38] Here the lacuna indicates the weariness of the scribe rather than the corruption of the text.

read aloud, With this seal which you have sent to me in intercession[39]
.... except myself and you and he who owns the palace and said,
"Take the key and whatever books you find on the throne and
whatever codices on the stone, take those. Take good care that the
officials do not take oil and grain." And I said to him, "Do you not
know that where the scriptures are found, the very house is
destroyed?" And you said, "What are we to do then?" And I said
to you, "Let one of you take them to the area where you make your
prayers and deposit them there, and I shall come with officials and
take them. And [we came there] and took everything according to
the agreement and burnt them according to the sacred command.

Maximus said, "Since the gist of this letter has been recited also in
the proceedings which he himself says he acknowledged and sent, we
request that this remain in your proceedings." Speretius said, "What you
have said has been written down". Caecilianus said, "From that point it
is false; my letter goes up to the point where I said, 'Farewell, most
beloved father.'" The proconsul Aelianus said, "Whom do you allege to
have added to the letter?" Caecilianus said, "Ingentius." The proconsul
Aelianus said, "Let your testimony remain in the proceedings."

10. The proconsul Aelianus said to Ingentius, "You will be tortured
to prevent you from lying."[40] Ingentius said, "I have made a mistake, I
added to this letter because of my grief over the cause of Maurus my
host." The proconsul Aelianus said, "[Constantinus] Maximus ever
Augustus and Licinius the Caesars have deigned to show such piety to
the Christians that they do not wish the way of life to be corrupted, but
rather desire that this form of worship be observed and practised.[41] So

---

[39] See n. 21 above; the words "except myself and you" appear here only, though Maier
inserts them in the previous passge. The author is enjoining secrecy on his correspondent.
[40] Torture was used regularly in Roman courts even under Christian Emperors: see
Augustine, *De Civitate Dei* XIX.6. Diocletian's law exempting decurions from the practice
is quoted at *Codex Justinianum* IX.47.11. Lactantius, *De Mortibus Persecutorum* 21.3
alleges that Galerius introduced new and less discriminating forms. See Corcoran (1996),
p. 104 n. 78 and pp. 250-252; and on the place of torture in Donatist martyrologies see
Tilley (1996), pp. xxxiii-xxxvi.
[41] Cf the letter of Licinius and Constantine at Lactantius, *De Mortibus Persecutorum* 48,
which constitutes the so-called "Edict of Milan" in 313. Aelianus here makes no
distinction between the terms Caesar and Augustus; cf the edict of Galerius, Licinius and
Constantine at Eusebius, *HE* VIII.17.

do not flatter yourself that when you tell me that you are a worshipper of God you cannot therefore be tortured. You will be tortured to prevent you from lying, which appears to be foreign to Christians.[42] And so speak straightforwardly, so that you will not be tortured." Ingentius said, "I have already confessed without torture." Apronianus said, "May it please you to inquire of him by what authority, what treachery, what madness, he went around all the Mauritianian provinces and the Numidian ones too; for what cause he excited sedition against the catholic church. The proconsul Aelianus said, "Were you in Numidia?" He replied, "No, My Lord; let someone prove it." The proconsul Aelianus said, "Nor in Mauritania?" He replied, "I was on business there." Apronianus said, "And here too he lies, My Lord, insofar as he says that he was in Mauritania but not in Numidia; for one cannot reach the Mauritianian territory except through Numidia."

The proconsul Aelianus said to Ingentius, "What is your rank?" Ingentius replied, "I am a decurion of Ziqua".[43] The proconsul Aelianus said to his officers, "Let him down." When he had been let down, the proconsul Aelianus said to Caecilianus, "What you have said is false". Caecilianus said, "No, My Lord. The one who wrote the letter, bid him come; he is a friend of this man, let him say himself up to what point I dictated the letter." The proconsul Aelianus said, "Who is this whose presence you desire?" Caecilianus said, "Augentius, with whom I was aedile." I cannot prove it except through Augentius himself, who wrote the letter. He himself can say up to what point I dictated it to him." The proconsul Aelianus said, "Then it is maintained that the letter is false?" Caecilianus replied, "It is maintained, My Lord, I do not lie, on my life!" The proconsul Aelianus said, "Since you exercised the *duovir*ate in your own territory, your words ought to be trusted."

Apronianus said, "It is nothing new for them to do this; on the contrary they have added what they wanted to proceedings also. They

---

[42] Possibly an ironic taunt, rather than, as Maier suggests, a pagan testimony to Christian virtue. Cf n. 36.

[43] That is, a *duovir*. While this may exempt him temporarily from torture, it does not lead his word to be valued equally with that of Caecilianus, as he has already admitted a lie. Donatists cited the torture of Ingentius as an example of catholic brutality (Augustine, Epistle 43.13).

have a lot of skill. The proconsul Aelianus said,[44] "From the testimony of Caecilianus, who says that the proceedings have been falsified and many things added to his letter, it has been made plain what Ingentius intended by doing this. And so let him be remanded in prison, for he requires a stricter interrogation. As to Felix the most pious bishop, it is plain that he is acquitted of burning the holy instruments, as no-one has been able to prove anything against him as to his handing over or burning the most sacred scriptures. For the interrogation of all [witnesses] recorded above has made it plain that no scriptures were found or damaged or burnt. The record in the acts is that Felix the pious bishop neither was present nor took cognizance nor ordered anything of the kind to be done."

Agesilaus said, "What does your highness command concerning those who came as instruments of your authority?"The proconsul Aelianus said, "Let them return to their own abodes.

---

[44] For this summary cf Augustine, *Cresc.* III.80.

APPENDIX THREE:

Constantine Augustus to Aelafius[1]

Already before this, when it had been brought to my knowledge that many in our province of Africa had started to separate, with rabid anger and vain recriminations against one another, over the observation of the most sacred catholic religion, I had decreed, in order to put an end to such dissension, not only that the Carthaginian Bishop Caecilian, who had in all cases been the particular object of the frequent approaches to me, should come to Rome, but also that some of those who believed that certain charges ought to be made against him should appear in person. For I had already commanded certain bishops to come to the aforesaid city of Rome from among the Gallic provinces, so that not only these, on account of their integrity of life and praiseworthy teaching, together with seven of the same communion,[2] but also the Bishops of the city of Rome[3] and those who would undertake the inquiry with these, should be able to bring the proper honesty to an affair which seemed to be in turmoil; whatever had been done in the presence of these men, they brought the whole of it to my knowledge,

---

[1]Aelafius is otherwise unknow, his name is curious, and it is hard to find place for him among the known *vicarii* of Africa. For the view that his name is impossible, and a corruption of Aelius Paulinus, see Barnes (1982) p. 145 n. 18. Against this see now Corcoran (1996) p. 331, citing the name Elaphius from a later inscription. For other discussions see Mazzucco (1993), pp. 50-4. The overt Christianity of the last sentence should be contrasted with the discretion of the closing words in Appendix 7; Aelafius, if this letter is genuine, must have been a Christian.

[2] Turner (1925-6) p. 286 makes the plausible suggestion that this phrase should be transferred to an earlier sentence, so as to read "Caecilian, and seven others of his own communion, but also" etc. This would imply that each party was represented by seven Bishops, just as Constantine's letter to Miltiades announcing the convention of the previous council (Eusebius, *HE* V.21) refers to ten on each side.

[3] Maier (1987) p. 154 n. 9 endorses the conjecture of Calderone (1962), pp. 234-41, that this refers to all the bishops who assembled at Rome in 313. Rome itself had (by this time) only one Bishop, yet Constantine's letter to Miltiades (Eusebius, *HE.* X.21) also addresses a certain Marcus, who may be a suffragan or a successor. Turner (1925-6) p. 285, adds the suggestion that the bishops of the Roman city may be those ordained in Rome.

having also compiled proceedings and furthermore giving their sworn word that their verdict had been given in accordance with the equitable judgment of the case, and they said that those who had thought good to raise certain charges against Caecilian were so much the more guilty that they were forbidding these men to return to Africa after this verdict had been pronounced.[4] Therefore after all this I had hoped, on a plausible reading of the matter, that the proper end had been imposed on the seditions and contentions which appeared to have been excited in an instant by other men.[5]

But when I had read what was written about these intrigues at your dictation,[6] which Your eminence had thought proper to send to Nicasius and others,[7] I found it evident that they declined to have before their eyes either respect for their own safety or, what is more, the worship of Almighty God, seeing that they persist in those actions which not only bring themselves dishonour and infamy, but also give occasion for detraction to those whose thoughts are known to be turned far away from this most sacred form of religion. For it behoves you to know also that certain of these men came asserting that the same Caecilian should not be deemed such a worthy minister of the most sacred religion, and after I replied to them that they made these representations in vain, since the same case had been decided in the city of Rome by competent and very honest men of episcopal status, they saw fit to reply to this, in a stubborn and pertinacious manner, that the whole case had not been heard, and that the same bishops had rather locked themselves up in a certain place and reached the verdict most amenable to themselves.

---

[4] Maier (1987) observes that there is no record of this prohibition elsewhere. According to Augustine, Epistle 43.16, "Melchiades" (sc. Miltiades) had ruled at Rome that whichever Bishop was appointed first in a given diocese should remain there while the other was given a bishopric elsewhere.

[5] Cf Constantine to Chrestus, Eusebius, *HE* X.5.21.

[6] Corcoran (1996) p. 168 notes this as an unusual testimony to dictation by an official; Turner (1925-6) p. 287 suggests, however, that *dictationis* should read *dicationis*, i.e. "the letter belonging to your jurisdiction". Aelafius is not addressed by any title at the opening of the letter, but Constantine now goes on to address him as *Gravitas tua*, which, as Corcoran (1996) pp. 329-30 shows, is frequent in Constantine's letters of this period to prefects and *vicarii*, though it is also used to lesser functionaries, including Numidian Bishops in Appendix 10.

[7] Nicasius has been identified as an imperial notary, a deacon at Arles and a Bishop at Nicaea: Corcoran (1996) p. 168 n. 217.

When, therefore, I saw that the number and magnitude of these claims was prolonging the disputes with such excessive stubbornnness that it seemed in no way possible to put an end to them unless both the said Caecilian and some three of those who are in disagreement with him should consent to come to the Council at Arles for the judgment of those who are hostile to Caecilian: I thought that I should enjoin on your attention that, as soon as you receive this letter, not only the aforesaid Caecilian with some of those whom he himself may choose - together with several persons from the provinces of Byzacena, Tripolitana, Numidia and Mauritania, who should also bring some of their own party with them, whom they themselves think fit to choose - but also some of those who are in disagreement with Caecilian, public transport having been provided throughout Africa and Mauritania, should at your instance sail thence to Spain in a short space of time, and that thereafter you should nonetheless furnish several modes of transport for these bishops severally, so that they may be able, before the first of August, to arrive at the aforesaid place; and that you should quickly admonish them that they ought, before they set out, to arrange that in their absence an adequate discipline shall be maintained, and that there shall be no chance of any sedition or controversy caused by certain persons in dispute, which tends to the greatest dishonour.

Let an end be made in secret after full discussion,[8] that when all have made their appearance, the things which are now known to be in dispute and fully deserve to receive a timely end, may be finished and settled with all dispatch. For since I have been informed that you are also a worshipper of the Most High God,[9] I confess to your eminence that I think it in no way right that such disputes and altercations should be concealed from us, when they might perhaps arouse the highest deity not only agsint the human race, but also against myself, to whose care he has by his celestial nod committed the regulation of all things

---

[8] Translating Ziwsa's *de secreto*; but his *apparatus* suggests *de cetero*, "as to the rest". The text could also be rendered "Let an end be made after full discussion has been held in secret".

[9] It is wrong to say, with Maier (1987) p. 157 n. 19 that Constantine is not yet a Christian. At this point he might be appealing merely to common ground between himself and a pagan magistrate; but the last sentence makes his motives, and the (supposed) religion of his correspondent, plain enough.

earthly,[10] and might decree something different if so provoked. For only then shall true and full security be possible for me, and a hope of the best and most prosperous outcome always and in everything from the unstinting benevolence of the most almighty God, when I am aware that all men worship the most holy God by the due rites of the catholic religion in harmonious and brotherly observance. Amen.

---

[10] Ever since Homer (*Iliad* I.528) the *nod* had been the attribute of divine command. *Panegyrici Latini* VII (VI) had ascribed the commanding nod to Constantine's (then senior) partner Maximian in 308 A.D. In his panegyric of 336 A.D. on Constantine, the *Triacontericus*, Eusebius insinuates identity between God's rule and that of Constantine by ascribing it both to God (p. 198.12 Heikel, 251.11) and to Constantine (217.14).

APPENDIX FOUR:

Letter from the Council of Bishops at Arles to Silvester of Rome[1]

Eternal greetings in the Lord to Pope Silvester from Marinus, Acratius, Natalis, Theodorus, Proterius, Vocius, Verus, Probatius, Caecilianus, Faustinus, Surgentius, Gregorius, Reticius, Ambitausus, Termatius, Merocles, Pardus, Adelfius, Hibernius, Fortunatus, Aristasius, Lampadius, Vitalis, Maternus, Liberius, Gregorius, Crescens, Avitianus, Daphnus, Orantalis, Quintasius, Victor, Epictetus.[2]

Having been summoned to the city of Arles by the will of the most pious Emperor, remaining in the common bond of love and linked by the unity of the catholic church our mother,[3] we therefore greet you, most exalted Pope, with becoming reverence. When we suffered the great and pernicious injury to our religion and tradition, and men of unbridled mind, who were so abhorrent both to the present sovereignty of our God and the tradition and rule of truth that they neither had any rational ground of speech or any proper mode of accusation of proof: so it was that by the judgment of God and the mother Church, who knows and approves her own,[4] they have been either condemned or expelled. And we wish, most beloved brother, that you had thought so important a spectacle as this important enough for your attendance! We do indeed believe that a more severe sentence would have been passed upon them, and that if you had given judgment along with us our assembly would have rejoiced with more delight!

---

[1] Silvester, supposed recipient of the forged "Donation of Constantine" which granted land and authority to his church, was Bishop from 31 Jan 314 to 31 Dec 335. Maier (1987), p. 161 n.5 suggests that his recent succession was the cause of his absence; more probably, like many Popes after him, he declined to submit his rulings to a council. He was also absent from the Council of Nicaea in 325.

[2] Marinus, as Bishop of Arles, would be president; cf Optatus I.25, where Reticius, Maternus and Merocles also appear as members of the previous Roman session. The list does not include Chrestus of Syracuse, though the letter summoning him is recorded by Eusebius, *HE* X.5.

[3] For the church as mother cf Optatus II.9. The title Papa ("Pope") was also given to holders of such patriarchal sees as Carthage and Alexandria at this time.

[4] Cf 2Tim 2.19; John 10.14.

But seeing that it was quite impossible for you to leave that region in which the Apostles sit daily and their blood incessantly testifies to the glory of God,[5] we have not, however, seen fit to treat only those matters for which we were invited, most beloved brother, but we reckoned that we should to take counsel among ourselves also, and since the provinces from which we have come are diverse,[6] equally various are the matters on which we reckoned that there ought to be a ruling. We therefore decided, in the presence of the Holy Spirit and his angels,[7] that we should bring forth for adjudication in the present time of peace[8] those matters which were of concern to each several person; we also decided that before this we should write to you, who hold the major dioceses,[9] that your voice would be most effectual in inducing a common decision. What our own opinion was we have, however, subjoined, in all humility, to our record.

And it seemed that with regard to our life and welfare the first matter to be treated was when one alone had died and risen for all,[10] this time should be observed by all with pious minds in such a way that neither divisions nor dissensions would be able to arise in such a great duty of

---

[5] On Rome's apostolic status see Ignatius, *Romans* 4.3, Irenaeus, *AH* III.3.2 etc. The veneration of Apostles there is emphasised in Pope Celestine's letter to the Ephesian Council of 431.

[6] Enumerated in the previous letter: Byzacena, Numidia, Tripolis, Mauritania, Africa, the Spains, the Gauls.

[7] Cf Acts 15.28.

[8] So Ziwsa. Maier (1987) reads *quasi te consistente*, "as if you were here". But it seems to me that the bishops are reminding their obstinate brother that synodal discussions may be rare. (They were abolished in 321 by Constantine's eastern rival Licinius).

[9] Spelt in Latin *dioceses* transliterating the Greek. But this term, originally denoting a group of provinces governed by a *vicarius*, still signifies a group of ecclesiastical provinces in the second and sixth canons of Constantinople (381-2 A.D.). Here, if the text is good, it means a single province, and Miltiades governs a collection of such areas. Turner (1925-6) p. 286 proposes instead to read *annuente qui maiores dioceses tenet*, a reference to the approbation of the *vicarius*, or Constantine as "holder of the main [secular] dioceses of the Empire".

[10] 2Cor 5.14-15.

devotion. We therefore decree that the Lord's pasch should be celebrated on one day throughout the whole world.[11]

Also, concerning those who in each place have been ordained as ministers, they shall remain in the same place.[12]

Now concerning those who brandish arms in peacetime; we decided that they should be barred from communion.[13]

As to the drivers in circuses who are believers, as long as they drive, they are to be separated from communion.[14]

As to theatre-performers, we decided that they should be separated from communion as long as they perform.[15]

Concerning those who are in an infirm condition and wish to profess belief, we decided that hands should be laid upon them.[16]

Now as to magistrates who are believers and accede to the magistracy,[17] our decision was that when they have been appointed, they should

[11] Pasch, the Jewish name for the passover, was applied to Easter, often with a false etymology from the Greek *paskhein*, "to suffer". On the importance of the Easter question to Constantine, and its settlement after the Council of Nicaea in 325, see Eusebius, *VC* III.5 and 14. Constantine's councils always favour the Roman date, whereas Irenaeus (Eusebius, *HE* V.24) had advised Pope Victor to respect the Asiatics.

[12] Cf canon 15 of Nicaea (325), where translation of bishops is said to contravene an ancient rule and excite disorder. Such canons aimed both at suppression of ecclesiastical strife and at the restraint of worldly motives. See Bright (1882), pp. 47-51.

[13] As Maier (1987), p. 164 n. 15 notes, this passage has often been rendered, "those who lay down their arms in a time of peace", i.e. it is taken as condemning Christian pacifism in a time of religious toleration. But Constantine had not fought a campaign since becoming a Christian, and in the light of the Donatist troubles, I prefer a different rendering.

[14] Constantine allowed circuses in Constantinople, and later councils do no more than restrict celebration and attendance (e.g. Trullo (692), canons 34 and 66). But this canon is in keeping with Tertullian, *De Spectaculis* 7.2, where the circuses are denounced as seats of idolatry, and with Hippolytus, *Apostolic Tradition* p. 25 Chadwick and Dix, where even those who attend the circuses are excommunicated.

[15] Cf Tertullian, *De Spectaculis* 10 and canon 51 of Trullo (692), forbidding clerics and laymen to perform theatrical dances. No doubt the reason was that they provoked sexual immorality.

[16] No doubt because they could not undergo the rigours of a baptism by immersion and would lack time for preparation.

[17] Maier (1987) p. 164 n.17 remarks that this canon applies especially to one who leaves his own province to become governor of another. While it was the duty of a magistrate to swear by pagan gods and administer brutal laws without God's sanction, the exercise of such office could hardly be free of sin.

indeed receive a communicatory letter from the clergy, but on the understanding that, in whatever place they exercise offcie, they should be supervised by the bishops of the same place, and if they begin to flout discipline, only then they should they be excluded from communion. And likewise as to those who wish to hold state offices. Now as to Africa, we decided that they should use their own custom of rebaptizing in such a way that, if any heretic comes to the church, they should ask what his creed is: and if they see that he was baptized in (the name of) Father and Son and Holy Ghost,[18] they should merely lay hands upon him; but if on being asked his creed he does not affirm this Trinity in reply, let him rightly undergo baptism and the rest.

Then {?the Emperor},[19] growing weary, bade all return to their own abodes. Amen.

---

[18] The "seventh canon" of Constantinople (381) implies that the Trinitarian formula is sufficient to constitute a valid baptism, even at the hands of heretics. However, Bright (1882) pp. 104-8, shows that this ruling may be no earlier than the 95th canon of Trullo (692). In view of the counter-precedent set by Cyprian, it is remarkable that the west should receive this principle before the east.

[19] The official is not named, but Eusebius, *VC* I.44, speaks of the Emperor sitting in the midst of a synod, surrounded by his friends and rejoicing in the concord of his Church.

APPENDIX FIVE:

Letter of Constantine to the catholic Bishops[1]

Greetings from Constantine Augustus to the Bishops his most beloved catholic brethren! The eternal and incomprehensible goodness of our God will by no means allow the human condition to carry on straying in error, nor does it permit the abhorrent wishes of certain men to prevail to such a degree that he fails to open up for them with his most brilliant beams a way of salvation by which they may be converted to the rule of righteousness. This indeed I have learnt by many examples, but I measure these by myself.[2] For there were initially in me many obvious defects in righteousness, nor did I believe that the supernal power saw any of those things that I did in the secrecy of my heart. So then, what lot awaited these offences of which I have spoken? Obviously that which abounds with all ills. But Almighty God who sits in the vantage-point of heaven bestowed upon me what I did not deserve; it is certainly impossible to tell or enumerate those benefits that his heavenly benevolence has vouchsafed to his servant. Most reverend bishops of Christ our Saviour[3], beloved brethren![4] I therefore rejoice indeed, and rejoice especially that, after having at last delivered your most righteous verdict, you have recalled to a better hope and destiny those whom the malignity of the devil seemed to have diverted by his contemptible persuasion from the exceeding brilliance of the catholic religion.

Oh truly victorious providence of Christ our Saviour, that it should even care for those who, repudiating truth and in a manner taking up

---

[1] Written after the Council of Arles, in connexion with the intended appeal to Constantine against Felix (Appendix 2.4). Augustine records that Caecilian was called to Rome, then to Milan when he failed to appear (Epistle 43.20; cf Optatus 1.25).

[2] Cf *Orat.* 11, where Constantine expresses the wish that he had been raised a Christian.

[3] Maier (1987) p. 168 n.5 remarks that this is the earliest appearance of Christ's name in a letter of Constantine. The word for "bishops" is *antistites*, used in the Vulgate (2Chron 29.34) of Israelite priests.

[4]. The address *fratres carissimi* ("beloved brethren") is typical of, but not unique to, Constantine's correspondence with Christian dignitaries: see Corcoran (1996) p. 336.

arms against it, coupled themselves with the heathen;[5] in that, if even now they should wish by simple faith to take up the obligations of the most sacred religion, they may learn how much has been provided for them by the fiat of God. And this indeed, most reverend brothers, was my hope, that even where the greatest obduracy of mind was implanted, it would be susceptible of admonition.[6] But the equitable judgment was of no use to them, nor did the propitious divinity enter into their senses; for in very truth it was not without good cause that the mercy of Christ withdrew from these, in whom it is as clear as day that their madness is of such a kind that we find them abhorrent even to the heavenly dispensation; so great a madness persists in them when with incredible arrogance they persuade themselves of things that it is not right either to say or to hear, repudiating the equitable judgment that had been given, so that by the will of heaven, I have discovered that they demand my own judgment! So strong and persevering is the wickedness of these men! How often already have I myself suppressed their shameless approaches with the answer that they deserved! If they had kept this before their eyes, they would certainly not have made this application! They demand my judgment, when I myself await the judgment of Christ.[7] For I tell you, as is the truth, that the judgment of the priests should be regarded as if God himself were in the judge's seat.[8] For these have no power either to think or to judge except as they are instructed by Christ's teaching.

What then are they thinking of, these wicked men who, as I have truly said, are officers of the devil? Oh raging temerity of madness! Just as is wont to happen in the cases of the heathen,[9] they have made an application of appeal! It is true that the heathen, fleeing from a lesser tribunal, where justice can be soon obtained, are wont to betake themselves to an appeal, since authority intervenes more for greater

---

[5] Cf. Ezekiel 16.1ff etc. for this typical prophetic image.
[6] Cf. the complaints of obduracy before Arles: Appendix 3 n.4.
[7] Quoted inaccurately and out of place at Optatus I.23. Augustine, Epistle 43.13 regrets the Emperor's modesty.
[8] Cf Ignatius, *Trallians* 3.1 for an early anticipation of this view; the company at Arles had claimed the presence of the Spirit.
[9] Following 1Cor 6.1ff.

tribunals.[10] What are they doing, these slanderers of religion, who refusing the judgment of heaven have thought fit to demand my judgment? Is that what they think of Christ our Saviour? See they are already traitors, without any further examination they themselves, and through themselves, have betrayed their own offences. What is their opinion of humanity,[11] when they have ruthlessly assaulted God himself?

And yet, most beloved brethren, albeit they are openly convicted of these things, you who follow the way of the Lord must none the less exercise patience, giving them even now the choice of what they think should be preferred. And if you see that they persist in these ways, set out forthwith with those whom God had adjudged worthy to revere him, and return to your own abodes, and remember to pray for me that our Saviour will always have mercy on me. I, however, have directed men of mine to bring these unspeakable deceivers of religion to my court, so that they may stay there and there learn that death is worse for them.[12] I have also given an official letter to the man who maintains the prefecture in Africa as *vicarius*,[13] saying that, whatever men he finds to be of a like insanity he should send on to my court, so that, when our God has made the case so clear, they will not continue to do those things which may provoke heavenly providence to the greatest anger.[14] May Almighty God grant my prayers and yours for your safety through the ages, most beloved brethren.

---

[10] Emperors of this period preferred to have deputations addressed initially to provincial magistrates, but did not allow these magistrates to refuse appeal. See Millar (1977) p. 381ff.

[11] Or possibly: "what human feeling is left to them?".

[12] Literally, "see for themselves death worse". Maier translates, "learn that there is something worse than death for them".

[13] That is, Aelinus Paulinus, as in Appendix 2.

[14] Cf the comments to Aelafius at the end of Appendix 3.

APPENDIX SIX:

Constantine's letter to the Donatist Bishops[1]

Constantine Augustus to the bishops. In accordance with your request, I had decided after a few days that you should return to Africa, that there the whole case which you believe to stand against Caecilian may be investigated by friends of mine, whom I shall choose, and receive its due conclusion. But as I have considered long and turned the matter over in my mind as it deserves, it seemed to me best that - since I know that some of your party are great troublemakers and in your obstinacy of mind have very little respect for equitable judgment and the spirit of upright truth, coming here perhaps in the hope that, if the investigation takes place here[2] the end of the matter will not be that which is proper and demanded by the spirit of truth, and that through your excessive obstinacy the event will be such as displeases the heavenly divinity and greatly impair my own judgment, which I hope will remain forever unblemished - my decision, as I have said, is that it would be better for Caecilian to come here with regard to the issue previously handled, and I believe that in accordance with my letter he will soon arrive.[3] To you, however, I promise that if in his presence you by yourselves prove anything with respect to even one crime or offence, I shall act as though all the things that you allege against him were seen to be proved. May Almighty God give perpetual safety.[4]

---

[1] Maier (1987) refers to this letter, not to the immediate aftermath of Arles, but to the events described in Augustine, Epistle 43.20; it would appear that Caecilian is being summoned to Rome. Constantine may be responding to the Donatist appeal against Felix (see Appendix 5). He now renounces the project of travelling to Africa, mentioned in Appendix 7, and this letter is therefore to be dated later than August 315.

[2] *ibidem* ("there") refers to Africa.

[3] Augustine, *loc. cit.*, indicates that Caecilian stayed in Africa.

[4] Or "health". It is not clear to me whether Constantine is praying for his correspondents or his empire. The precept that the gods must be placated for the sake of the world is stressed in the rescript of the persecuting pagan Emperor Maximinus Daia (Eusebius, *HE.* IX.9.12), though in *Orat.* Constantine argued that the harmony of the world depends on there being only one divine being.

APPENDIX SEVEN:

Constantine to Celsus

To Celsus the *vicarius* of Africa.[1]

Maenalius,[2] who has long been in the grip of insanity, is obdurate, as are others who have departed from God's truth and given themselves most basely to error: so too your Eminence's most recent letter has testified, in which you have reported, most beloved brother,[3] that you were adhering to our orders concerning the proper handling of their contumacy and had been impeded by the tumult which they raised. Therefore - since their malignant intention is evident from the fact that, when I had decided to demand a full inquiry into the various charges at issue between them and Caecilian, they strove to make good their escape from my presence - they have confessed by this vilest of deeds that they were hurrying to those acts which they had both committed before and now continue doing. But, as it is patent that not one of them truly profits by his own crimes, even if there was a temporary delay in restraining them, I thought fit to command Your Eminence that you should meanwhile ignore them and accept the necessity of dissimulation with regard to them. But when you have read this letter, please act as openly toward Caecilian as toward them because when, by God's gracious favour, I come to Africa, I shall, by reading a very plain verdict, fully demonstrate to all,[4] as much to Caecilian as to those who are seen to be acting against him, what sort of devotion should be paid to the highest deity and what kind of cult he would seem to delight in.

I shall also, be applying a diligent examination, fully discover and cause to come to light those facts which certain people presently believe themselves to be hiding from now on in the mental labyrinths of ignorance. Those same people who incite and do things of this nature,

---

[1] Domitius Celsus, *vicarius* of Africa from April 28 315 to Jan 11 316, according to Barnes (1982), p. 146. His letter to Constantine is not preserved.

[2] Maier (1987) p. 194 n. 6 suggests that this is the Maenalius who at Optatus I.13 is among the consecrators of Silvanus.

[3] On this form of address see Corcoran (1996) p. 336.

[4] This journey would appear never to have been made (see n. 1 to Appendix 1).

so that the supreme God is not worshipped with the requisite devotion, I shall destroy and scatter. And as it is sufficiently apparent that no-one can obtain the blessings of martyrdom in a manner that is seen to be foreign to and incompatible with religious truth,[5] those whom I find to be opposed to right and religion itself, and apprehend in the violation of the due form of worship, these, without any doubt, I will cause to suffer the due penalties of their madness and their reckless obstinacy.[6] I will also make them know for certain what respect they owe to the most perfect faith, swearing also on my salvation[7], as much with regard to the people as to those clerics who hold first place, that I will be most diligent in inquiring and in rendering the judgment which is manifestly the truest and most pious, while I demonstrate also to these men what sort of worship should be given to the deity. For I believe that in no other way at all shall I be able to escape the greatest guilt, than by reckoning it intolerable to conceal what is scandalous. What greater obligation is imposed on me by my own intent and the bounty of my sovereign, than that, dispelling errors and cutting short all rashness, I should bring it about that everyone displays true piety, simple concord and the worship fitting to God Almighty

[5] Cf Augustine, *Cresc.* III.56 etc
[6] For the same language applied to the African schismatics, cf Eusebius, *VC* I.45.
[7] Christians continued to pray for the Emperor's safety (Athanasius, *Apologia* 60 etc.)

APPENDIX EIGHT:

Petronius to Celsus[1]

Petronius Annianus and Julianus[2] to Domitius Celsus, *vicarius* of Africa. Seeing that Bishops Lucianus, Capito, Fidentius and Nasutius, and the presbyter Mammarius,[3] who at the heavenly bidding of the Lord Constantinus Maximus Invictus[4] ever Augustus had come to Gaul with others of that religion,[5] have been ordered by his Highness to return to their own abodes, we have given to these men, brother, in accordance with the bidding of the same eternal and most clement sovereign, a vessel with sufficient provision to reach the port of Arles[6], so that they may sail from there to Africa, as this letter should apprise your Vigilance. With our best wishes, brother, for your utmost welfare and happiness. Hilarius, chief of staff, wrote this on the fourth of May from Trier.[7]

---

[1]Dated to 28th April by the final sentence. The year must therefore be 315 (see Appendix 7 n. 1 on the dates of Celsus) and this letter precedes Appendices 6 and 7 chronologically. The dislocation my be accidental, or the catholic archivist may have made it follow Constantine's concessions to the Donatists, as though to mark the point at which his patience had expired.

[2] The praetorian prefects: see Maier (1987) p. 188 n.5. Barnes (1982) pp. 95 and 100 notes that, while the prefecture of Petronius is attested from 315 to 317, he is likely to have held it also before his consulship with Volusianus in 314. On the prefecture of Julius Julianus (313-324) see *ibid.*, pp. 102-3.

[3] The signatories of the letter to Constantine at Optatus I.22, together with an unknown presbyter.

[4] This pagan title gave way to the humbler *Niketes/Victor* after 324. See Ehrhardt (1980) on this title and the frequency of triumphal appellations for Constantine in African inscriptions.

[5] The prefects dissociate themselves from the Christian religion.

[6] Arles, being at the mouth of the Rhone, was the obvious port for voyages from and to Africa, and, as one of the first four Roman *coloniae* in Transalpine Gaul, was also a natural site for Constantine's first synod. On its later importance as a centre of christian culture and discipline, see Turner (1916).

[7] Trier in Germany was the usual seat of Constantine from 310 to 316: see Barnes (1982) pp. 70-73.

APPENDIX NINE:

Constantine to the catholics[1]

Constantine Augustus to all the bishops throughout Africa and the people of the catholic church.

You know well that I have attempted to fulfil the debt of faith, so far as my wisdom prevailed and my integrity sufficed, through all the offices of humanity and moderation, so that through the authority of our law[2] that peace of holiest brotherhood, the grace of which the Most High God has suffused in the hearts of his servants, might be steadfastly maintained with the utmost concord. But since our policy was not able to tame that power of ingrained wickedness, deep-seated though it be only in a few minds, and in this depravity they continued to plead on their own behalf, so as in no way to allow the object of their criminal delight to be wrested from them,[3] we must take measures, while this whole business concerns but a few, that the mercy of Almighty God towards his people should be temperately applied. For we ought to expect the remedy from him, to whom[4] all good prayers and deeds are dedicated.

But while the heavenly medicine does its work, our policy is to be so far regulated that we practice continual patience, and, whatever their insolence tries or does as a result of their customary intemperance, all this we are to tolerate with the virtue of tranquillity. Let nothing be done to reciprocate an injury; for it is a fool who would usurp the vengeance which we ought to reserve to God,[5] particularly when our faith ought to be confident that whatever suffering result from the

---

[1] Dated to c. 321 by Maier (1987), p. 240 n.6. Constantine had now commenced a war against his former colleague, Licinius, which in 324 was to make him sole monarch of the Roman Empire. The African *vicarius* at this date, Verinus, is named by Augustine, *Post Gesta* 56. Cf. also Eusebius, *VC* I.45.

[2] Or "the teachings of our religion". Constantine saw each as the support of the other.

[3] Cf the reluctant toleration of Christian obstinacy by Galerius, Licinus and Constantine at Eusebius, *HE* VIII.17.

[4] Reading *quo* with Ziwsa and Von Soden, though Maier (1987) p. 241 n. 19 prefers the MS *cum*.

[5] A perverse construction of Romans 12.20-21.

madness of people of this kind will have value in God's eyes by the grace of martyrdom.[6] For what is it in this age to conquer in the name of God, if not to bear with unmoved breast the lawless attacks of those who harry the people of the law of peace? If you sincerely observe this, you will soon see through the grace of the Most High Deity that, as the practices and ways of those who present themselves as standard-bearers in this most wretched quarrel lose their power, all will know that they ought not to give themselves to everlasting death, perishing by the persuasion of a few people, and so they will be able by the grace of penitence to correct their errors and ingraft themselves in eternal life. Farewell, most beloved brethren, by the common prayer that God decrees through the ages!

---

[6] To judge by this letter, the "martyrs" were victims of riots rather than legal penalties.

APPENDIX TEN:

Constantine to the Numidian Bishops[1]

Constantinus Victor[2] Maximus and ever triumphant Augustus, to Bishops Zeuzius, Gallicus, Victorinus, Sperantius, Januarius, Felix, Crescentius, Pantius, Victor, Babbutius and Donatus.

Since Almighty God, who is the maker and father of this world,[3] by whose bounty we enjoy life, look up to the heavens and rejoice in human society also, is known to will this, that the whole human race should consent as one community and be held fast together by a certain social affection as though by mutual embraces, there is no doubt that heresy and schism proceeds from the devil, who is the fount of evil; and thus there is no doubting that whatever is done by heretics occurs at the instigation of him who has occupied their sense and reason. For when he has brought such people under his power, he rules over them in all respects. Now what good can be done by one who is mad, treacherous, impious, sacrilegious, opposed to God and an enemy of the Church,[4] one who withdrawing from the holy, true, righteous and Most High God who is Lord of all - who created us and brought us forth into this light, who gave us the spirit for life that we enjoy and who by his own will made us that which he wanted to be his own, together with all things - and runs with headlong error to the devil's party?

---

[1] Dated to Feb 5, 330 A.D. See Maier (1987), pp. 246-252. The letter shows that Constantine's position has not changed, and confirms his financial support for the catholics in an area where the power of the opponents had seemed likely to prevail.

[2] The title adopted after 324; see Appendix 8 n.4.

[3] A Platonic phrase (*Timaeus* 28c); cf *Orat.* 10. The *Divine Institutes* of Constantine's friend and adviser Lactantius would have introduced him, not only to Plato, but to the Ciceronian sentiment that all humans are united by a common sympathy, and to the commonplace that humans are born to look up at the heavens (*DI* II.1). On Constantine and Lactantius see Bolhuis (1956), Barnes (1973), and Edwards (1995). On the possibility that Constantine read Chalcidius' Latin version of the *Timaeus* see Waszink (1962) and Barnes (1981) p. 74.

[4] Cf 2 Tim 3.1ff for a similar catalogue of vices which oppose themselves to the rigour of the church.

But since a mind once occupied by evil - it must necessarily set about the works of its teacher - performs those things which are seen to be contrary to equity and righteousness, for that reason those who are occupied by the devil follow his falsehood and iniquity. I am not indeed surprised that shameless men should shun the good, for so the proverb rightly indicates: "like gathers with like".[5] When people are infected by the evil of an impious mind, it is necessary that they should separate from our society. "An evil man", as the scripture says, "brings forth from his evil treasury evil things, but a good man brings forth good from the good".[6] But since, as I have said, heretics and schismatics who leaving the good and pursuing evil perform those things that are displeasing to God, and are agreed to adhere to the devil who is their father,[7] Your Eminences have acted most rightly and wisely, and according to the sacred precept of faith by abstaining from their perverse quarrels and pardoning them the fact that they arrogate what is not due to them and belongs to others, lest, in their evil and treacherous perversity, they should break out into sedition and in crowds and assemblies stir up people like themselves and therefore something should break out which cannot be put down.

Their depraved intention is always in need of devil's work to perform. And thus when thanks to the patience of the priests of God they survive along with that very father of theirs, those who are worshippers of the Most High God obtain glory for themeslves, but these damnation and condign punishment. Indeed it is by this that the judgment of God appears manifestly more great and righteous, that he bears them with equanimity and condemns by his patience, enduring all the things that come from them. God indeed promises to be the avenger of all;[8] and thus when vengeance is left to God a harsher penality is exacted from one's enemies. This, I know, you servants and priests of God have done, and I am highly gratified that you demand no vengeance on those who are impious and depraved, sacrilegious and

---

[5] Maier (1987) p. 248 n.8 notes that this phrase occurs in Cicero, *De Senectute* 3.7. Like the statement that God designs us for social affection, this quotation reflects Lactantius' influence.

[6] Matthew 12.38.

[7] Cf John 8.44.

[8] Cf . Deuteronomy 32.35, Romans 12.19 etc.

profane, treacherous and impious and ungrateful to God and enemies of
the Church, and rather request that these men should receive pardon.
This is what it is to be fully and deeply acquainted with God, to do his
precepts zealously, to prosper in belief, to be aware of truth, to know
that a greater vengeance is provoked against the opponents of the
Church when they are spared in the temporal sphere.

Having, therefore, received the letter from your wise and eminent
persons, I have learnt that the heretics or schismatics have, with their
wonted shamelessness, thought fit to invade the basilica of that church
which I had ordered to be built in the city of Constantina,[9] and that -
though frequently admonished, not only by our judges on our orders but
by ourselves, to give back that which was not theirs - they refused,
while you, however, imitating the patience of the Most High God, have
with peaceable mind relinquished to their malice those things that are
yours and are rather requesting another place for yourselves, namely the
fiscal land. This petition, according to my customary policy, I have
gladly embraced and have immediately given an official letter to the
steward,[10] saying that he should transfer our treasury, with all his own
rights into the possession of the catholic church, which I have made a
gift with prompt generosity and have ordered to be handed over to you
forthwith.

However, as to the place in which I commanded a basilica to be built
with fiscal revenue, I have also written ordering the consular official of
Numidia[11] that he himself should aid your virtuous persons in the
construction of that church. Where readers of the catholic church and
subdeacons, and others too, who at the instance of the aforesaid persons
have on account of certain customs been called to public duties or the

---

[9] See Lepelley (181) p. 384. Maier (187) p. 250 n.10 and Schindler (1983) note that the
Donatists had control of Cirta, as Victor the grammarian implies in Appendix 1..

[10] The *rationalis rei privatae*, according to Jones (1964) Vol I p. 412 was a provincial
official charged with the disposal of the Emperor's personal property. This would include
confiscations from temples (Jones, p. 414), and on p. 424 Jones cites this passage as an
outstanding instance of imperial largesse. Like his previous bounty to Caecilian (Eusebius,
HE X.6) this testifies to Constantine's undivided sympathy with the catholics.

[11] The *consularis* is identified as M. Aurelius Valerius Valentinus by Barnes (1982) p.
173.

decurionate,[12] I have stated, by the statute of my law, that they are not to be called up for any duty; and those too, who were brought in at the instance of heretics, we have commanded to be absolved of their onerous obligations. For the rest, I have also ordered that the law that I issued concerning the catholic churches is to be observed; all which things are prescribed by the witness of this letter, so that they may be done in open view of your patient persons. And I wish indeed that heretics or schismatics would at some time provide for their salvation, and having cleansed the mists from their eyes would open them to the true vision of the light and secede from the devil and even so late flee to God, who is one and true and the judge of all! But since it is patent that they remain in their evil ways and wish to die in their misdeeds, sufficient for them are our admonition and the foregoing assiduous exhortation. For if they would submit to our bidding, they would be freed from every evil. Let us, however, brethren, pursue what is ours, be zealous in obeying commands, observe the divine precepts by good deeds, and acquitting our life of errors and by the favour of God's mercy hold a course for the right shore!

Given at Serdica on February 5[13].

---

[12] The exemption of Christian clergy from municipal duties is not securely attested before the reigns of Constantine's sons, but they certainly enjoyed immunity from many taxes. See Barnes (1981), pp. 50-1, and *Codex Theodosianus* XVI.2.2, which provides that readers, subdeacons and other clergy who have been maliciously brought before the secular magistrates should be acquitted, and should in future enjoy full immunity.

[13] See *Codex Theodosianus* XVI.2.7 and Barnes (1982) p. 78 for the residence at Serdica in 330. Constantine, having captured the city from Licinius in 316, called it his "second Rome".

Bibliography

1. Texts abbreviated in the footnotes.

AMBROSE (*Myst.*, *Sacr.*), *Sancti Ambrosii Opera*, including *De Mysteriis* and *De Sacramentis*, ed. O. Faller (Vienna, 1955).

AUGUSTINE, *Epistulae*, Vols I-II, ed. A. Goldbacher (Leipzig, 1885-7 = *Corpus Scriptorum Ecclesiasticorum Latinorum* 34).

_____ (*Parm.*, *Bapt.*), *Contra Parmenianum Libri Tres, De Baptismo Libri Septem*, ed. M. Petschenig (Leipzig, 1908 = *CSEL* 51).

_____ (*Petil. Cath.*, *Cresc.*) *Contra Litteras Petiliani Libri Tres, Epistula ad Catholicos de Secta Donatistarum, Contra Cresconium Libri Quattuor*, ed. M. Petschenig (Leipzig, 1909 = *CSEL* 52).

_____ (*Brev.*, *Post Gesta*), *Liber de Unico Baptismo, Breviculus Collationis cum Donatistis, Contra Partem Donati post Gesta. Contra Gaudentium* etc., ed. M. Petschenig (Leipzig, 1910 = *CSEL* 53).
Note: treatises of Augustine usually have two ways of numbering chapters. In every case I have used the sequence which produces smaller chapters.

EUSEBIUS (*VC, Orat.*), *Über das Leben Constantins, Constantins Rede an die Heilige Versammlung, Tricennatsrede an Constantin*, ed. I.A. Heikel (Leipzig, 1902)

_____ (*HE*) *Histoire Ecclésiastique*, ed. G. Bardy et al. (Paris, Sources Chrétiennes, 1952-65)

_____ (*VC*), *Über das Leben Constantins*, ed. F. Winkelmann (Berlin, 1975).

HILARY (*Myst.*), *Traité Des Mystères*, ed. J-P. Brisson (Paris, Sources Chrétiennes, 1947)

IRENAEUS (*AH*), *Contre Les Hérésies*, ed. A. Rousseau and L. Doutreleau, 10 vols (Paris, Sources Chrétiennes, 1965-82).

JEROME (*Alt.*), *Altercatio cum Luciferianis*, in J.-P. Migne, (ed.), Patrologia Latina 23 (Paris, 1845).

LACTANTIUS (*DI*), *Divinae Institutiones*

_____ (*Mort.*), *De Mortibus Persecutorum*, ed. J. L. Creed (Oxford, 1984).

OPTATUS, *De Schismate Donatistarum Libri Septem*, ed. H. Hurter (London, 1870).

_____ *Libri Septem*, ed. C. Ziwsa (Leipzig, 1893 = CSEL 26).

_____ *Contre les Donatistes*, Vol I (Livres 1-2), ed. J. Labrousse (Paris, Sources Chrétiennes, 1995).

_____ *Contre les Donatistes*, Vol II (Livres 3-7), ed. J. Labrousse (Paris, Sources Chrétiennes, 1996).

TERTULLIAN (*Bapt.*), *De Baptismo*, ed. E. Evans (Oxford, 1964).

Passio Abitinensium = Maier (1987), pp. 57-91.

Passio Donati = Maier (1987), pp. 198-211.

Passio Isaac et Maximiani = Maier (1987), pp. 256-75.

Passio Marculi = Maier (1987), pp. 275-281.

Passio Virginum = Maier (1987), pp. 92-105.

2. Relevant Books and Articles.

JRS = *Journal of Roman Studies*
JTS = *Journal of Theological Studies*

ABRAMOWSKI, L. (1977), "Irenaeus, *Adv. Haer.* II.2", *JTS* 28, 101-4.

ALEXANDER, D. S. (1980), "The Motive for a Distinction between Donatus of Carthage and Donatus of Casae Nigrae", *JTS* 31, 540-7.

ALFOLDI, A. (1948), *The Conversion of Constantine and Christian Rome* (Oxford).

BARNES, T. D. (1973), "Lactantius and Constantine", *JRS* 63.

_____ (1975), "The Beginnings of Donatism", *JTS* 26, 13-22.

_____ (1981), *Constantine and Eusebius* (Cambridge, Mass.).

_____ (1982), *The New Empire of Diocletian and Constantine* (Cambridge, Mass. and London).

_____ (1985) *Tertullian*, 2nd edition (Oxford).

BATIFFOL, P. (1914), "Filumenus ou Philoumenos, fonctionnaire de l'Empereur Constantin", *Bulletin de la Société Nationale des Antiquaires de France* (Paris).

_____ (1920), *Le Catholicisme de S. Augustin*, Vols I-II, 3rd edition (Paris).

BAYNES, N. (1931), *Constantine the Great and the Christian Church*, separately reprinted from *Proceedings of the British Academy* 15 (1929).

BENSON, E. W. (1897), *Cyprian, His Life, His Times, His Work* (London).

BÉVENOT, M. (1966), "Clement of Rome in Irenaeus' Succession List", *JTS* 17, 98-107.

BOLHUIS, A. (1956), "Die Rede Konstantins des Grossen an die Versammlung der Heiligen und Lactantius' *Divinae Institutiones*", *Vigiliae Christianae* 10, 25-32.

BRAKKE, D. (1995), *Athanasius and the Politics of Asceticism* (Oxford).

BRENT, A. (1995), *Hippolytus and the Roman Church in the Third Century* (Leiden).

BRIGHT, W. (1882), *Notes on the Canons of the First Four General Councils* (Oxford).

BRISSON, J.-P. (1958), *Autonomisme et Christianisme dans l'Afrique Romaine* (Paris).

BURCKHARDT, J. (1949), *The Age of Constantine the Great*, tr. M. Hadas (London).

CASPAR, E. (1927), "Die Römische Synod von 313", *Zeitschrift fur Kirchengeschichte* 46, 333-46.

CECCONI, G.A. (1990), "Elemosina e propaganda. un analisi della 'Macariana persecutio'", *Revue des Études Augustiniennes* 31, 42-66.

CHADWICK, H. and DIX, G. (1992), *The Treatise on the Apostolic Tradition of St Hippolytus of Rome* (London).

CHARLES, R.H . (1913), *The Apocrypha and Pseudepigrapha of the Old Testament. Vol II: Pseudepigrapha* (Oxford).

COLEMAN-NORTON, R.P. (1966), *Roman State and Christian Church*, Vol I (London).

CORCORAN, S. (1996), *The Empire of the Tetrarchs* (Oxford).

COURCELLE, P. (1957), "Les exégèses chrétiennes de la quatrième éclogue", *Revue des Études Anciennnes* 59, 294-319.

DANIÉLOU, J. (1961), *The Origins of Latin Christianity*, tr. J. A. Baker (London).

DAVIES, P. S.(1989), "The Origins of the Persecution of 303", *JTS* 40.

_____ "Constantine's Editor", *JTS* 42 (1991), 610-618.

DAVIS, R. (1989), *The Book of Pontiffs* (Liverpool).

DE DECKER, D. (1978), "'Le Discours à l'Assemblée des Saints' attribué à Constantin et l'oeuvre de Lactance", in J. Fontaine and M. Perrin (eds) *Lactance et son Temps* (Paris), 75-87.

DIESNER, H.-J. (1961), "Volk und Volksaufstände bei Optatus von Mileve", *Wissensschaftliche Zeitschrift der Martin-Luther Universität Halle* 10, 63-6.

DILLON, J. (1977), *The Middle Platonists* (London).

DIX, G.P. (1945), *The Shape of the Liturgy* (London, 2nd edn.).

DOLGER, F. (1932), "Das Kultvergehn der Donatistin Lucilla von Karthago", *Antike und Christentum* 3.

DUCHESNE, L. (1886), *Le Liber Pontificalis,* Vol I (Paris).

EDWARDS, M. J. (1995), "The Arian Heresy and the Oration to the Saints", *Vigiliae Christianae* 49.3, 379-387.

EDWARDS. M. J., with GOODMAN, M. D., PRICE, S.R . and ROWLAND, C. (1997/8), *Apologetic* (Oxford).

EHRHARDT, C. (1980), "'Maximus', 'Invictus' und 'Victor' als Datierungskriterien auf Inschriften Konstantins des Grossen", *Zeitschrift fur Papyrologie und Epigraphik* 49, 177-181.

ENO, R.B. (1973), "The Work of Optatus as a Turning-Point in the African Ecclesiology", *The Thomist* 37, 668-85.

——————— (1993), "The Significance of the Lists of Roman Bishops in the Anti-Donatist Polemic", *Vigiliae Christianae* 47, 157-70.

ERRINGTON, R.M. (1988), "Constantine and the Pagans", *Greek, Roman and Byzantine Studies* 29, 309-18.

FOWDEN, G. (1991), "Constantine's Porphyry Column: the Earliest Literary Allusion", *JRS* 81, 119-31.

——————— (1994), "The Last Days of Constantine: Oppositional Versions and their Influence", *JRS* 84, 146-70.

FREND, W. H. C. (1940), "The *Memoriae Apostolorum* in Roman North Africa", *JRS* 30, 32-49.

——————— (1952a), *The Donatist Church* (Oxford).

——————— (1952b), "The *Cellae* of the African Circumcellions", *JTS* 3, 87-9.

——————— (1961), "The *Seniores Laici* and the Origins of the Church in North Africa", *JTS* 12, 280-4.

——————— (1965), "A Note on the Great Persecution in the West", in G.J. Cuming (ed.), *Studies in Church History* ii (London), 141-8.

——————— (1969), "Circumcellions and Monks", *JTS* 20, 542-9.

FREND, W.H.C and CLANCY, K. (1977), "When did the Donatist Schism Begin?", *JTS* 28, 104-9.

GIRARDET, K. M. (1989), "Die Petition der Donatisten am Kaiser Konstantin (Fruhjahr 313)", *Chiron* 19 185-206.

GARDUCCI, M. (1982), *La Cathedra di S. Pietro nella scienza e nella fede* (Rome).

GRASMÜCK, E. L. (1954). *Coercitio. Staat und Kirche im Donatistenstreit* (Bonn).

HANSON, R. P. C. (1985), "Eucharistic Offering in the Pre-Nicene Fathers", in his *Studies in Christian Antiquity* (Edinburgh), 83-112.

JONES, A. H. M. (1948), *Constantine and the Conversion of Europe* (London).

——————— (1964), *The Later Roman Empire,* Vols I-III (Oxford).

JONKERS, E. J. (1954), *Acta et Symbola Conciliorum quae Saeculo Quarto Habita Sunt* (Leiden).

KELLY, J. N. D. (1972), *Early Christian Creeds,* 3rd edition (London).

KRIEGBAUM, B. (1986), *Kirche der Traditoren oder Kirche der Märtyrer? Die Vorgeschichte des Donatismus* (Innsbruck-Wien).

——————— (1989), "Ein neuer Lösungsverschlag fur ein altes Problem: die sogennanten preces der Donatisten (Optatus I.22)", *Studia Patristica* 22, 277-82.

——————— (1990), "Zwischen den Synoden von Rom und Arles. Die donatische Supplik bei Optatus", *Archivum Historiae Pontificae* 28, 23-61.

LANCEL, S. (1979), "Les débuts du Donatisme", *Revue des Études Augustiniennes* 25, 217-229.

——————— (1988), "Le dossier du Donatisme", review of Maier (1987), *Revue des Études Latines* 66, 37-42.

LANE FOX, R. (1986), *Pagans and Christians* (Harmondsworth).

LEPELLEY, C. (1979-81), *Les cités de l'Afrique romaine au bas-Empire,* 2 Vols (Paris).

——————— (1983), "Chrétiens et païens au temps de la persecution de Diocletien: le cas d'Abthugni", *Studia Patristica* 15, 226-32.

LIEBENAM, W. (1897), "*Curator rei publicae*", *Philologus* 10, 290-325.

LIEU, S. N. C. and MONTSERRAT, D. (1996), *From Constantine to Julian: Pagan and Byzantine Views* (London).

LOCKWOOD, R. (1989), "*Potens et Factiosa Femina*", *Augustinian Studies* 20, 165-82.

LUCAS, C. (1940), "Notes on the *Curatores Rei Publicae* of Roman Africa", *JRS* 30, 55-74.

MACCARRONE, M. (1976), *Apostolicità, episcopato e primato di Pietro: Ricerche e testimonianze dal II al V secolo* (Rome: Lateranum 42).

MAIER, J.-L. (1973), *L'Episcopat de l'Afrique Romaine* (Rome).

——————— (1987), *Le Dossier du Donatisme*, Vol I (Berlin: *Texte und Untersuchungen* 134).

MANDOUZE, A. (1960), "Encore le Donatisme", *L'Antiquité Classique* 29, 60-107.

——————— (1982), *La Prosopographie Chrétienne du bas-Empire: I. Afrique* (303-533) (CNRS, Paris).

MARCELLI, P. (1990), "La simbologia delle doti della Chiesi in Ottato di Milevi", *Studi e materiali di storia delle religione* 14, 219-44.

MAZUCCO, C. (1993), *Ottato di Milevi in un secolo di studi* (Turin).

MAZZARINO, S. (1974), *Antico, Tardoantico ed Era Constantiniana* (Bari: *Storia e Civiltà* 13).

MERDINGER, J. (1989), "Optatus Reconsidered", *Studia Patristica* 22, 294-99.

MIHALIC, P. M. (1982), *Constructive Confrontation. The Approach of Optatus the African towards the Donatists* (Rome: Pontifical University Dissertation).

MILLAR, F. (1971), "Paul of Samosata, Zenobia and Aurelian", *JRS* 61, 1-17.

——————— (1977), *The Emperor in the Roman World* (London).

MOLLAND, E. (1950), "Irenaeus of Lugdunum and the Apostolic Succession", *Journal of Ecclesiastical History* 1, 12-28.

MONCEAUX, P. (1912), *Histoire littéraire de l'Afrique chrétienne* (Paris), esp. 487-510.

——————— (1913), "Sur la date du Traité de Saint Optat contre les Donatistes", *Comptes Rendus de l'Académie des Inscriptions et Belles-Lettres*.

MUNIER, C. (1972/3), "La tradition manuscrite de l'Abrègé d'Hippone et le canon des écritures des églises africaines", *Sacris Erudiri* 21, 43-55.

MUSURILLO, H. (1972), *Acts of the Christian Martyrs* (Oxford).

NASH, E. (1976), "*Convenerunt in domum Faustae in Laterano.* Optati Milevitani I.23.", *Römische Quartalschrift fur Christliche Altertumskunde und fur Kirchengeschichte* 71, 1-21.

NICHOLSON, O. P. (1994), "The Pagan Churches of Maximinus Daia and Julian the Apostate", *Journal of Ecclesiastical History* 45 (1994), 1-12.

PARKER, W. H. (1887), "Optatus", in *Dictionary of Christian Biography*, ed. W. H. Smith and H. Wace, Vol IV (London), 90-93.

PERCIVAL, H. R. (1899), *The Seven Ecumenical Councils of the Undivided Chrurch. together with the canons of all the local synods which have received ecumenical acceptance.* (Edinburgh: *Library of the Nicene and Post-Nicene Fathers* XIV).

PIETRI, C. (1976), *Roma Christiana. Recherches sur l'Église de Rome, son organisation, sa politique, son idéologie de Miltiade à Sixte III* (Rome).

PIGANIOL, A. (1932), "Dates constantiniennes", *Revue d'Histoire et de Philosophie Religieuse* 13, 360-372.

PINCHERLE, A. (1925), "L'ecclesiologia nella controversia donatista", *Recherche Religiose* 1, 35-55.

PULLER, F. W. (1893), *The Primitive Saints and the See of Rome* (London).

RANKIN, D. (1995), *Tertullian and the Church* (Edinburgh).

RATZINGER, J. (1954), *Volk und Haus Gottes in Augustins Lehre von der Kirche* (Munich).

RIVES, J. B. (1995), *Religion and Authority in Carthage from Augustus to Constantine* (Oxford).

ROETHE, G. (1937), *Zur Geschichte der römischen Synoden im 3. und 4. Jahrhundert*, Vol 2 (Stuttgart).

ROUTH, M. (1846), *Reliquiae Sacrae*, Vol. 4 (Oxford).

RONDET, H. (1972), *Original Sin, The Patristic and Theological Background*, tr. C. Finegan (Shannon, Ireland).

RUYSSCHAERT, J. (1973), "La légendaire 'sedes' petrinienne du Majer", *Rivista di archeologia cristiana* 49, 293-9.

SAGI-BUNIC, Th. (1962), "Controversia de Baptismate inter Parmenianum et S. Optatum Milevitanum", *Laurentianum* 3, 167-209.

STE.-CROIX, G. E. M. de (1954), "Aspects of the 'Great' Persecution", *Harvard Theological Review* 47, 75-109.

SALZMAN, M. (1993), "The evidence for the conversion of the Roman Empire in Book XVI of the Theodosian Code", *Historia* 42, 362-78.

SCHINDLER, A. (1983), "L'Histoire du Donatisme considéré du point de vue de sa propre théologie", *Studia Patristica* 17, 1306-15.

SCHMIDT, J. (1892), "Uber die alba des ordo von Thamugadi und das flamonium perpetuum", *Rheinisches Museum* 47, 114-129.

SCHÜRER, E. (1979), *The History of the Jewish People in the age of Jesus Christ,* revised by G. Vermes, F. Millar and M. Black, Vol II (Edinburgh).

SHERWIN-WHITE, A. N. (1939), *The Roman Citizenship* (Oxford).

SIMMONS, M. B. (1995), *Arnobius of Sicca* (Oxford).

SMITH, R. (1995), *Julian's Gods* (London).

TEUTSCH, L. (1982), *Das Städtewesen in Nordafrika in der Zeit von C. Gracchus bis zum Tode des Kaisers Augustus* (Berlin).

THORNTON, C. G. T. (1986), "Destruction of Idols- Meritorious or Sinful?", *JTS* 37, 121-9.

THUMMEL, H. G. (1992), *Die Frühgeschichte der Ostkirchlichen Bilderlehre* (Berlin: Texte und Untersuchungen 139).

TILLEY, M. (1996), *Donatist Martyr Stories* (Liverpool).

TOUTAIN, J. (1896), *Les Cités Romains de la Tunisie* (Paris).

TURNER, C. H. (1916), "Arles and Rome", *JTS* 17, 236-47.

——————— (1917), "The Episcopal Lists, III, IV", *JTS* 18, 103-134.

——————— (1925-6), "Adversaria Critica: Notes on the anti-Donatist Dossier and on Optatus, Books I, II", *JTS* 27, 283-296.

VASSAL-PHILLIPS, O. R. (1917), *The Work of St Optatus, Bishop of Milevis, Against the Donatists, with Appendices* (London).

VIDMAN, L. (1969) *Sylloge Inscriptionum Religionis Isiacae et Serapicae,* Vol I (Berlin).

VON SODEN, H. (1950), *Urkunden zur Entstehungsgeschichte des Donatismus,* 2nd. ed. revised by H. Von Campenhausen (Berlin).

WASZINK, J. H. (1962), *Timaeus a Calcidico translatus commentarioque instructus* (Leiden: *Plato Latinus* 4).

Glossary and Index

This index contains the names of persons and places referred to by
Optatus or in his appendix and directly involved in the Donatist
controversy, together with historical and Biblical citations which are
important to the argument of Optatus. The names of Roman Bishops
and Italian bishoprics can be found in the lists at the end.

Aaron, prototype of priesthood: 20.
Abthugni (Hr es Souar), see of Felix: 17, 27, 170-80.
Adam, first man, and the effect of his sin: 133.
Aelafius (?Elaphius), recipient of Appendix 3:181.
Aelianus, proconsul of Africa: 26, 172.
Aelius Paulinus (?Verus), *vicarius* of north Africa: 170-171.
Africa, Roman province (= modern Tunisia): *passim*.
Agesilaus, witness at trial of Felix of Abthugni: 172-80.
Antiochus IV (Epiphanes), Hellenistic ruler, persecutor of Jews c.167
B.C.: 136.
An(n)ulinus,proconsul of Africa and persecutor of Christians in 303/4
A.D.: 76.
Apronianus, witness in trial of Felix: 170-80.
Arius, Alexandrian presbyter, condemned at Nicaea: 89.
Arles, Gaulish colony, scene of council in 314: 183-5, 195.
Athenius, Mauretanian magistrate: 46.
Augentius, colleague of Ingentius: 179.
Axido, circumcellion leader: 69.

Bagaia (Ksar Baghai), Numidian town and scene of major Donatist
rising: 57, 68. 70..
Baruch, scribe to Hebrew prophet Jeremiah: 130-131.
Boniface, Donatist Bishop of Rome:34.
Botrus, aspirant to succeed Mensurius in Carthage: 17.
Brixia, north Italian city (Brescia), where Caecilian was detained: 25.
Byzacena, province in north Africa: 183.

Caecilianus, Alfius, pagan magistrate and witness in case of Felix: 87,
170-80.
Caecilian, Bishop of Carthage, successor to Mensurius.

Korah, opponent of Moses and Aaron: 20, 117..

Lateran, place of Roman council of 313: 24.
Lemellef (Bordj Rhedir), site in Mauretania Sitifensis: 45.
Leontius, *comes* and oppressor of Donatists: 57, 71, 80.
Lebanon, metaphor for Roman Empire: 63.
Licinius, co-Emperor and consul with Constantine: 24.
Limata/Liniata, Numidian seat of Bishop Purpurius: 13.
Lucian, Bishop of Carthage after Cyprian: 19.
Lucianus, signatory of Donatist petition: 22-3, 195.
Lucilla, calumniator of Caecilian: 15, 18.
    Her conspiracies: 19, 157, 166-9.

Macarius, *comes* and oppressor of Donatists with Paulus: 57, 68, 71, 80, 82.
    Attacked and defended: 73-4, 145-9.
Macrobius: Donatist Bishop of Rome: 34.
Maenalius, Donatist troublemaker: 13, 193
Majorinus, precursor of Donatus: 10, 12. 19, 144, 157.
Mambres, Egyptian opponent of Moses: 144-5.
Mammarius, presbyter, friend of Capito etc.: 195.
Marcion, second-century heretic: 8, 88, 102.
Marculus, false martyr of Donatists: 72.
Mars, deacon of Cirta: 152.
Marinus, Bishop of Aquae Tibilitanae, collaborator: 13.
Mascul(ul)a (Khenchela), Numidian see of one Donatus: 13, 20.
Mauretania (Tingitana, Caesariensis, Sitifiensis), group of provinces upset by Donatists:45-6, 176, 179.
Maurus, Bishop of Utica: 178
Maxentius, Emperor in Italy and Africa 306-312:16.
Maximian, colleague of Diocletian, then Maxentius: 75, 153.
Maximus, witness at trial of Felix of Abthugni: 170-80.
Mensurius, Bishop of Carthage, 303-311 A.D.: 16-17.
Miccius, scribe, witness at trial of Felix of Abthugni: 171.
Milevis (Milev), town associated with Purpurius: 13.
Miltiades/Melchiades, Bishop of Rome and president of council in 313: 24.
Montenses (Hillmen), Roman Donatists: 35.

Moses, author of Jewish Law: 74, 123, 129-38, 144 etc..
Munatius Felix, *flamen perpetuus* of Cirta: 153-5.
Mutus, gladiator who supported Silvanus' election: 165.

Naaman, Syrian leper, as symbol of baptism: 157.
Nasutius, signatory of Donatist petition: 22-3, 195.
Nicene Council, of 325, condemned Arius: 89.
Nicasius, recipient of letter from Aelafius: 182.
Noah, ark as symbol of baptism: 97-8, 131.
Numidia, Roman province, homeland of Donatism: 13, 183, 200 etc.
Nundinarius, deacon to Silvanus: 14, 150-69.
    Letters concerning him: 160-9.

Octav(i)ensis/Octabensis locus, place in Numidia: 69.
Olympius, companion of Eunomius:26.

Parmenianus, Donatist Bishop of Carthage, answered by Optatus as a
brother:3, 6, 10, 20, 28, 40, 47, 95 etc.
    His book on the gifts of the Church: 3, 31-2.
    On symbols for baptism: 4, 93-8
    Proved schismatic: 10, 12, 32 etc.

Part(h)enius, catholic bishop molested by Donatists: 55.
Paul, Apostle to Gentiles and author of New Testament letters: 62, 81,
102, 113, 134, 140, 144 etc.
    His baptism of the Ephesians: 106-9.
    On the two testaments and virginity: 120-1.
Paulus, colleague of Macarius: 62, 67, 71,.82.
Paul, Bishop of Cirta under the persecution: 153-4.
Peter, chief of Apostles, first Bishop of Rome:10, 12. 32-4.
    On foot-washing: 100.
    His sin and restoration: 139-41.
Petronius Annianus, Roman official in Appendix 8: 195.
Phine(h)as, Biblical character who obeyed God: 72-4, 147.
Photinus, contemporary heretic: 89.
Praxeas, second-century heretic: 8, 88, 98.
Primosus, catholic Bishop of Lemellef: 45.
Primus, deacon killed by Donatists: 45.

Appendix 1: the Roman Bishops to Siricius

Readers may wish to compare the list of the Roman pontiffs given by
Optatus at II.3 with that in the *Liber Pontificalis*. The dates in the latter
are taken from Davis (1989). I reproduce the Optatan list without
Ziwsa's "corrections".

Liber Pontificalis	*Optatus*
Peter (64/67)	Peter
Linus (c.70)	Linus
Cletus (c.85)	
Clement (c.95)	Clement
Aneclitus	Anacletus
Evaristus (c.100)	Evaristus
Alexander (c.110)	
Xystus (c.120)	Sixtus[1]
Telesphorus (c.130)	Telesphorus
Hyginus (c.140)	Hyginus
Pius (c.145)	Anicetus
Anicetus (c. 160)	Pius[2]
Soter (c.170)	Soter
Eleutherius (c. 180)	
Victor (c. 195)	Victor
Zephyrinus (197/8-217)	Zephyrinus
Callistus (217-222)	Calixtus
Urban (222-230)	Urban
Pontianus (230-235)	Pontianus
Anteros (235-236)	Anterus
Fabian (236-50)	Fabian

---

[1] The Latin form of the name means 'sixth", and if it were the original, would be
evidence for a shorter list than that in the *Liber Pontificalis*, even if it meant sixth *after*
Peter. The tradition that he styled himself thus because he was the sixth Pope is, however,
unreliable.

[2] The Liberian Catalogue supports Optatus: see Davis (1989), p. 94.

Cornelius (251-253)[3]	Cornelius
Lucius (253-254)	Lucius
Stephen (254-257)	Stephen
Xystus (257-258)	Sixtus
Dionysius (260-267)	Dionysius
Felix (268-273)	Felix
Eutychian (274-282)	
Gaius (282-295)	
Marcellinus (295-303)	Marcellinus
Marcellus (305/6-306/7)[4]	
Eusebius (308)[5]	Eusebius
Miltiades (310=314)[6]	Miltiades
Silvester (314-335)	Silvester
Marcus (336)	Marcus
Julius (337-352)	Julius
Liberius (352-366)	Liberius
Felix (355-365)	
Damasus (366-384)	Damasus[7]
Siricius (384-399)	Siricius

---

[3] A longer interregnum than usual may have been created by the disputes between the lax and rigorous parties that martyrdom of Fabian; these led after Cornelius' election to the damaging schism of Novatian. See Davis (1989), pp. 8-9.

[4] The succession to Marcellinus was disputed, and Marcellus banished by Maxentius; hence (perhaps) his absence from the Optatan list.

[5] The Liberian Catalogue regards the period from 304 to 308 as an interregnum, assigning both Marcellus and Eusebius to 308: see Davis (1989), p. 95.. If this is true, it may give further evidence that Maxentius extended peace to Christians in that year: see Optatus I.17 and notes.

[6] The apparent interregnum is explained by Eusebius' exile, not his death. The *Liber Pontificalis* allots six years to Eusebius, no doubt to make it possible for him to baptize Constantine after his capture of Rome in 313: see the *Inventio Sanctae Crucis*, Davis (1989), p. 13; Fowden (1994).

[7] According to the *Liber*, the years of Felix are included in those of the exiled Liberius: see Davis (1989), p. 28.

Appendix 2: The Italian Bishoprics at I.23

Bishop	See	Equivalent
Miltiades	Roma	Rome/Roma
Merocles	Mediolanum	Milan
Florianus	Sinna	Siena
Zoticus	Quintianum[8]	
Stennius	Ariminum	Rimini
Felix	Florentia Tuscorum	Florence/Firenze
Gaudentius	Pisa	Pisa
Constantius	Faventia	Faenza
Proterius	Capua	S. Maria di Capua Vetere
Theophilus	Beneventum	Benevento
Sabinus	Terracina	Terracina
Secundus	Praeneste	Palestrina
Felix	Tres Tabernae[9]	
Maximus	Ostia	Ostia
Evandrus	Ursinum[10]	
Donatianus	Forum Claudii	S. Maria di Foro Claudii

---

[8] The Quintiana statio is an otherwise obscure site, some miles west of Tarquinia in Tuscany.

[9] This too is merely a station on the Appian Way, about thirty miles from Rome.

[10] Possibly Urvinum (modern Urbino), though there is an Ursinis in Gallia Narbonensis.

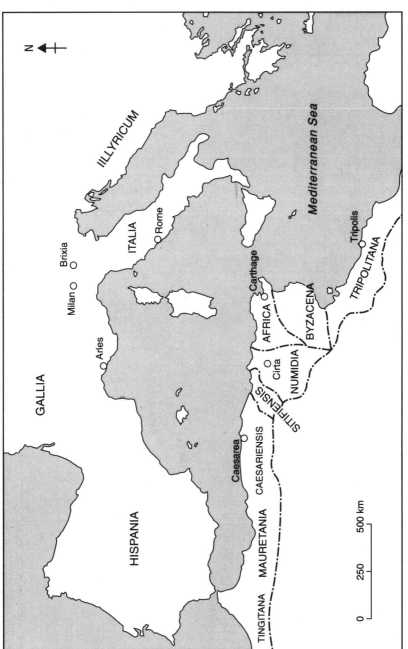

Map 1 The African Provinces after Diocletian (drawn by Stephen Ramsay)

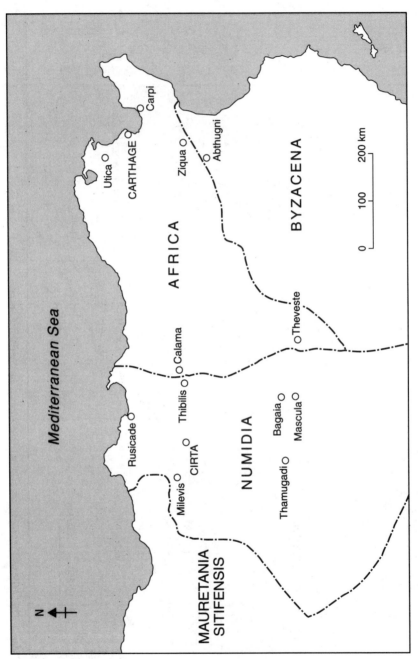

Map 2 Numidia and Africa (drawn by Stephen Ramsay)